ABOUT THE A

Carl McColman is an independent scholar and student of the Celtic mysteries. He is a freelance writer and spiritual teacher based in Atlanta, Georgia. He is the author of numerous books, including *The Complete Idiot's Guide to Celtic Wisdom* and *The Aspiring Mystic: Practical Steps for Spiritual Seekers*. Visit Carl online at www.carlmccolman.com.

Go Muireann na nGael

366 Celt

A YEAR AND A DAY OF CELTIC
LORE AND WISDOM

BY

CARL MCCOLMAN

Element
An Imprint of HarperCollins*Publishers*
77–85 Fulham Palace Road
Hammersmith, London W6 8JB

The website address is: www.thorsonselement.com

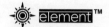

and *Element* are trademarks of
HarperCollins*Publishers* Limited

First published 2005

1 3 5 7 9 10 8 6 4 2

© Carl McColman 2005

Carl McColman asserts the moral right to be
identified as the author of this work

A catalogue record for this book
is available from the British Library

ISBN 0 00 719309 2

Printed and bound in Great Britain by
Clays Ltd, St Ives plc

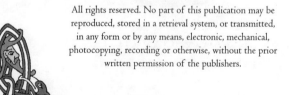

CONTENTS

INTRODUCTION

"IN CONVERSATION THEY SPEAK IN RIDDLES, FOR THE
MOST PART HINTING OF THINGS AND LEAVING A GREAT
DEAL TO BE UNDERSTOOD."

Thus did the classical writer Diodorus Siculus describe the druids, the original keepers of Celtic wisdom and lore. What we mostly know about the druids reveals just how much we do not know: we know they did not write down their lore, we know that they were not only spiritual leaders but also scientists/intellectuals; and yet even so we know that they were the ritual priests, the soothsayers, and the interpreters of omens. And apparently, they did it all with a rollicking good humor, and uncanny ability to speak in oblique and mysterious ways.

The Celtic world is a world of poetry before philosophy; of mysticism before theology; of magic before logic. Storytelling matters more than the ability to explain something in dry, step-by-step detail. The Celts are, and always have been, a people with one foot in the otherworld, and thus are governed by the enigmatic conventions and customs of that spiritual realm: where time is meaningless, love is forever, and dancing just might never ever end.

The book you're holding is written with the spirit of the old druids in mind. Riddles and hints matter more here than direct explanations or matter-of-fact descriptions. This is a book of meditations, but what does that mean? Some of the pages that follow invite you into a world of fairies and goddesses; others sneak significant symbols past you in the guise of a summary description of this or that aspect of the tradition. There are 366 pages of thoughts and ideas and invitations into the inner world—read them a day at a time, or get wild and swallow up a week or even a month at a single sitting. I decided to number the entries, rather than date them—daily meditation books seem so structured and tight, if you read "May 17" on any other day it's just, well, wrong. That, of course, is an invitation to utter chaos, at least as a riddle-talking Celt sees it. So I decided to circumvent the chaos and give each reader the freedom to explore these 366 "morsels" in whatever way works best for you.

The entire collection is organized in 40 different "paths," each one consisting of 3, 9, or 21 meditations. No one path is required as a prerequisite for any of the others. Once in a while paths crisscross and you'll encounter the same figure or event that you bumped into three or four paths back. The Celtic tradition just kind of works that way.

Feel free to jump around between the paths, or even within any one path. Read these pages in order, or not. The choice is yours. 366 pages later, you'll have covered a nice slice of the Celtic terrain. And you'll still be an absolute beginner in the world of the Celts. Listen to the druids: they'll have more riddles to offer you. Some will open up amazing shafts of light that will illuminate and inspire you. Others will leave you scratching your head and wondering, "Huh?" That, too, is part of the territory.

May the blessings of the four directions, the three realms, the two worlds, and the one source fill all your days with laughter and joy.

Carl McColman
Summer Solstice 2004

Note on spelling: *The names of Celtic deities and heroes can be spelled many different ways. For the sake of simplicity, I have chosen to conform to the spelling found in MacKillop's* Dictionary of Celtic Mythology *(Oxford University Press, 1998). Brigit poses a unique problem since both a goddess and a saint bear the same name. Following MacKillop, in this book I have identified the goddess as "Brigit" and the saint as "Brigid."*

THE PATH OF APPROACH

The Celts are the people of the end of the world. Just as the tip of the Cornwall peninsula is called Land's End, so too has Ireland been regarded since ancient days as the last stop before the mysterious otherworld located over the waters. Today that sense of mystery has been lost by knowledge of global geography—a traveler leaving the British Isles heading west arrives not at Tír na nÓg but rather comes to Boston or New York. But if we insist on approaching Celtic wisdom with a purely materialistic sense of things, then we run the risk of missing out on the glory and grandeur of their mystical sensibility. Britain and Ireland and Brittany may no longer be the ends of the physical earth, but they can still represent for us a final stopping place before that immense and mysterious journey to the spiritual world that lies just beyond the reaches of the senses.

THE PATH OF APPROACH

Who are the Celts? Are they simply the people of Ireland, Scotland, Wales, Cornwall, the Isle of Man, and Brittany (with Galicia thrown in for good measure)? Or does the Celtic world include anyone who can trace his or her ancestry back to one of these lands? For that matter, may we suppose that the Celtic experience also embraces anyone who comes to live in a Celtic land, or even anyone (of any ancestry or ethnicity) who feels called to explore the wisdom and spirituality of this ancient family of cultures and languages? Maybe the question needs to be put another way. What makes the Celtic world Celtic? What separates Celt from Saxon, or Roman, or Slav? Ah, but these are not the questions to be asking. Celtic wisdom (and spirituality) invites us to come together, not be separated off from one another. The Celtic way is the way of hospitality and of convivial fellowship— worrying about the impertinent details of life that separate us can wait for another day.

So if we need a definition of the Celtic world, let's leave it at the world that has its roots in languages such as Gaelic, Irish, Welsh, Breton, Cornish, and Manx. But although the Celtic experience begins with language, it doesn't end there. Culture, nature, a sense of place and tradition, and a deep love for Spirit all contribute to forging the Celtic identity.

THE PATH OF APPROACH

How can we approach Celtic wisdom today? Especially for those of us who live far away from the islands of our ancestors, what does it mean to walk a Celtic path? There is no single or straightforward answer to a question like this. The Celts are not so much philosophers as poets, not so much architects as artists. Celtic lore invites us to discover meaning through myth and symbol and dream; to celebrate life through the crashing of wave on rocks or the whisper of a winter wind. There can be no "Point A to Point B" logic behind following the Celtic way. Surely, we can study the bards and the druids and the saints, learn their stories, and consider how their lives illuminate our own. Indeed, no better way to embrace Celtic wisdom exists, at least as far as I can tell. But keep in mind that you or I can hear the same stories or ponder the same legends and draw quite different conclusions about the heart of the path we are called to walk. This is as it should be. For the Celtic path is not one of corporate standardization, but rather celebrates the same kind of abundant diversity that characterizes the natural world.

4

THE PATH OF SOVEREIGNTY

A part-historical, part-legendary Irish hero named Niall is said to have encountered a goddess who called herself Sovereignty. He was in the wilderness hunting with his brothers, and they stumbled across a sacred well attended by an ugly old hag. Thirsty, the oldest brother approached the water, but the crone blocked his way. "You can drink all you desire, young man, but first you must give me a kiss." Revolted at the mere thought, he backed away. The second oldest stepped forward, but received a similar challenge from the hideous woman. Each brother in turn declined the request for a kiss, until the youngest, Niall, stepped forward and offered the hag a full embrace. Their lips locked, and magic happened. When Niall stepped back, he found that the old crone had transformed herself into a radiant, lovely lady. "I am Sovereignty," she said, "and since you alone of your brothers has accepted me in my dark aspect, now I accept you as the king." And so it was that Niall became the king of the land.

THE PATH OF SOVEREIGNTY

Why was it important for Niall—or for any king, actually—to accept the ugly side of Sovereignty as a prerequisite to enjoying her beauty? Perhaps this story contains an ancient truth. Sunlight only shines for half of a day. Light emerges out of darkness, and so to reject darkness means to reject the original state of all things. Niall's brothers made the mistake of passing judgment on someone they deemed as ugly, repulsive, unattractive. Only the youngest brother could see that a kiss was a small price to pay for the nourishing waters. So what if the old woman wasn't so much to look at? And of course, by accepting her, he proved himself worthy to see that her decay is only part of her story.

There's a phrase for you: "only part of her story." Each one of us is a magnificent story, filled with heart, emotion, dreams, and desires. We also have our share of loss, disappointment, and sorrow. Think of when you encounter someone: an angry person standing in line at the post office; a harried mother with rude, bawling children; a government employee who's not interested in all the reasons why your taxes were paid late. When we encounter such people, we only encounter part of their stories. Sometimes, the parts we see are not to our liking. Perhaps we can take a lesson from Niall, and remember that there's more to them than meets the eye.

THE PATH OF SOVEREIGNTY

Irish myth tells how when the first Celts came to Ireland with the intention of settling, they met three goddesses—Banba, Fódla, and Ériu—each of whom offered to help the Celts in their quest to conquer the land, if only they would name the land after her. Ériu was the last of the three that they encountered, and they met her at the spiritual center of the land, and she offered the greatest amount of help to the invaders. So they promised her primacy in terms of the land bearing her name. And indeed, to this day Ireland (in Irish, Éire) takes its name from this goddess. The suggestion is clear: the land is divine, and the land is not only named for a goddess, but in a very real way the land embodies the spirit of the goddess. It's the spirit of Sovereignty, encoded in the very land.

THE PATH OF SOVEREIGNTY

The crone whom Niall kissed may be the most obvious example of a mythological figure in the Celtic tradition linked with the concept of Sovereignty—after all, she described herself as such. But she is hardly the only figure in the tradition who embodies this powerful spirit. Indeed, many goddesses in Celtic lore have a profound connection with the land, or with the king, or with the relationship between the two. Meadbh, who appears in Irish literature as a mythic queen, may have originally been a goddess linked with Tara, the traditional seat of the high king of the land. Meadbh's name means "she who intoxicates" and she may be linked with ancient rituals that conferred kingship onto a new leader through ritualized marriage with the goddess. Other Irish goddesses are associated with traditional seats for regional kings: the king of the northern province of Ulster ruled from Emain Macha, a site associated with the goddess Macha; while the royal seat of the western province of Connacht was associated with the Mórrígan, a goddess whose name means "great queen." Again and again, political authority and the relationship between the king and the land all points back to a profound spirituality—where the freedom of the people is bound up with the spirit of the Feminine Divine.

THE PATH OF SOVEREIGNTY

Why does Celtic spirituality draw this unusual link between the goddesses of the land, and the concept of Sovereignty? Maybe it has something to do with power. A king, after all, is a powerful person. A society can only function if its members are willing to support their leaders. But where does a king derive his power and authority? Most monarchies, at least in the Christian world, have suggested their royal power comes from God. Here, Celtic spirituality offers a radically different perspective. To the Celts, royal authority comes from the goddess: from the spirit of sovereignty, the spirit of the land. This is not meant to undermine belief in God in a traditional or Christian sense. But it does imply that the God of monotheism shares divine power, at least in the Celtic world. He shares power with the goddess, who is as connected to the earth and the land as surely as God is associated with heaven above. So the goddess is Sovereignty as a subtle way of saying that she answers to no one—not even God. She is God's partner in ordering the universe—not his slave.

THE PATH OF SOVEREIGNTY

The Irish language does not have a word for the coronation of a king; instead the ceremony by which a new king was installed was called the *banais righe*, or the wedding-feast of the king. Who was the king marrying? The goddess, of course: Sovereignty herself, in one of her various forms. Ancient annals describe this wedding-feast as involving two elements: the goddess (or a priestess assuming the role of goddess) offering a sacred drink to her new "husband"— perhaps mead, from which the goddess Meadbh takes her name; and then the consummation of the marriage itself, symbolizing a sacred union between the land and the people—land symbolized by the goddess, and people symbolized by their king. So here is a profound clue into the heart of Celtic wisdom: life is lived truly and bountifully out of a harmonious, marriage-like relationship between humanity and nature. Nature is not some inert resource for us to exploit as we wish, but rather is divine, and can be related to as a Divine Feminine: a goddess.

THE PATH OF SOVEREIGNTY

The Irish word for sovereignty is *flaitheas*. It is related to *flaithiúil*, a lovely word that means "generous." To understand the Celtic concept of sovereignty, consider how generosity can be related to it. The goddess of Sovereignty is, in essence, a generous, abundant, and nurturing spirit. The hag by the well was perfectly willing to share of her water. All she asked in return was one loving kiss.

As most people understand it today, sovereignty is not so much a topic related to generosity, but rather has to do with dominion (lordship). The sovereign is the lord, the one who gets to make all the rules and tell everyone else what to do. But that is hardly a Celtic understanding of the concept. Sovereignty in the Celtic world is the spirit of authentic freedom, which extends not only to the political freedom that an independent state enjoys, but also the empowered ability to relate to others out of a profound inner-directed liberty. This includes, of course, the power to be giving (generous) as circumstances dictate. The goddess can only be giving because she is free. This is a point well worth considering. Perhaps we can only be free to the extent that we are generous.

THE PATH OF SOVEREIGNTY

The fact that sovereignty is related to generosity contributes to one of the most powerful themes of Celtic wisdom: the importance of hospitality as a social virtue. Hospitality is basically the generosity shown to strangers and guests in our midst. Mythology abounds with stories that suggest a king rules well when his court is filled with hospitality—that a visitor must eat till satisfied before even beginning to discuss whatever business brought him to the royal hall. By contrast, kings who do not practice hospitality are satirized, the land goes barren under their rule, and ultimately they are forced to abandon the throne. Sovereignty is not only related to generosity, but to a specific type of generosity: hospitality, through which any and all may benefit from the land's abundance and the king's largesse. From this we can get a clear sense that, to the ancient Celts, the goddess is more than just a kind of female version of the Almighty—she is a powerful presence who stands for the spirit of charity, generosity, and care for others, qualities that lead in turn to the blessings of abundance and prosperity from the land.

THE PATH OF SOVEREIGNTY

Why does the link between the goddess, the concept of sovereignty, and the concepts of generosity and hospitality matter to us today? After all, no society today (Celtic or otherwise) inaugurates its leaders by performing a symbolic sacred union with the goddess! But the importance of these concepts resides not so much in their political implications, as in their spiritual relevance to each of us as individual persons. After all, I may never be the leader of a nation, but I have "sovereignty" over my own life. As a follower of Celtic wisdom, I can see that my personal freedom is related to how I choose to relate to my environment—to the land on which I live. I can also see that I am only truly free if I can freely choose to be generous and practice the virtue of hospitality. In other words: in today's world, each one of us can be called to the role of "king"—to enter into intimate relations with the goddess of the land, and find in her spirit of Sovereignty the power to foster a life that is spiritually meaningful and rewarding; in other words, a life of generosity and hospitality.

THE PATH OF THE DRUID

If there's one word firmly associated with Celtic mysticism, it is "druid." And yet probably no other concept connected with the spirituality of the Celts is less understood, or more frequently consigned to the mists of fantasy. We have only a handful of written records from ancient times (when the original druids were still active in the Celtic lands, prior to the coming of Christianity), and the druids themselves wrote none of these. Instead, Greek and Roman authors like Julius Caesar and Pliny have given us what little information we have about the earliest druids—and when you consider how some of these classical authors were biased against the Celts, it's easy to see how this source material is not only scanty, but unreliable.

We're not even entirely sure what the word druid means, although the popular notion that it has to do with "oak wisdom" is as good a theory as any. Seen this way, a druid is a natural philosopher, one who discerns the innate wisdom of the earth and interprets it for the good of the community. So when modern folks dismiss the druids as "tree huggers," they're probably not too far from the truth. But a druid would reply in an ironic tone of voice, "You say that like it's a bad thing?"

THE PATH OF THE DRUID

The ancient writers who comment on the druids say that they were the spiritual and intellectual leaders of the Celtic world, and that their function in society included not only presiding at religious ceremonies, but also serving as scientists, philosophers, counselors, mediators, and seers. In other words, they were not just otherworldly dreamers, but collectively served as the "think tank" of the ancient Celtic world. In the modern world, it's easy to forget the intellectual/scientific dimension of the druids, but in ancient times such mental skill would have been an essential part of a druid's life. The druids were not driven by intuition or psychic hunches (attending to those kinds of stimuli would have been the job of the seer, another specific function in Celtic society), but by knowledge, reason, and wisdom. That this mental agility was embedded in spiritual activity would not have been considered odd, for throughout the ancient world, science and religion had not yet undergone the divorce that would separate them at the dawn of the modern world. In the world of the druids, true wisdom meant being knowledgable about inner matters and external realities in a holistic and integrated way.

THE PATH OF THE DRUID

Much of what the classical writers had to say about the druids smacks of propaganda that would have been useful to Roman generals seeking support for their military excursions in the Celtic world. After all, if the druids are really so barbaric as to perform massive human sacrifices where dozens of hapless victims are burned alive, wouldn't it be a service to civilization to put them out of business?

Truth be told, it does appear that druids performed human sacrifice, although evidence is not widespread and so such practices may have been considered an extreme measure, at times of severe famine or imminent invasion. And it seems a bit disingenuous that representatives of a society that entertained itself with gladiators would dismiss the druids as barbaric!

So at the end of the day, we really know very little about the ancient druids, their beliefs, and their rituals. Later folklore and mythology of the Celtic world offers some ideas as to what these ancient philosopher-priests (and -priestesses) would have been like, but these sources date from a time when druidism had already been extinct for centuries. Meanwhile, a colorful assortment of "revivals" of druidism over the last 250 years tell us more about modern spirituality (and romanticism) than about the ancient wisdom they are supposedly reconstructing.

THE PATH OF THE DRUID

The Roman historian Pliny provides us with one of the most memorable of images associated with the druids—the collecting of mistletoe. On the sixth day after the new moon, the druid would climb into an oak tree and cut the mistletoe with a golden sickle, dropping it onto a white cloak held by others on the ground—it was unlucky for the mistletoe to touch the ground. It would then be prepared and used as a healing herb. Meanwhile, the ceremony would culminate with the sacrifice of two white bulls. This unusual ritual has become one of the most popular images of ancient druidry, and I know of at least one organization of modern druids that duly performs a "Mistletoe Rite" every month on the sixth night of the moon. But no one other than Pliny discusses the ceremony, leading some to question whether it had any grounding in reality. Perhaps it was a one-time event that Pliny witnessed, or for that matter, perhaps he (or his source) fabricated the entire affair. The take-away: we never know how others will view us. We never know how accurate our perception of others really is. These are points worth keeping in mind.

THE PATH OF THE DRUID

The ancient druids were said to believe in reincarnation. They were soothsayers and diviners, and were as necessary for the performing of ancient Celtic sacrifices as a Catholic priest is to the consecration of the Eucharistic host. They were knowledgable about the planets, and the natural world, and moral philosophy, and yet they taught by the use of riddles and enigmas. If all of this is beginning to sound like a hodge-podge, well, it is. So little information is available to truly shed light on the earliest Celtic priests. In her book *Druid Shaman Priest*, scholar Leslie Ellen Jones suggests that succeeding generations have reinvented the ways we think about the druids, in ways that make this mysterious order of magical intellectuals relevant to our modern world.

There's a lesson in there. It's not only the druids that we constantly reinvent. We reinvent God (such as the notion of the Divine Feminine—the Goddess). We reinvent our understanding of what it means to be Celtic, or to be spiritual, or to be wise. There's not necessarily anything wrong with this—but it seems like it would be a good idea to remember that such processes of revising how we understand our world and ourselves are perpetually going on.

THE PATH OF THE DRUID

Beginning in the sixteenth and seventeenth centuries, antiquarians and amateur archaeologists began to explore theories about the prehistoric stone circles and other ancient monuments in the British Isles. Their pet theory? That such sites were originally the temples of the druids. Today we can easily dismiss the inaccuracies of such speculation—we know that Celtic culture only arrived in the British Isles around 500 BCE, centuries after sites like Stonehenge and Newgrange were constructed. But within the framework of the world-view of three centuries ago, such ideas were electrifying. Western society was moving out of the middle ages and into the modern world; nations were being formed and the soul of the modern, secular, scientific age was being born. In this epochal age, people sought their roots, and a vision of druids constructing or using the megalithic sites seemed as good an entry as any into the dreams of the past.

Are earlier notions of who the druids were mere folly and fantasy? Yes, perhaps. But if we learn one thing from the errors of the past, let it be this: we have no more of a lock on the "truth" about the druids today than the antiquarians of the seventeenth century had in their time. Perhaps our image of the shamanistic nature-loving priests will someday be just as quaint as the druids-as-stone-age-engineers.

THE PATH OF THE DRUID

A legendary meeting of druids is said to have taken place at a London tavern in 1717, attended by delegates of druidic and bardic orders from throughout the Celtic world. Scholars today doubt that such a meeting ever really occurred, but it lives on as a myth in the traditions of several modern druid groups—and what a singularly appropriate myth, seeing the rebirth of druidry not in a stone circle or sacred grove, but at a pub! Some sixty-four years later, a secret society called the Ancient Order of Druids was founded, and this marks the reliable history of druidism reborn (and yes, this order's organizational meeting took place in a pub). For almost two hundred years, druidism was a blend of fraternal organization and national identity (especially in Wales, where bardic competitions became popular beginning in the nineteenth century). Many of the stereotypes that dog druidism today arose from the fraternal druid orders, which consisted of English gentlemen, wearing white robes and performing ceremonies in London parks as well as more traditionally sacred sites like Glastonbury or Stonehenge. For these druids, the Celtic wisdom-keepers of old were revered not so much for their religious beliefs or intellectual function as for their symbolic value as the cultural forefathers of the land.

THE PATH OF THE DRUID

J the eighteenth century druid revival began in a pub, another humorous chapter in the history of the druids dates to 1960s North America. At Carleton College in Minnesota, students were required to attend chapel regularly—unless they were participants in the regular religious ceremonies of a non-Christian religion. So in 1963 a group of clever students organized a "druid grove," mainly so that they could skip chapel and hang out in the woods. The college, perhaps sensitive to the satirical nature of this assembly, dropped the chapel requirements shortly thereafter—but the druids found that their organization thrived, no longer as a form of ironic protest but as a genuine (if somewhat anarchic) spiritual movement. This organization, known as the Reformed Druids of North America, eventually inspired other, more earnest druid groups, such as the Henge of Keltria or Ár nDraíocht Féin. Meanwhile, across the ocean, British druids were undergoing a similar process of transformation from the secular fraternal groups of old, to younger, hipper, more pagan-identified communities that characterize the new face of druidry for tomorrow.

And so the druids continue their process of reinvention. What will the future hold?

THE PATH OF THE DRUID

Neopagan ("new pagan") druidry is a creative spiritual force, combining knowledge of myth and folklore with a body of ritual designed to honor the earth and celebrate community. Leaders of neopagan druids speculate on the spirituality of polytheism and pantheism for today, and consider the implications of deep, nature mysticism for today's urbanized society. Of course, not everyone with an interest in Celtic matters will embrace the new druidism, if for no other reason than the ongoing vitality of the Christian faith, especially in Ireland and North America. In some ways, the druids of old really are lost—druidism has not been an independent and socially influential intellectual or philosophical movement for at least 1500 years. But the attempts at reviving druidism, even as a minority cultural or spiritual movement, speak to the ongoing need for Celtic wisdom—even if its influence is marginal rather than mainstream.

In thinking about druidism for today and tomorrow, bear in mind what the word druid probably means: "oak wisdom." Whether you see druids as a long-lost priesthood, or a symbol for Celtic shamanism, or a doorway into a nature-based spirituality, keep wisdom in mind as the essential element for the druids. You don't have to join a druid group, wear a white robe, or collect mistletoe in order to celebrate the spirit of the druids. All that is required is a commitment to wisdom.

THE PATH OF NATURE

Perhaps the single most attractive element of Celtic wisdom and spirituality is its link with nature. Celtic mysticism is the mysticism of the earth. This crosses religious lines—Christians embrace the Celtic love of nature as fully as do neopagans. From the windswept islands of the Hebrides, to the lush verdant fields in Ireland, to the panoramic coastlines of Cornwall, the Celtic world is brimming with the majesty of nature—and this has, from the beginning, shaped the Celtic soul.

The sense of nature as divine or holy is hardly unique to the Celts. Native American wisdom is clear in its respect for Mother Nature and insistence that a balanced life means walking in harmony with the environment. Similar themes may be found throughout primal and shamanistic cultures worldwide. For that matter, the Jewish tradition has a strong history of insisting that the earth be cared for—the commandment to remember the Sabbath is not just a religious directive, but also implies that society needs to refrain from over-working the land.

So the Celtic tradition of venerating nature is not alone. Which is another way of saying that the profound earth mysticism of the Celts is, ultimately, of universal importance.

THE PATH OF NATURE

Why is Celtic nature mysticism so attractive? To begin with, the culture of the West—which traces its roots back to the Roman Empire and its reliance on centralized, urban government—seems to have lost its way regarding nature. The political and business climate throughout Europe, America, and increasingly the rest of the world, regards the environment as a resource, and efforts at conservation or environmental protection are chiefly designed to preserve those resources for long-term usage. Rarely is a sense of nature as divine, as sacred, as valuable in itself, seriously considered. And yet this is the heart of the Celtic understanding of nature. Nowhere is this seen more clearly than in the link between the goddess, the land, and sovereignty. A king does not assume the right to manage the land, or exploit, or utilize its resources. Rather he marries the land, in the persona of the sovereign goddess. Goddess and king are partners—what we know of pre-Roman Celtic law suggests that marriage was often seen as a joining of equals. What would our world look like today, if we could begin to see the environment as our partner, rather than our resource?

THE PATH OF NATURE

The connection between humankind and nature was, to the ancient Celts, an essentially moral relationship. If a king ruled with wisdom and justice, the land responded with abundance and prosperity—cows gave plentiful milk, the land yielded bountiful harvests, and the trees were laden with fruit. But under a king whose reign was unjust or inhospitable, the land withdrew her blessings. Crop failure, drought, and meager harvests were linked not to the arbitrary whims of capricious nature, but rather to the failings of a king (and, by extension, to the people he governed). Mythically speaking, the remedy of such a problem was to find a new king—symbolic of establishing a new, and healthier, relationship with the sacred land. Simply put, when nature is encountered relationally, then nature has a claim on how she is treated. It matters what we do in regard to our environment. This is the heart of Celtic mysticism.

THE PATH OF NATURE

For many people, Celtic nature spirituality is mostly a romanticized kind of thing. We can travel to Tintagel or Glendalough or Iona and be enraptured by the many faces of the goddess—lush or austere, majestic or severe. We can find peace by a holy well or ponder the mysteries in a ring of standing stones. Our imaginations can be beguiled by stories of the fairy folk—never mind the ominous or dangerous edge to the fairy faith; we'll just enjoy the idea of spirits inhabiting our gardens. It's all lovely, poetic, and beautiful. But does it really make a difference in our lives? How does Celtic nature spirituality *matter*?

The question is a subtle pun. For "matter" comes from the same Latin root as does "matrix" (womb) and "mother." To make something matter—anything, not just nature mysticism—means to imbue it with relationship, meaning, purpose, as symbolized by the most primal and powerful of all relationships, that between mother and child. Catholic Ireland is full of imagery of the madonna and child, but this is far more than just religious artwork. It's truly an icon of the most profound relationship of all, that between the earth and her children. So how do we find, in our sentimental love for the glorious beauty of nature, a genuine relationship between humanity and the environment? As we answer that question, we will be taking an important step toward making the Celtic tradition come alive in our midst.

THE PATH OF NATURE

Saying that the ancient Celts were pagan is kind of like saying that they were Celts: we're using a word to describe them that did not originate with them. It was the Greeks who named the Celts, and the Roman Christians who coined the religious meaning for the word *pagani*, which originally suggested civilian or country-dweller. But the country-dweller sense of the word means that it is not entirely inappropriate—after all, the Celts had no cities until the Romans or Vikings or Normans came along and built them. As a rural people, they naturally found their spiritual compass in the waters of the sea, the whispers of the wind, the fertility of the land. Their faith certainly was not "pagan" in the later pejorative sense of amoral or superstitious, but rather embodied a profound sense of being held in the embrace of the wild earth, her raging seas, and her abundant life. The pre-Christian Celts were likely animistic—regarding everything as imbued with spiritual presence. This survived after the arrival of Christianity, where heaven and the presence of God were seen not as removed from the natural world, but intimately interwoven within it. Nature was seen not just as an image of beauty—she truly embodied Divine love and grace.

THE PATH OF NATURE

The pagan spirituality of the Celts has been a significant inspiration to the neopagan ("new pagan") movement that began in England in the mid-twentieth century and has since spread throughout the English-speaking world, as well as Europe and beyond. Although much of the modern pagan movement is undermined by an uncritical overemphasis on magic and psychic phenomena, the heart of the new paganism reflects a sincere effort to re-sacralize nature, to awaken the sleeping goddess of the land and restore a sense of humanity as living in relationship with her. Since this is such an integral, if not always conscious, part of the Celtic world, neopagans have embraced many elements of Celtic wisdom, from the myths, to the gods and goddesses, to Gaelic folk holidays and ceremonial customs. Some modern pagans carefully seek to integrate Celtic culture into their spirituality in respectful and considerate ways; others simply treat the Celtic tradition as a consumable resource (ironic, given how its greatest strength may be in the way it can teach us alternatives to the consumer lifestyle).

THE PATH OF NATURE

The great achievement of Christianity in the Celtic world came not from how it triumphed over the pagan spirituality that existed prior to its arrival, but—on the contrary—how it more or less seamlessly integrated the earth-honoring traditions of the pagan Celts into its singular vision of faith. Celtic Christianity is nature Christianity. Nowhere is this more clearly set forth than in the *Lorica* of Saint Patrick, a poem-prayer that invokes Divine protection:

> *I bind unto myself today*
> *The virtues of the star-lit heaven,*
> *The glorious sun's life-giving ray,*
> *The whiteness of the moon at even,*
> *The flashing of the lightning free,*
> *The whirling wind's tempestuous shocks,*
> *The stable earth, the deep salt sea*
> *Around the old eternal rocks.*
>
> (Translated by Cecil F. H. Alexander)

The entire poem is primarily about protection in Christ (as befits a Christian poem). But as the above stanza clearly shows, the grace of Celtic Christianity is mediated as fully through nature as through church or word or sacrament.

THE PATH OF NATURE

In the *Carmina Gadelica*, an anthology of Scottish folk prayers and poems collected in the late-nineteenth century, we see how Celtic Christianity carried its nature-positive spirituality into the modern world. The ordinary Christian folk of Gaelic-speaking Scotland offered prayers and the poetry of praise at every moment of the day, and in every setting—from rising out of bed, to stoking the fire, to milking the cow, to traveling or fishing or spinning thread. "Nature" in this rich spiritual tradition means more than just the environment. Arising out of the essential truth that all things are part of nature—including humanity and the culture of the world we've created—the *Carmina Gadelica* sings of the natural presence of God and Mary and all the saints (with the occasional pagan god or goddess thrown in) throughout the daily rhythm of life. There is no separation between nature and grace, or between nature and humanity—or between nature and the divine. All is interwoven. And that tapestry is held together in the language of devotion and praise.

THE PATH OF NATURE

Relating to nature as a Sacred Other, not as an exploitable resource ... allowing nature to function as a means of grace in our lives ... recognizing that nature means more than just the unspoiled wilderness, but in a deeper and more real sense encompasses all aspects of the material world—these are but a few of the treasures revealed to us by the simple yet richly-textured tradition of Celtic nature mysticism. And as we conclude this path within the Celtic tradition, bear this in mind: just as you are not separate from God, or not separate from nature, or not separate from grace, so too are you not separate from the rich tradition of Celtic wisdom. Whether you are a Celt by ancestry or by the stirrings of your heart, if you embrace the Celtic tradition, you are part of it. Which means that the choices you make, the poems you write, the decisions you come to in your life to honor the natural world, are all part of the ongoing symphony of Celtic mysticism. Celtic spirituality is not a museum installation; it is a living path of insight and illumination. Consider how you can honor the goddess of the land and allow the grace of nature to flow in your life. Then you will become a living conduit of the Celtic way.

THE PATH OF THE BARD

The tale is told that long ago, with the transition from oral tradition to the preservation of lore in medieval manuscripts, somehow the great Irish epic *The Tain* (the Cattle-Raid of Cooley) had been lost. Sadly, no one survived who knew the tale. Like a language that had died, the rich stories and myths surrounding the tale of the war in Ulster had disappeared, seemingly forever.

But not so fast. Around the year 600 CE, a great Irish bard named Senchán Torpéist attempted to gather the missing strands of the story together, so that it might be remembered and handed down to future generations. He consulted with various bards and poets and scribes, all of whom knew part of the story, none of whom knew the entire narrative. When it seemed futile and he was on the verge of giving up, the bard received a vision. In it he was visited by Fergus mac Róich, one of the great mythic kings and heroes of Ulster, and a tutor to the young hero, Cúchulainn. In the vision, Fergus carefully recounted every detail of *The Tain* to Senchán Torpéist, and so the story was saved. The bard saw to it that it was written down, and so the epic survives to this very day.

THE PATH OF THE BARD

The story of Senchán Torpéist and the remembering of *The Tain* provides an important glimpse into the role of the bard in Celtic society. To begin with, the bards were the keepers of history. Far more than mere poets, their job was to preserve the memory of the people, by safeguarding the genealogies and stories of great and valorous heroes, from the recent to the distant past. Clearly, if a tale as noble and heroic as *The Tain* had been lost, there had been a breakdown in the bardic system. In our world of Hollywood-style adaptations of stories, it might seem like no big deal if a story is lost—just make up a new one. But this would have been unthinkable to a bard. Any story worth telling is a story worth remembering—it is an aspect of the lore of the people. So the bard's role was not only to entertain and inform, but perhaps more importantly, to archive and preserve.

THE PATH OF THE BARD

So what could a bard do when an important element of the lore had been lost? In a way, the loss of *The Tain* is a metaphor for the loss of the entire pre-Christian Celtic tradition. We see how Senchán Torpéist attempted to remedy the problem: first, by gathering what fragments existed and by attempting to reconstruct the story from them, almost as one would try to repair a broken piece of fine crystal by reassembling the various fragments. So the bard's role as archivist could extend to being a historical detective, looking at all that we do know as a way of trying to close the gap on what we don't know. After all, to understand who we are today, and to guess where we're going, it's fairly important to recognize who we've been and where we're coming from. So by carefully preserving (or investigating) the past, the bard gives us in the present perhaps the most valuable gift possible: self-knowledge.

THE PATH OF THE BARD

In the end, Senchán Torpéist revived *The Tain* not by detective work or by educated guesswork—he received supernatural assistance. The spirit of one of the ancient heroes visits him, and sets the record straight. And thus, the seventh-century bard is able to preserve a story that probably dates back some five to six hundred years before his time. So we come to another important characteristic of the bards. Their skills and training extended beyond those of a mere journalist or historian—their poetry was regarded as having a spiritual component, making them not only poets, but prophets as well (prophecy meaning not only the ability to speak of the future, but in its broader sense of the ability to speak any spiritually-sourced truth). In Ireland, the bards were known as the *filidh*, a word best translated as "seer-poet." The eloquence of the bard came not only from their own training and natural abilities, but also from their abilities to communicate with the otherworld. As a weaver of words and a preserver of memories, the bard also played a necessary third function: as a spokesperson for Spirit. Indeed, the *filidh* were regarded as having magical abilities. Which is not too surprising, considering that the order of bards probably originated in the ancient priestly function of the druids.

THE PATH OF THE BARD

The bard's magic could be described in a single word: enchantment. Chanting, of course, is related to song, but an enchantment is a song with something extra: an altered state, a doorway to the spiritual realm. Enchantment is what separates garden-variety entertainment from the true bard's art, where his or her talents are used to bring divine transformation into the world.

Think of Gregorian chant. It's a style of music that has been used in Christian monasteries for a thousand years, and yet in the late twentieth century several CDs of such unadorned singing were bestsellers, with millions of copies sold to people who had little or no connection with organized religion. Why? Naturally, because the music was enchanting. People described it as soothing, relaxing, peaceful, meditative—all words that speak of a mild altered state of consciousness that the music helped foster. Herein lies another clue to the power of the bards. Much Celtic music, from airs on a harp to lively jigs played on a fiddle, embodies a similar ability to entrance the listener—to snap him or her into a sonically-induced mystical state. In the hands of a true bard, such musical magic is not merely an impressive show, but a ceremonial means of finding inner transformation.

THE PATH OF THE BARD

The bards of old did not merely sing praises and recite poetry of glorious and mighty deeds. Granted, that may have been their stock in trade when working for a wealthy patron, but legend insists that the bards could curse as well as charm. Indeed, Irish myth clearly describes how a talented bard's satire could raise blisters on a previously unblemished face—a not inconsiderable feat, with profound implications for a king whose right to rule lay partially in his flawless physique. Indeed, much of the dramatic tension of the earliest cycle of Irish myths comes when the bard Cairbre satirizes the inhospitable Fomorian king Bres, causing boils to erupt on his face and thereby setting into motion the forces which would depose him—and lead to the greatest of legendary battles.

Cursing is not something that we moderns like to think of as a "spiritual" activity. Yet the interesting part of Celtic cultural history is that cursing is found among both the pagans and the Christians of old. Perhaps we don't like cursing because we secretly wish to believe that the world is a benign place where no hostile forces exist. The ancients certainly knew better, and wanted their spiritual leaders to have a psychic arsenal ready to protect themselves from malevolent energies.

THE PATH OF THE BARD

One way we can find meaning in the bard's ability to satirize an unjust or inhospitable king would be to think of the bard's vocation in terms of helping people to see things from a new angle. Sure, to the extent that the bard praises the worthy king, it's a straightforward job. But sometimes, it is the job of a poet or a storyteller to make sure we see things from an alternative perspective. In ancient times, this meant presenting the actions of the unjust leader in a humorous or ironic way. Nowadays, we no longer have poet-historians, but we do have storytellers, journalists, essayists, and other contributors to the public debate. For these modern "bards," it might simply mean refusing to buy in to the "official" way of seeing things. No, what the government says is not the only way the world is. No, what religious leaders, or scientific leaders, or business leaders have to say is not necessarily the ultimate truth. A gifted bard may not speak words of such satirical potency that they cause blisters to burst forth, but he or she may nevertheless invite listeners to consider choices and possibilities that might otherwise go unnoticed and unexamined.

THE PATH OF THE BARD

Can the ordinary person be a bard? Well, maybe few of us will ever master the intricate knowledge of history and lore that an ancient bard was required to know; after all, the bards of old, like their druidic peers, had to study anywhere from twelve to twenty years before they were considered masters of their craft. In our day, such training does not exist; let alone opportunities for anyone to ply the bard's trade. Even so, this does not mean that the spirit of the bard is lost. Anyone who tells stories with a dash of magic or mythology is walking in the path of the bards. Anyone who integrates poetry, music, history, and prophecy into their way of seeing the world and sharing it with others is living as an aspiring bard. And anyone who uses their skills as a communicator to invite others to consider alternative ways of seeing the world— especially in regard to those who wield power—is certainly on the bardic path.

So don't think of the gifts of the bard as unattainable to you today. Maybe the deep secrets of Taliesin (the greatest of Welsh bards) are lost, but there are other, humble ways to do your part to keep the spirit of the bard alive.

THE PATH OF THE BARD

What would it take to be a bard today? First of all, give up on the idea of calling yourself a bard. For starters, if you haven't studied for over a decade or mastered at least several hundred mythic poems or tales, you don't deserve the title. But it's okay to describe yourself as an *aspiring* bard. Now, what exactly do you aspire to? Poetry. Music. Song. Story. Alternative ways of seeing the world. Consider how you can integrate these art forms into your spirituality and your daily life. Remember what separates a bard from an entertainer: look at how you can use language and music not merely to show off how clever you are, but to truly bring joy and meaning to the world of spirit, and likewise to help bring the world of spirit to those who hear your artistry. Finally, if you do not wish to explore the path of the bard for yourself, then find ways to cultivate and nurture such skills in others. Listen to their stories, dance to their music, comment on their perspective. Allow the (aspiring) bards in your life to transform you.

THE PATH OF MYTHOLOGY

Perhaps no single element is more important to the spirit of Celtic wisdom than myth. I don't mean myth in the sense of "something that people falsely believe to be true" like the many urban legends that circulate around the Internet. No, the streets of America are not filled with kidney thieves, nor did Nostradamus predict the 9/11 disaster. Rather, the myth that is so essential to the Celtic world is the matter of mythology— the stories, legends, poems, ballads, and folklore that speak to a world beyond space and time, where gods and goddesses, heroes and heroines, warriors and bards dwell—and where in their magical and dramatic lives, we can find insight into the mystery and majesty of our own.

Some aspects of Celtic myth and lore are commonplace: just about anyone who's heard of Ireland has heard of banshees or leprechauns. Most everyone knows that Patrick evicted the snakes from Ireland, and that King Arthur's knights spent the better part of their careers searching for the Holy Grail. But the layers of myth go far, far deeper. And what is often ignored when mythic stories are told or retold is what they mean—why they're so important. Of course, sometimes such meaning is best left unsaid, so that each person may discover anew how the myths speak to him or her.

THE PATH OF MYTHOLOGY

The single best collection of myths in the Celtic world comes from Ireland; the other significant body of myth was preserved in Wales. Both Irish and Welsh myth were committed to written form in the Middle Ages, by Christian scribes, most if not all of whom were monastic. This leads to a number of unanswerable—yet difficult—questions. Are the myths simply the product of imaginative storytellers, or do they hearken back to an ancient, pagan belief system? How many of the myths have been lost? Of the ones that survived the ages, how much pagan lore did the Christian scribes who preserved them censor, consciously or unconsciously? Of course, we'll never be able to answer these questions definitively, although scholars have made a number of educated guesses. The good news? The written myths do seem to point to an earlier time; some of the stories preserved may have originated as early as the first century CE. The bad news: yes, there's a lot missing. Yes, there's no doubt that the Christians tampered with their pagan source material (the damage was worse in Wales than in Ireland). But the extent of this loss is itself shrouded in mystery. All we can do is take what we have, and attempt to understand the grandeur of the Celtic past based on fragmentary evidence. And then keep the myths alive, by telling the stories, and identifying ways to apply this ancient wisdom today.

THE PATH OF MYTHOLOGY

As the stories, particularly in the Irish tradition, have come down to us, they are organized neither by chronology nor by key characters, but by theme. The myths include battles, invasions, wooings, visions, cattle-raids, adventures, voyages, feasts, deaths, and so forth. Modern storytellers, however, have tended to try to put the tales into some semblance of order, and so have developed a series of cycles that cover the sweep of Irish mythic history, from the first inhabitants of the land up to the semi-legendary tales of early historical kings. As might be expected, the myths begin with the exploits of gods and godlike beings; eventually such supernatural figures are reduced to fairies. But even the mortal heroes have a larger-than-life quality about them, a theme that plays out in several tales that involve time-travel: someone from the mythic era, upon encountering mortals from a later age, always finds them as small and weak compared to the robust heroes of old.

THE PATH OF MYTHOLOGY

We have no Celtic creation myth. That may be because the Christians who preserved the myths felt it improper to recount a story that contradicted the book of Genesis. But it may also say something about the Celtic understanding of the universe—not as a stage that at some original moment was fashioned *ex nihilo*, but as an endlessly woven knot or spiral of existence, without beginning, without end. Irish myth begins with a series of "invasions"—stories about the first inhabitants of Ireland, who came in wave after mythic wave of settlers, invaders and conquerors. The drama mounts with each new tribe or family, culminating in three climactic battles, in which gods, heroes, demons, and finally, mortals, fight for sovereignty and ascendancy. The last of these battles sets the stage for the ongoing relationship between mortals and spirits—we humans live above the surface, while the gods/fairies/ancestors dwell in the underworld.

That first sequence of stories is called the Mythological Cycle. Next comes the Ulster Cycle, so called because most of the action takes place in Ireland's northern province. The Ulster Cycle tells the story of Cúchulainn, the greatest of Celtic warriors, and his mighty exploits, particularly during the cattle raid of Cooley when Queen Meadbh attempts to steal a great brown bull—and Cúchulainn single-handedly opposes her.

THE PATH OF MYTHOLOGY

In the Heroic Cycle of Irish myth we meet Fionn mac Cumhaill, who is not a god, or the son of one, but rather an ordinary boy who gains his supernatural skills by eating a magical fish. Fionn becomes the leader of a legendary band of hunter-warriors called the Fenians, whose job it is to serve as guardians of the land. Such guardianship could have spiritual as well as military implications—indeed, Fionn proves himself to the high king by successfully defeating a fairy monster that had taken to burning the great hall at Tara to the ground every year at Samhain. The tales of Fionn and the members of his war band, however, have as much to do with their own interpersonal dynamics as with enemies they must vanquish.

Then comes the Historic Cycle, fourth and final of the Irish mythic cycles. These tales are the least otherworldly of the myths, although enough interaction between the human and fairy realms takes place in these adventures to make them worthy of the best storyteller. Actual historical figures begin to show up, although often with mythic elements interwoven into their stories—like George Washington throwing the coin across the river, these tales represent the rubbing places where myth and history meet. A favorite theme in the Historic Cycle involves human encounters with otherworld beings—setting the stage, naturally enough, for the rich legacy to follow in the centuries-old fairy tradition of the common Celtic people.

THE PATH OF MYTHOLOGY

Welsh mythology, unfortunately, is neither as comprehensive nor as coherent as its Irish counterpart. Although the oldest manuscripts are about the same age as those preserved in Ireland, the stories they contain seem either younger, or more thoroughly tampered with. Post-Celtic religious and social ideas permeate the Welsh tradition, making these tales an interesting bridge between the more purely pagan myths of Ireland, and the high chivalry of the Arthurian legends—which grew out of Welsh myth but found their fullest expression in the courts of medieval France.

The key story cycle in the Welsh tradition is the Four Branches of the Mabinogi, often misspelled as Mabinogion, thanks to an error on the part of one of the first translators to render these tales into modern English. In this collection of myths we meet goddesses like Rhiannon, gods like Bran, heroes like Pwyll, and druids like Gwydion. The tales of the Mabinogi repeatedly explore mother–son relationships, leading many to feel that it represents an initiation into a cult of the mother goddess and her beloved son–god. Often included in modern translations of the Mabinogi are several other stories and romances, including one of the earliest tales of the Holy Grail, several heroic quests, and the moving, shamanistic tale of the birth of the great bard Taliesin.

THE PATH OF MYTHOLOGY

It's great fun to explore history with an eye to discovering the fate of the "real" Arthur. Probably a tribal chieftain in the chaos of Britain after fifth-century Roman troops suddenly withdrew, he may have been a leader in fighting against the encroaching Saxon presence on the island. Our knowledge of the historical figure—assuming he ever existed—can only be speculative, but the development of the mythic King Arthur is far easier to trace. He began as a shadowy figure in Welsh poetry and Romance, only to become something of a literary sensation after being exported to Brittany and France. The marriage of Celtic myth and medieval courtly literature proved powerful enough to still arouse our hearts and imaginations a thousand years later. The Arthurian cycle grew in the telling, combining shadowy figures like Merlin and Morgan LeFay, whose origins clearly lie in Celtic myth, with more purely literary creations like Lancelot. Ironically, the tales of King Arthur have long eclipsed all other forms of Celtic mythology as the image of Celtic romance that most people would first think of—ironic because the Arthurian saga is the least authentically Celtic of any myths associated with this heritage.

THE PATH OF MYTHOLOGY

In our modern efforts to understand the wisdom and lore of the ancient Celts, we have other resources besides just the stories of myth. A wonderful collection of "triads"—a literary form used as a tool for memorizing key information—provides glimpses into the lore of the ancients, as does a charming Irish anthology called the *Dindshenchas* ("the lore of prominent places"), which collects legends and poems that explain the names of natural features in the landscape. Many such names have mythical origins, and so the stories in the *Dindshenchas* provide as much of an insight into myth as into the history of names.

Finally, there is the vast body of folklore: oral (and more recently, written) traditions of tales, poems, and ballads, some of which have fascinating similarities to the old myths, all of which provide insights into how the Celtic mind works and how Celts, from ancient times to the present, have made sense out of the world in which they live.

Both Irish and Welsh myth come to us in fragmentary form, a frustrating matter for the modern seeker of wisdom. But remember what was said of the druids: "they speak in riddles ... hinting of things and leaving a great deal to be understood." In a way, the mythic tradition is the greatest riddle of all.

THE PATH OF MYTHOLOGY

Mythology lives. Sure, there may not be as many traditional storytellers as there were a century ago, and fewer people may speak the old Celtic languages, but the tales have a way of reinventing themselves or adapting for a new generation. Many Celtic authors, poets, and illustrators have reinterpreted the old tales in new ways, whether directly (as in the retelling of myths by Lady Gregory) or obliquely (as in the way James Joyce wove Fionn mac Cumhaill into his dark and puzzling masterpiece *Finnegans Wake*). Meanwhile, the explosion of interest in Celtic spirituality among the neopagan community has ensured that the old stories will continue to be told, perhaps with more feeling than has been the case for 1500 years. What's important to remember is that the stories do not have to conform to a canon or critical edition of any sort. They are tales that live and breathe, and every storyteller who recounts these old adventures, whether aloud or in print, will put his or her own spin on how the tale is told. Details will change, plotlines will evolve, and characters will mature. It's a mistake to worry about getting myth "right." Far more useful is to continually ask, "What can this story tell me about myself, and my world?" For that is the mark of a true myth, even when the details are fuzzy.

THE PATH OF THE SEER

Aside from the druids and bards, the third kind of Celtic wisdomkeepers according to ancient tradition consisted of the seers, or ovates. Classical writers referring to the Celts of mainland Europe indicate that seers, bards and druids were three distinct communities; while in other areas these categories may have been more integrated. For example, in Ireland we find the tradition of the *filidh*, or visionary-poets—a kind of wisdomkeeper who combines the qualities of bards and seers.

What makes a seer? Begin with the word itself: one who sees. So the seers were the visionaries, the mystics and psychics who were able to receive information from the otherworldly realms. The seers were gifted at interpreting the signs of nature—the omens that could be discerned in the patterns of birds in flight or of clouds overhead. As diviners, the seers were gifted at scrying—the ability to tease meaning and wisdom out of the patterns of a burning flame or a convulsing sacrifice. Whatever the medium, the seer was responsible for receiving raw data, interpreting it, and communicating its meaning to others as messages from the spirit world.

THE PATH OF THE SEER

One gifted seer from Irish myth, the druid Cathbad, uttered a prophecy concerning the birth of a girl who would be named Deirdre. His gloomy prediction foretold of great suffering that would ensue thanks to her (or rather, thanks to stupid things the king would do in regard to her). Need I say that the Ulster Cycle tale known as "Deirdre of the Sorrows" is little more than a detailed recounting of how the seer's prophecy came to be fulfilled?

Any competent seer possessed the ability to get out of the way of a message coming through from the spirit world. In other words, an essential part of the seer's role in society entailed his or her ability to prophesy. Among the seers of old, such inspired information may have come from a variety of otherworldly sources—from ancestral or natural spirits as well as from any of a variety of gods or goddesses.

Prophecy is often understood as predicting the future, but that is only a small part of the prophetic function. The best prophecy is not about understanding the future so much as about living well in the present. Master the present, and the future takes care of itself. So even if a seer could predict the future, his primary value would still have been his ability to speak spiritual knowledge and wisdom, as it had more of an immediate use.

THE PATH OF THE SEER

Like Cathbad, at least some seers did enjoy a reputation for prophecy in the popular understanding of revealing the future. Two of the best-known prophetic seers, both from Scotland, were Thomas of Erceldoune (also known as True Thomas or Thomas the Rhymer) and Coinneach Odhar, better known as the Brahan Seer. Thomas lived in the thirteenth century, and according to legend was a bard whose skill with the harp caught the attention of the fairy queen. She approached the harper, beguiled him into being her lover, and whisked him away to the otherworld for seven years—and in return for his being a good sport, gave him the "gift" of an ever-true tongue (in other words, of being forever unable to tell a lie). Four centuries later, the Brahan Seer made a series of predictions about everything from technology to politics; but after telling a local noblewoman about her husband's infidelity, he was repaid with accusations of witchcraft that led to his execution. Obviously, a seer's life comes with its share of danger!

THE PATH OF THE SEER

A colorful assortment of seers dance through the world of Celtic myth. Merlin the Magician and Taliesin the Bard were both renowned for their prophetic gifts, while the Mórrígan—one of the most frightening of Celtic goddesses— speaks about a grim future in one of the most chilling passages of Irish myth. A seer named Finnéces spent years trying to catch and eat the salmon of wisdom thanks to a prophecy that a person named Finn would gain the world's wisdom from eating the fish; unwittingly, he sets the stage for the prophecy to come true—only it would be his servant boy, Fionn mac Cumhaill, who would eat the salmon and gain the wisdom. Later stories recount one of Fionn's comrades in the Fianna, Diorruing, as a seer gifted not only with prophecy but also clairvoyance that he accessed merely by closing his eyes. This gift was not always a blessing, however: once when Diorruing commented to Fionn about the one woman who would be a worthy mate for him, great tragedy ensued when she chose to give her love to another member of the Fianna.

Such prophecies could be in the myths only as literary devices—to help move the stories forward. But it's just as easy to see in them how they indicate the importance of prophecy—and therefore, of the seer—in the world of Celtic wisdom.

THE PATH OF THE SEER

Especially in Irish tradition, the roles of the seer and the bard are closely related. In Irish society even after the arrival of Christianity, the *filidh* or "seer-poet" provided both spiritual guidance and artistic vision to the community. Modern artists, whose work today is aimed at making people think, or inspiring revolution, or otherwise impacting society beyond the sheer aesthetic value of the work, are continuing this tradition of visionary creativity.

So when we consider the function of the seer in the world of Celtic wisdom, bear in mind that the seer's role may extend far beyond the trade of psychics and soothsayers. Sure, you can visit your local metaphysical bookstore and book a session with an astrologer, clairvoyant, or tarot reader, and if the person has a whit of talent you'll get an insightful and perhaps even healing reading. But they are not the only visionaries who embody the living tradition of the seer. You can cultivate the spirit of the seer within yourself even if you have no desire to practice divination or fortune telling. Perhaps in today's societies, seers can be found everywhere: as schoolteachers, librarians, software designers, nurses, engineers ... yes, even politicians and lawyers could be susceptible to the power of the spiritual world to erupt into their lives and provide guidance and insight into the direction best for them (and others) to follow.

THE PATH OF THE SEER

Among shamans of old, it was sometimes believed that a person didn't opt to be a shaman, but rather became one when they were so chosen by the spirits. I think it may be wise to keep this in mind, and always allow for the possibility that the true seer is not made, nor necessarily even born, but is chosen.

Thanks to an ancestor, an angel, a spirit guide, or a fairy presence, we might find doors into eternity opened for us not of our own choosing, and signifying a path which no one else can see, let alone follow. Especially for a child or a teenager, such unfolding of visionary or spiritual talent can be unsettling and could be mistaken for madness. To become a seer requires not only a gift for spiritual insight (what has been called "second sight" or simply "the sight"), but also a mentor, a guide, who can help that budding visionary discern their singular destiny. This is not to say that one who desires to serve Spirit as a visionary might not also be called. If you should feel such a yearning, then it only makes sense to learn all you can about psychic and intuitive skill, to develop a meaningful, committed practice of prayer and meditation, and to develop your mental capacities to the fullest. All this, and then asking for spiritual guidance. In other words—perhaps you cannot choose to be a seer, but you can always ask to be chosen.

THE PATH OF THE SEER

One might well ask, why would anyone want to be a seer? Consider the life of poor Thomas the Rhymer: he could not say anything other than the truth. One hopes that he was gifted at keeping his mouth shut, for otherwise he would be forever getting into all sorts of trouble, by both frightening and angering those who may not appreciate the truthful words spoken by him. Such a person might not always make for cheerful dinner conversation, and could certainly gain a reputation as being dour and pessimistic! Of course, with the discipline of a well-shut mouth, he could learn to speak only about the good things due to happen, but even that would exact its toll—for, after all, we cannot always tell if something is good or bad, even as it happens, and perhaps not even for years afterward. A seer like Thomas could survive only by warning his listeners that, like a good referee, "he calls them likes he sees them"—and leave the value-assessment up to others.

The role of a seer is essentially social. There's no point in visionary ability strictly for yourself (sure, there's the idea of being able to clean up at the stock market, but what good is that, if there's no one to share it with?). The only sustainable and meaningful reason to access hidden wisdom and spiritual vision would be to give it away.

THE PATH OF THE SEER

Scientific tests have revealed that if subjects who are familiar with a standard deck of playing cards are given a deck with a "wrong" card (such as a red ace of spades or a black queen of hearts), only a small number of those who examine the cards quickly will catch the mistake. Apparently, we are such creatures of custom and convention, trained to see what we expect to see, that even an erroneous playing card can slip by our powers of observation. So how many other anomalies or "paranormal" (beyond normal) events simply fail to catch our eye? Herein enters the true task of a seer: to be the one who sees the wrong-colored card at first glance, who notices the glitches and gaps that invite us into the places where "reality" is simply not so tightly sewn up as we might wish to believe. This function of the seer is not meant to foster chaos, but rather, liberation. We catch what Joseph Chilton Pearce called "cracks in the cosmic egg" so that we might be more truly faithful to things as they are—not as we might wish, hope, or be trained to believe they are.

THE PATH OF THE SEER

The concept of the seer ought not to be taken too literally. One might "see" mystical and extraordinary things, but there are many ways to approach the threshold of spiritual mystery. The French word *clairvoyant* is familiar to most people with an interest in psychic phenomena—it is basically the French equivalent of seer, meaning "clear watcher"—but there are also *clairaudients* (clear hearers), *clairsentients* (clear feelers), and even *clairscentrists* (clear smellers), *clairgustants* (clear tasters) and *clairtangents* (clear touchers, or psychometrists). Many ways to access spiritual information exist; and anyone who is chosen to be a seer may find that their guidance comes in any of a variety of (extra) sensory ways.

The key point here is for all of us—even if we have no concept of ourselves as "seers" or "psychics"—to remain open to receiving guidance and insight through intuitive means that can reach us in an almost endless variety of ways. Celtic wisdom reminds us that the spirit world is always nearby—and so, the ways of communicating with it are always within reach.

THE PATH OF NEART

In MacLennan's *A Pronouncing and Etymological Dictionary of the Gaelic Language*, the word *neart* is defined as "force, pith, power, might, energy, vigor; vast quantity; number, superabundance." As the dictionary attests, it's a wonderful word that represents how a variety of spiritually-meaningful concepts intersect within the Celtic mind. Neart represents the life-energy of abundance. It signifies the fundamental energy that flows at the heart of all things—an energy that not only keeps things going, but also fills everything with potential and possibility. If you want to look at it spiritually, it is the energy of Divine love. If you prefer a more non-theistic approach, neart could symbolize something akin to the impersonal "Force" of *Star Wars* fame. Except that there's no dualism within neart—no "light side" and "dark side." In the words of a new and delightful idiom that has surfaced in contemporary American speech: "It's all good." Neart is the energy of Celtic non-duality: it holds all things together in its flow of power and prosperity.

THE PATH OF NEART

In his book *Where Three Streams Meet: Celtic Spirituality*, Irish monk Seán Ó Duinn suggests that neart could be thought of as *mana*, the Polynesian concept of "life-force." Which brings to my mind a variety of other ways of thinking about neart: it is *reiki*, the Japanese concept similar to *mana*—of "Universal Life-Force." It is *prana*—a similar concept found in the Sanskrit tradition. Sure, it's dangerous to draw sweeping parallels like this that blithely hop across cultures and their distinctive ways of understanding the cosmos—and yet, one of the treasures of neart is how it offers us both a sense of the energy that pulsates through all things, *and* how that energy is a source of plenty. In this way of seeing things, neart may not be exactly the same as similar concepts from other cultures, but it is close enough to celebrate common ground. We can leave it to the academics to split the hairs that separate reiki from neart, and so forth. In the meantime, Celtic spirituality can join numerous other wisdom traditions in affirming that the world we live in is not a place of scarcity and hardship—at least not essentially. No matter what material challenges we face, we are all custodians of immense spiritual wealth.

THE PATH OF NEART

So how does neart function in our ordinary lives? Let's begin with faith. Believing something can often be the very essential key to making it so. People who believe in the power of prayer are far more likely to report it making a real, observable difference in their lives. For those who don't believe, maybe it's just a matter of prayer not being given credit where it's due—or perhaps, lack of faith can be an obstacle to the flow of energy (read: neart) in our lives. You want a miracle? Begin by believing it. No, not just paying it lip service; but choosing to live your life in a way that creates the amazing open-minded possibility that a four-alarm way-too-big-to-be-a-coincidence miracle just might manifest for you. Sure, not everyone gets miracles: as a friend of mine put it, "the Goddess is not in the habit of breaking her own laws." But once in a while, it seems that the laws of nature do get bent, or slipped around. And it's neart that's doing the bending and slipping.

THE PATH OF NEART

Choose to open your mind and heart and soul to the power and flow of neart. It's exciting to believe that, at any moment in time, at any place anywhere, something amazingly wonderful, entirely unexpected and undeserved may possibly happen. With a belief like that, it's so much, much easier to live by hope, rather than to sink in cynicism and despair. Yeah, sure, the odds may be against a miracle—well, the odds are against winning the lottery, too, and how many of us pop a dollar (or five) across the counter at the gas station, "just in case?" Belief in neart doesn't even cost us anything! My father is the kind of guy who never spends more than a dollar a week on the lottery—but he does it every week, fifty-two bucks a year (cheaper than going to a rock concert). And he says, "as soon as I buy that ticket, I just assume I'm a millionaire. And if I don't win, well, I'll just buy another ticket. Then I'm a millionaire all over again." Dad doesn't live extravagantly—he's a stickler for paying the credit card off in full every month, no exceptions. But he lives by faith. And so the neart flows through him.

THE PATH OF NEART

Opening up to the flow of neart is a lot like believing in God (or the Goddess, or the gods and goddesses. Choose the way of describing Ultimate Reality that is most in keeping with your religious or spiritual viewpoint). It's a decision, a choice, a commitment. It's saying "YES" to the universe, to possibilities, to hope. It's deciding that it's a whole lot more fun, effective, and meaningful to live from a sense that the cosmos is good and nurturing and plentiful, than to shrink within a self-armoring idea that there's never enough, every one is out for themselves, ultimately there is no meaning. Sure, when life kicks us in the teeth it's so very tempting to become cynicism's lover. But ultimately that's one affair that just leads to an ever-yawning downward spiral of despair. It can be cool, hip, intellectual, ironic, fashionable to be the cynic, the skeptic, the professional doubter. But at the end of the day, it really doesn't feel very good. Meanwhile, my dad's just as happy as can be—carrying his million-dollar lottery ticket around. Sure, call him naïve or even Pollyannaish. But who's got the smile— the real smile, that goes way down deep inside?

THE PATH OF NEART

Take this question of believing in neart a step further ... once we choose to believe in a force for life and power and miracles, then we actually are capable of experiencing that energy flow through us. Maybe it's a physical sensation—similar to reiki, which can be experienced as a warmth or tingling sensation flowing through those who use the energy when doing healing-touch work with others. Or maybe it's not so much a feeling, but a telltale pattern of serendipity and good things that flow through our lives and the lives of those we know and love. In other words, we can recognize it by the trail it leaves behind—a trail of happiness, of satisfaction, of a sense of Divine presence moving through the world. It creates a swath of joy, and anyone who believes that such a thing exists can start to see the evidence for it. A teacher of mine instructs her students to look for three miracles in their lives every day. Inevitably someone asks for a definition of "miracle." Must it be something supernatural? Well, not necessarily—"miracle" is related to "mirror," and refers to a reflection of Divine power in our lives; a reflection of neart. And that can come in small as well as huge ways. At least three times a day.

THE PATH OF NEART

The Celtic tradition has a reputation for being optimistic. Certainly Celtic Christianity is a remarkably positive expression of the Christ path, and Celtic paganism (with its emphasis on the beauty of nature, the nobility of the hero, and the immortality of the soul) has its clear positive orientation as well. I rather think this upbeat characteristic of the Celtic path begins with the reality of neart. If we live in a universe pulsating with power and abundance, then ultimately our problems are solvable, surmountable—there's nothing to fear. It's reminiscent of Jesus' overarching message: Be not afraid. How sad that so many of his followers are wracked with fear, fear of offending God, fear of damnation, fear that others will be lost just because they live or think differently!

Optimism is a choice. It's the product of faith, for it requires a hopeful approach to life. Faith says "I believe in neart," while optimism says "I'll experience its blessings most any day now." They go hand-in-hand for those seeking to live a life of spiritual wisdom.

THE PATH OF NEART

Neart is more than just a psychological strategy for cultivating hope and faith and optimistic thinking. It's also a cause for living a life according to the dictates of those positive values. If you want water to flow through a pump, you have to prime it. If you want neart to flow through your life, you "prime the pump" by creating the space for the abundance to manifest. That space is created through hospitality, generosity, and charity—good Celtic virtues, all! The only way for neart to flow *to* us is by creating the means for it to flow *through* us, which means finding ways to give it to others. Funny—the same thing is often said of love: the best way to find it is to give it away. It has been said that in heaven and hell, we have no elbows. Those who suffer in hell struggle with their inability to feed themselves, since an arm that won't bend cannot bring food up to the mouth. But in heaven, this same physical circumstance is no problem: for you see, everyone feeds someone else. *And no one gets left out.*

THE PATH OF NEART

Celtic folks love to talk of "the thin places," those places where the veil separating the physical world from the otherworld are even thinner than normal. Examples of thin places include churches, holy wells, sacred sites like stone circles or old monasteries, and places of great natural beauty and power. I first heard of this concept from a priest in Glendalough (a thin place if ever there was one). But I've come to think that the thinness of a thin place doesn't just provide access to an unseen inner world. Perhaps more important, it provides access to neart. Call it energy, call it hope, call it a fuel of miracles. For those who choose to see, it's as plain as the noses on our faces. Thin places are places of nourishment and rejuvenation—for they provide us with ready access to that energy that keeps us connected to blessings. The energy is more than just the bringer of blessing—it is blessing itself.

THE PATH OF THE SAINTS

Ireland has been called "the island of saints and scholars." But the other Celtic lands have produced their share of holy people as well. The coming of Christianity to the Celtic world was revolutionary on more than one level: not only did it forever change the way that the Celts viewed spirituality and the cosmos, but perhaps even more importantly, the Celtic tradition influenced how Christianity was practiced, giving birth to a unique expression of that faith, marked by optimism, mysticism, and deep love for nature.

Saint Patrick is probably the only Celtic "super-saint," which is to say a saint whose fame and popularity extends well beyond the Celtic world. But other saints, like Brigid, Columcille (Columba), Brendan (called "the Navigator" because of the legend that he and his companion monks sailed from Ireland to North America—in the sixth century!) and Columbanus all have enjoyed their own measure of fame. And what's truly lovely about the Celtic world is the abundance of lesser known (and in some cases only regionally venerated) "saints." Many of these folks have never been officially canonized, but that never stopped their small-scale cults from flourishing. In a way, the Celtic veneration of saints echoes the older veneration of pagan deities—the emphasis was not on the big names that everyone knew, but on the local figure, who may never have been famous but who gave a particular place its own unique sanctity.

THE PATH OF THE SAINTS

The monk and evangelist Mungo, also known as Kentigern, lived in the sixth century. Of noble British birth, he became a missionary in northwest England and Scotland, and is today perhaps best known as the founder and patron saint of Glasgow. The city's Coat of Arms includes four symbols associated with Mungo: a bird, a fish, a bell, and a tree. The bell commemorates a legend in which the saint received a bell as a gift from the pope, while the three symbols from nature each correspond to a miracle associated with Mungo: the bird symbolizes a robin that Mungo raised from the dead; the tree represents a miraculous fire he kindled with frozen wood; while the fish depicts a salmon he caught which had the queen's lost ring in its belly, thereby saving her from her husband's wrath.

The nature symbols correspond to the three great realms of nature: the fish represents the lower regions of water (sea, river, lake, well); the bird represents the upper regions of the atmosphere (the sky), while the tree symbolizes the land herself. Land, sea, and sky: one of many sacred Celtic trinities.

Mungo spent time in Wales but eventually returned to Glasgow and was buried at the site of Glasgow Cathedral, where today the crypt is still said to house his remains.

THE PATH OF THE SAINTS

Ita is a lesser-known Celtic saint, remembered today mainly through her pupil: Brendan the Navigator, one of Ireland's most colorful and renowned of early saints. Ita was the abbess (the leader of a monastery) of a community located in County Limerick. She was often described in early biographies as the "Brigid of Munster," suggesting that she played a role in the south of Ireland similar to that held in the east by her more famous contemporary. It's a marketing trick that is as dangerous today as it was a thousand years ago: compare yourself to someone more famous, and you're at risk for never getting out of their shadow. Even so, Ita remained a popular saint in the south of Ireland and has been immortalized for her role as Brendan's first teacher. The Navigator continued to seek her counsel long after leaving her fosterage. Unlike the many Celtic saints who were famed for their travels, Ita apparently loved the place where she first put down roots, and remained in Limerick until her death in the year 570.

It is said that one of the most important things any of us can do is raise or teach a child well. Perhaps Ita should be the patron saint of those who nurture greatness among those of the next generation.

THE PATH OF THE SAINTS

Piran is the patron saint of Cornwall and of tin miners (the tin trade being particularly important in Cornwall); he is possibly the same figure as the Irish saint Ciaran, the founder of the monastery at Clonmacnoise. Legend holds that Piran once escaped from captivity in Ireland and sailed to Cornwall using a millstone for a raft! Apparently the good saint had quite the capacity to work miracles—after all, sailing a stone boat makes even walking on water seem, well, easy. Today, scholars question just how historical a figure he is, wondering if, like other Celtic figures such as Brigid and even Patrick, his story may actually reflect more myth than fact. Well, maybe it does. But in the Celtic world, myth matters. Celtic spirituality envisions a world where anything is possible: where saints can cause a millstone to float or perform all sorts of other miracles. Why believe in such impossible tales? What good can possibly come out of crazy tales of miracles and floating rocks? We know that the human mind is an amazing instrument, and that often the key to miracles such as healing serious diseases, or summoning superhuman strength at a moment of crisis, begins with the power to believe. When we consider how a saint could make a millstone float, it opens up just a glimmer of possibility—Pearce's "the crack in the cosmic egg"—that allows miracles to really happen. Just because we believe.

THE PATH OF THE SAINTS

If Ireland had produced Saint Francis, he probably would have been named Kevin. The reclusive founder of Glendalough has numerous legends and stories associated with him that underscore his reputation as a friend of nature and a lover of animals.

One tale recounts how the saint was praying by one of the lakes near his hermitage, but his prayer book slipped and fell into the water. Even today such a turn of events would be an annoyance, but consider how valuable books were in ancient times; this would have been quite a problem. But before Kevin could even jump in after the book, an otter, sensing the sanctity and compassion of the man, grasped the book and returned it to its owner. Other stories tell of bears seeking refuge from hunters in the cave Kevin used as his hermitage, and of birds coming to perch on his shoulders or his head while the saint stood quietly at prayer. One day while praying, Kevin discovered that a blackbird had begun to build a nest on his outstretched hand. Filled with compassion, he could not bear to disturb her motherly work, and so stood still as she completed her nest, laid her eggs, and eventually hatched and raised her young. Finally, when the babies were old enough to fly, Kevin at long last allowed his arms to rest.

THE PATH OF THE SAINTS

March I is the feast day of the patron saint of Wales, Dewi (or David), who died on that day in 588. Known for his austerity and simplicity, Dewi founded a monastery where no wine was drunk nor meat consumed, and work was largely done in silence. As a bishop, Dewi worked hard to preserve the autonomy of the Celtic church in Wales from the encroaching power of the more Roman-style Christians of Saxon England; he is also credited with refuting the Pelagian heresy during his ministry (Pelagius was a Celtic theologian whose ideas were eventually denounced as heresy, particularly by Saint Augustine). It is said that he founded twelve monasteries, and that he traveled to Jerusalem where he was consecrated an archbishop. But these stories may well be little more than legend. Despite his reputation as a strict and austere monk, David's dying words may be the best insight into his character, and clearly reveal how the saint embodied the delightful charm of the Celtic spirit: "Brothers and sisters, be joyful and keep the faith."

THE PATH OF THE SAINTS

Cuthbert of Lindisfarne was a visionary from early in his life; according to the English historian Bede, Cuthbert's gift began with a vision he received the night of Aidan of Lindisfarne's death. At the request of a Northumbrian king, Aidan had left the monastery at Iona to found a Celtic community at Lindisfarne, the holy isle off the coast of northeast England. At the time of Aidan's death in August of 651, Cuthbert was a shepherd; while watching over his flock, he saw the angels escorting Aidan to heaven. This inspired him to enter the monastic life as well. In due course, his journey took him to Lindisfarne, where he eventually served as prior before retreating to a nearby island to live a hermit's life. But like Kevin of Glendalough, he would not be left alone, and so eventually he accepted the call to be consecrated bishop of the holy isle. Also like Kevin, he had a reputation as a friend of animals; his ministry was characterized by gentleness and care for the poor. He died only two years after his consecration as a bishop; today his remains are buried in Durham Cathedral, after having been relocated repeatedly to hide them from the Vikings.

THE PATH OF THE SAINTS

The patron saint of Scotland is Saint Andrew, who of course was one of Jesus' disciples and never set foot in the British Isles. Andrew is associated with Scotland because, according to legend, a ninth-century Scottish king, preparing to go to war against his English rival, received a vision of Saint Andrew's cross. The king promised to make Andrew the patron of Scotland if he emerged victorious that day, which he did. But if there were to be a Celtic contender for the position of Scotland's patron, it would likely be Columcille (Columba), an Irish-born missionary who founded the legendary monastery of Iona, a small island in the Hebrides. Columcille came from a prominent Irish family, and had a distinguished career as an Irish monk; but when a conflict over a manuscript that Columcille secretly copied led to violence, the mortified priest chose exile and, following the dictates of his spiritual mentor, dedicated his life to evangelism. Iona became a leading spiritual center in Scotland, and a site where many Scottish kings were buried (including Shakespeare's Macbeth). True to his Celtic blood, Columcille once said that he feared the sound of an axe in the woods of Derry more than he feared hell itself.

THE PATH OF THE SAINTS

So many saints populated the Celtic church in the centuries when it existed independent of Rome: Colman, of Iona and Lindisfarne, who retreated to a remote foundation in Ireland rather than submit to Roman authority; Enda of Inishmore, one of the earliest of Irish monks who mentored Ciaran of Clonmacnoise and advised Brendan the Navigator; Yves Hélory, a Breton lawyer who became canonized because of the kindness he showed to the poor; Maughold, a pirate converted to Christianity who established a great monastery on the Isle of Man; Adomnan, who became a soul friend to Irish kings and the best-known biographer of Columcille. And on the list could go. Every Celtic saint, famous or humble, stands for celebrating the rich tradition of spiritual devotion, and reminds every one of us, ordinary mortals though we might be, to live a life of sanctity and spiritual virtue—yes, even now. Celtic spirituality is the spirituality of intimacy and closeness between the mortal and heavenly worlds. If the spiritual realm is so available to us, then also holiness is within each person's grasp. You don't have to be as famous as Patrick or Columcille to manifest the life of devotion. Simply choosing to do it is all it takes to get started on the journey. It's a long and arduous journey, mind you—but a path that has been trod by many worthy feet before us.

THE PATH OF THE FAIRIES

In 1911 a young American scholar named Walter Evans-Wentz published a book developed from his dissertation at Oxford University, called *The Fairy-Faith in Celtic Countries.* The book recounts the extensive collection of folklore that the young scholar made throughout the six regions in western Europe where Celtic languages survived until modern times: Ireland, Scotland, Wales, Cornwall, Brittany, and the Isle of Man. All the stories and legends and personal experiences that Evans-Wentz documents involve belief not only in the existence of fairies, but also in the many ways in which fairies can interact with the physical world. The author goes on to put forward several dated, but nonetheless fascinating, theories as to why it is scientifically plausible to believe in the fairies.

I don't know if Evans-Wentz proved his case or not, but he certainly did anchor the link between the Celts and the fairies that seems to go back to the days of myth. Celtic wisdom takes many forms and speaks to us in many different ways. But the fairy faith knits the many strands of Celtic spirituality together. It is an integral part of the Celtic mystical world.

THE PATH OF THE FAIRIES

In Welsh they are called *Y Tylwyth Teg*, which means "the fair folk." In Irish they are the *Daoine Sídhe*, or "people of the fairy mounds," referring to the cairns, raths, and other prehistoric monuments that have been traditionally seen as homes for the fair folk. Euphemisms for these mysterious otherworldly beings abound—they are called the other crowd, the good people, the gentry, and sometimes just "them." Typical of Celtic wisdom, the fairies are seen as best spoken of in oblique and roundabout ways—so as not to upset them, you see.

But no matter how firmly the fairy-faith may seem to be part of Celtic consciousness, it is not in any way unique to the Celtic world. Many of the popularized notions of the fairies (such as can be found in Shakespeare or Walt Disney) come from English, rather than Celtic, sources. The word "fairy" itself is French in origin, etymologically linked with the concept of fate. So why are the Celts popularly seen as the believers in a much more universal spiritual phenomenon? Not hard to answer—given the Celtic love for spirituality and mysticism, it's no wonder that the Celts would be among the last to maintain credence in the existence of such inexplicable and mysterious beings as the fairies.

THE PATH OF THE FAIRIES

Mind you, the fairies as the Celts have traditionally understood them have hardly anything in common with the fairies as they are typically portrayed in popular culture (or in the modern media). Tinkerbell may be a cute little sprite with some connection to traditional beliefs, but it is a real mistake to see in her diminutive petulancy the sum total of the fairy world. Similarly, the Victorian-era notion of fairies as garden-resident Thumbelinas is charming in its own way (and has spawned a vigorous industry of gift items now available at your local new age shop), but it's not a very good representation of the good people as the Celts knew them—and, often as not, feared them.

Yes, the fairies have always been known for how little they are. But such spiritual beings could also appear as big as, if not larger than, a typical man or woman. Since so many stories in the tradition talk of fairy lovers, or fairies exchanging their babies for human infants, it's clear that the little people have not always been the tiny people. But that's what they've become. And in the world of Victorianesque flower fairies and post-modern knickknacks, the fairies just keep getting smaller and smaller. Which is a metaphorical way of saying that our society has taken a belief that has long been trivialized and is making it more marginalized than ever.

THE PATH OF THE FAIRIES

Where do the fairies come from? Many stories relate them to tales of angels fallen from heaven. A kind of "Switzerland" of God's court, the beings who would become the fairies sided neither with God nor with Lucifer when the latter revolted against the Almighty. They didn't exactly deserve the punishments of hell, but neither were they in a position to remain in heaven—so the Archangel Michael sent them to the earth to live in the twilight state of fairyland.

But a more compelling theory about the origin of the fairies comes from Irish myth. It seems that the Celts, as the first mortals to arrive in Ireland, engaged in battle with the Tuatha Dé Danann (the legendary tribe of gods, goddesses and heroes) when they arrived. The battle left no conclusive winner, so the Celts and the Tuatha Dé Danann struck a deal: the mortals would live above ground, while the magical beings would retreat to a subterranean (subconscious?) world beneath the surface of the land. Hence, they become the *Daoine Sídhe*, the people of the fairy mounds. So here we see the fairies not as some morally questionable heavenly rejects—but as the ancient ancestors, the shining and divine and immortal beings of the Celtic lands.

THE PATH OF THE FAIRIES

Nowadays, when most people think of fairies, neither fallen angels nor ancient gods come readily to mind. Many people today regard the fairy phenomenon as the conscious intelligence of the spirits of nature—whether that means spirits associated with specific plants or animals, or spirits linked to a place, or simply spirits who are somehow more linked to the natural world than we clumsy humans are. Given their history of living underground, the fairies appear to be chthonic spirits, that is to say, spirits of the deep earth—not to be confused with the celestial spirits of the sky and beyond, traditionally seen not as fairies but as angels. Fairy theorist R.J. Stewart suggests that fairies are the next step up the evolutionary ladder beyond humans; presumably one of the benefits of occupying a higher rung on the Darwinian ladder is a natural ability to live in closer harmony with nature. At any rate, just as angels are the messengers from the heavenly realm, fairies seem to play an oblique latter-day role as the messengers from mother earth.

THE PATH OF THE FAIRIES

But if fairies are the ambassadors who can help human beings to live in greater harmony with our natural environment, what does that say about how we have commercialized and trivialized the good people? Perhaps the process of transforming fairies from fearsome otherworldly spirits to charming garden sprites coincided with the changing way that modern humankind has regarded our habitat. To the pagan Celts, nature embodied the sovereignty of the Goddess; in the Christian view, nature has often been seen as something amoral and fearsome that needed to be mastered; while in today's post-modern, secularized world, nature has become our neglected mother, whom we ignore to our peril. And just as we have tamed nature from powerful goddess to mistreated earth mother, so we have tamed the fairies, reducing them to plastic statues available for thirty dollars at your neighborhood boutique. Granted, angels have suffered a similar fate. Maybe we need to reconsider: it won't be until we respect the spiritual beings in our cosmos again, that we will likewise truly respect the nature that sustains us.

THE PATH OF THE FAIRIES

The question of respect for the fairies is well illustrated by the popular folktale of the fairies and the hunchbacks—which is not unique to Celtic lands, but is certainly a favorite among Irish storytellers. The tale recounts how a hunchback falls asleep one night on a fairy mound, only to encounter the good people; he is kind to them and helps them compose a song, and for his civility they magically remove his hunchback. He wakes up a healed man, and cheerfully makes his way to town. Another, more naturally mean-spirited hunchback sees him, and learning what happened to him goes and spends the next evening on the fairy mound. He encounters the same troupe of fairies, but treats them abusively and makes poor suggestions on how to improve their songs. Angered, the gentry "reward" him by taking the hump from the first man and adding it onto the back of the second, making his back far more hunched than before. It's a story with an apparent enough moral: treat the fey folk well, and be treated well yourself. The implications for how we relate to nature are not hard to discern.

THE PATH OF THE FAIRIES

Belief in fairies might be a lovely and charming aspect of the Celtic tradition, but it is something that can be taken too far. Dozens of children in the nineteenth century were burned or even killed when their superstitious parents held them over the fire, certain that they were "changelings" or fairy imposters, left behind when the gentry had kidnapped their actual babies. Supposedly the way to make such a changeling admit the truth would be to hold it over an open fire—a foolhardy practice with often disastrous results. Nor was this torture limited to babies; in 1895 a group of men in County Tipperary were arrested after they had killed a woman named Bridget Cleary, burning her to death in a misguided effort to purge her of malignant fairy influence. In the twenty-first century, it is easy to distance ourselves from such superstitious crimes; but we shouldn't be too smug. Most people today have just as many irrational, superstitious, or scientifically unverifiable beliefs as did the peasants of Ireland a century ago. We need to be clear that, no matter what we believe, some things are non-negotiable—such as treating others with dignity and kindness. "Thou shalt not kill" is not an optional mandate, after all!

THE PATH OF THE FAIRIES

What is the future of the fairy-faith? Like so many aspects of the Celtic world, it is an endangered thing, thanks to the march of secular beliefs and the mass media into every corner of rural life. Today it seems that more upper-middle-class new age consumers are likely to believe in the fairies than their rural forebears. And while the Irish farmers of old basically tried to keep from running afoul of the gentry, our postmodern shamans eagerly seek to contact them through guided meditations and trance journeys. That may not be such a bad thing, especially if it leads to a greater sense of the dependence that humankind has on the environment. But it's a new chapter in the world of the fairies. Just as the Tuatha Dé Danann went underground and Celtic paganism changed forever, so now as the fairies are transformed from fearsome metaphors of the chaos in nature to charming spirit guides and purveyors of subjective wisdom, a transformation is happening from which there can be no return.

THE PATH OF THE WARRIOR

A significant theme in Celtic mythology involves the life of the warrior. Great battles of Tolkienesque proportions figure prominently in Irish myth, and arguably the single most dramatic and complex figure in that tradition is Cúchulainn, the greatest of Celtic warriors. Welsh and Arthurian legends also have a generous share of battles and conflict. Considering that until most of their lands fell to Roman occupation, the Iron Age culture of the Celts was very much based on a war society, this prominence in the myths is hardly surprising. But how does the Celtic warrior speak to us today, in a world where terrorists fight dirty and nuclear arsenals have forced us to reconsider the way we manage conflict?

Celtic lore is not just about war and the glorification of the hero. But it's a major enough theme in the tradition that we need to take it seriously. How does the warrior speak to us today? We need to ponder how the spiritual seeker in the twenty-first century may embody the warrior spirit; even if what we're fighting is not the heroes of the next tribe over, but rather the specter of environmental destruction and a society that has been rendered inhospitable by runaway consumerism.

THE PATH OF THE WARRIOR

One thing needs to be stated clearly about the warrior ethos in the Celtic world: it's not just about testosterone. Cúchulainn, incidentally, learned his skills from a female mentor, Scáthach. Perhaps even more important is a historical figure who embodies the spirit of a mother fighting fiercely to protect her young. The first-century Celtic queen Boudicca was queen of a tribe in eastern Britain during the time of the Roman conquest, whose honor was violated when the invaders killed her husband and raped her daughters. Thirsty for vengeance, Boudicca led an uprising that burned two Roman settlements before the conquerors could squash it. Eventually, facing certain defeat from the vastly superior Roman war machine, Boudicca poisoned herself rather than surrender to her enemies.

Boudicca was a pious woman, particularly devoted to a goddess named Andraste, whose name means "invincible." She represents a certain fierce nobility in the Celtic tribal soul, choosing to resist injustice even when the odds were so totally against her. We can see her as an icon of valor, who may have ultimately lost her personal freedom but who died with her dignity and inner freedom forever unconquered.

THE PATH OF THE WARRIOR

Irish mythology lionizes Lugh as a god of many skills—yet what makes him a true hero is his ability to lead his people to victory. At first he is an outsider, coming to the hall of the king of the Tuatha Dé Danann and having to talk his way into receiving an audience with the king. His selling point? That he is a possessor not just of one or two skills, but of many. Yet to impress the king, he must rise to three challenges—to demonstrate brute strength, mental skill, and musical artistry. Once he proves his mettle, Lugh is promptly given the resources to lead the Tuatha Dé Danann in battle against their archenemies, the Fomorians. This he does, leading to a dramatic moment when Lugh faces his own grandfather, a Fomorian giant. More loyal to his role as a warrior than as a grandson, Lugh slays his ancestor and wins the day.

Sure, Lugh is a hero, and his role as the war-god *par excellence* is strengthened by the fact that he is Cúchulainn's father. But all is not glory and light in Lugh's world. When Lugh's father is slain by the sons of Tuireann, Lugh demands that they perform a series of heroic tasks as punishment for their crime. Tuireann's sons complete the tasks, but are left mortally wounded in the process. One of the tasks involved procuring for Lugh a magical healing cloak; if he let them wear it, they would be spared death. But in Lugh's world, forgiveness is meaningless, and he responded to their begging for mercy by doing nothing.

THE PATH OF THE WARRIOR

For the warlike Celts, martial goddesses were just as important as martial gods—indeed, next to their role as personifications of sovereignty, one of the most common functions of Celtic goddesses was as warrior queens and inciters of battle. Meadbh, Andraste, Macha, Badb, and Brigantia all had aggressive characteristics; probably the most striking and notorious of Celtic war-goddesses was the Mórrígan, the phantom queen, who according to legend was sited at historical battlegrounds as late as the battle of Clontarf in 1014 CE! Like several of the other battle goddesses, the Mórrígan had an erotic/fertility side to her as well as her more notorious role as the harbinger of terror and death in war. She vigorously mates with the Irish father god, the Dagda, at Samhain—a festival that honors death. So she represents life in the midst of death, or the continual turning of the wheel. But she also represents death in the midst of life, a quality that she brought to bear on Cúchulainn at his tragic end. Like Lugh, the Celtic warrior goddesses were fierce, uncompromising, and powerful—but not exactly the kind of figure you'd turn to for mercy.

THE PATH OF THE WARRIOR

In many ways, Cúchulainn is a deeply tragic figure. As a child, he overheard a druid say that anyone who first picked up his arms on a certain day would lead a short but glorious life. The boy made sure to arrange with the king that he would receive his arms on that particular day. It is the first of a series of choices he made where he consistently chose glory or victory over alternatives that might be more humane, even if less valorous. Usually, his single-minded pursuit of the warrior ideal didn't particularly cost him—but not always. While studying martial arts in Scotland, Cúchulainn had an affair with his mistress's daughter, Aife. She bore him a son, Connla, who was born after Cúchulainn's return to Ireland. A decade later the boy traveled to Ireland in search of his father, but under a sacred vow not to reveal his name. When challenged to identify himself, he fought instead—and eventually this led to a fight between son and father. Cúchulainn wasted no time in killing the boy, and only after his death did he learn that he had killed his own (and only) son. Like fathers who send their sons to fight an unwinnable war, Cúchulainn paid for his single-mindedness with his own blood.

THE PATH OF THE WARRIOR

Killing his son is not the only tragedy to have visited the life of Cúchulainn. One morning, while preparing to do battle in the war between his native Ulster and the rival province of Connacht, a beautiful woman, dressed like a princess, approached the warrior. She made it clear that she had other things on her mind besides the upcoming fight, but Cúchulainn blew her off, insulting her by saying that the last thing he needed while preparing for battle was a woman! Anger flashed through her eyes, but she gave him one more chance, only to be rebuffed again. Then she revealed herself: and Cúchulainn discovered that he had just rejected the Mórrígan. So focused was he on his task as a warrior that he dismissed her threats, but he soon learned the price he must pay for rejecting the divine feminine. She relentlessly harried him, attacking him in a variety of shape-shifted guises—as an eel, a wolf, even a heifer. Each time she attacked he wounded her, but lost ground as the opposing army took advantage of the diversion. Meanwhile, she tricked him into blessing her, so that her wounds were easily healed. Whoever said that hell has no fury like a woman scorned could well have been thinking about the terrible consequences of a warrior rejecting the warrior goddess.

THE PATH OF THE WARRIOR

In the end, however, it wasn't the Mórrígan who presided over the death of Cúchulainn, but his nemesis Meadbh. She helped to arrange for a climactic battle where first his horse, then his charioteer were killed. Then the warrior himself was terribly wounded, and sensing that his time was at hand, Cúchulainn tied himself to a standing stone so that he could remain fighting even to the point of death. Even as his strength was ebbing, he was a formidable adversary, and soon no warrior would come near the dying hero, for fear of his lingering deadly might. Eventually, though, his head drooped, and finally a raven—the totem of the Mórrígan—landed on his shoulder. Only then would his adversaries approach his lifeless body.

It's a heroic end, but it also has an unmistakable whiff of tragedy about it. Cúchulainn was only 27 years old. He had dispatched countless enemies to the otherworld, and had single-handedly (but ultimately unsuccessfully) defended his home province from invasion. And yet, in the end he seems to be little more than a cartoonish superhero, worthy of a Hollywood special effects extravaganza. Lots of blood and gore, but surprisingly little soul.

THE PATH OF THE WARRIOR

The towering, tragic figure of Cúchulainn is not the last word in Irish—or Celtic—wisdom. As the old religion gave way to the new, the heroic ideal of the supermasculine warrior also gave way to a new model of might based on spiritual values and a commitment to values such as forgiveness, compassion, and peacemaking—hardly the perspectives of folks like Lugh or the Mórrígan. The new virtues of Celtic Christianity show up in Patrick, a former slave who opposed the slave trade; in Brigid, whose sacred oak would not tolerate a weapon set against it and who had once actually given her father's sword to a beggar that he might sell it to buy food; and Columcille, who voluntarily exiled himself to Scotland after conflict erupted over his actions in his native Ireland. Each of these figures was a warrior in his or her own right, but they were warriors of peace, wielding a bishop's or abbot's staff rather than a sword.

And so it is in the Christian "peaceful warriors" that we find a way to interpret the pagan warrior figures like the unforgiving Lugh or the tragic Cúchulainn. Their willingness to fight for their homeland and their people remains an inspiration. But unless this warrior spirit is married to eternal values, it runs the risk of imploding upon itself. And that, in the end, serves no one.

THE PATH OF THE WARRIOR

What can the Celtic tradition teach us about the spirituality of the warrior? I think we must look at the tradition as a whole, and imagine what kind of fruit a union between Cúchulainn and Brigid would bear. In other words, how do we integrate the fierceness of the archetypal warrior with the large heart and miraculous abundance of the archetypal Celtic saint? Brigid, of course, was no pushover—just as Cúchulainn was no blind aggressor. Even so, each seems to need the other. Peacemaking requires the courage and dedication of a warrior's heart, and that heart requires utter loyalty and obedience to values that transcend the mentality of I'm-right-you're-wrong. In short, the warrior of the future will, unlike Cúchulainn, fully embrace the spirit of the Divine Feminine. Even if it is the goddess in her warrior guise—after all, Brigid the peace-loving saint is not unrelated to Brigantia, a war goddess of Great Britain. But the point is to integrate. Know the limits, and know all the alternatives when it comes to upholding them. *All* the alternatives. This is the path of the Celtic warrior.

THE PATH OF THE OTHERWORLD

To the extent that the Celtic world-view has been shaped by Christianity, the cosmos may be seen as involving three tiers: the heavenly realm, where God is present as well as the saints and all others who enjoy the beatific vision; the earthly realm, essentially the physical universe of space and time; and hell, the realm of shadow and separation from the supernal light. It's a powerful map of reality, and its power derives not least from its similarity to the native Celtic pre-Christian world-view, as preserved in myth and folklore. Whether Christian or pagan, the Celts recognize the power and presence of a spiritual order somehow distinct from the knowable universe. Call it heaven and hell—or call it the otherworld, the Summerland, the land of youth—it is somehow separate from the measurable world of matter and energy.

Separate, but not immensely so. Christianity celebrates the infusion of heavenly energies into the ordinary world, and Celtic Christianity with its optimistic sense of Divine Presence particularly emphasizes such a theological view. But the pagan Celts were just as immanent in their perception of the connection between the ordinary world and the otherworld of spiritual presence. In some ways the otherworld might be far removed in space; but in other ways, it is as close to you as your mind or your heart. An entry point to the otherworld could always be just around the corner.

THE PATH OF THE OTHERWORLD

When the Tuatha Dé Danann came to Ireland, they came from four magical, otherworldly cities. The tradition vaguely suggests that these cities were "to the north" of Ireland, but it also hints that they are celestial cities in the sky. These mystical cities were called Finias, Gorias, Murias, and Falias. The tribe brought with them four astounding treasures, one from each city: from Finias came the great Spear of Lugh, which is said when used in battle would never miss its target; from Gorias came "the Answerer," the magical Sword of Nuadu which was invisible and could never be broken; from Murias came the Cauldron of the Dagda, which served endless supplies of food that could feed the entire tribe without emptying; and from Falias came the Stone of Destiny, which would emit a roar whenever the rightful king touched it. The symbolic echoes within the four treasures are rich and multilayered. They echo the four functions of traditional Celtic society: the spear represents the warriors; the sword's function as an "answerer" represents the mental skills of the druids; the cauldron represents the farmers and merchants, while the stone represents the king. So, from the otherworld come several key things: the gods themselves, the source of magic, and even the very structure of the cosmic order.

THE PATH OF THE OTHERWORLD

The otherworld shows up in Celtic lore under a variety of names, locations, and qualities. Perhaps the two best-known descriptions of the otherworld come out of the Irish tradition: Tír na nÓg, the land of youth (immortalized when Oisín was taken there by his fairy lover, Niam), and Tír Tairngire, or the land of promise (the object of several Celtic quests, including the famous voyage of the Christian saint Brendan—suggesting that the land of promise could transcend its pagan origin to function as the new religion's heaven). These two lands—of youth and promise—epitomize the Celtic otherworld as a realm of joy and delight. They are lands of beauty, happiness, and abundance, where love is eternal and inner peace reigns supreme. They are also magical places, where time and space do not obey the same rules as we experience in our mortal lives. A single day in the otherworld might correspond to a century or three back in the physical universe. And while the myths suggest that these magical lands lay to the west, over the ocean, the ocean can as easily be interpreted as a metaphor for the vastness of eternity that can separate the mortal world from the lands of light.

THE PATH OF THE OTHERWORLD

Just as the Tuatha Dé Danann first came to the land of Ireland from their four otherworldly cities, so they retreated into the otherworld after failing to vanquish the mortal Celts upon their mythic invasion of the island. Retreating from Ireland, they took up residence in a number of otherworldly abodes: the lands of youth and promise being among them. Another common theme in the lore holds that the tribes of Dana removed themselves from the surface of the land, only to take up residence in a subterranean underworld. This corresponds with their transformation from gods and heroes to fairies—in Irish, *sídhe*, or dwellers within the mounds. Various cairns and passage-tombs and other ancient burial sites were regarded by the Celts as power sites, where spirits dwelled; so naturally enough these sites became associated with the great figures of the myths. And so, not only was the otherworld seen as located over the water, but also as under the surface of the earth; not only were the prehistoric sites regarded as portals into the otherworld, but caves and possibly even holy wells also came to be regarded as gateways to the realms below.

THE PATH OF THE OTHERWORLD

Welsh tradition identifies the underworld as Annwn—the name literally means "in the world"—and recounts a dramatic story of a conflict between two otherworldly kings, in the middle of which a rather bumbling mortal named Pwyll gets involved. The two kings fight at a prescribed time each year; one year Pwyll, disguised as one of the kings, Arawn, kills the rival King Hafgan with a single blow, thereby cementing not only Arawn's claim as the ruler of all Annwn, but also creating bonds of friendship and exchange between Arawn's magical kingdom and Pwyll's own mortal province. It is from Arawn in Annwn that Pwyll receives a gift of pigs—the first of such animals to grace the land of Wales. Another treasure from Annwn was not given to the mortal world, but rather taken by force, when King Arthur raided the underworld to capture a sacred cauldron (a probable source myth for the grail legend). Arthur's thievery did not come without a price—he lost almost three shiploads of men during the raid.

If Annwn seems less friendly and hospitable than Tír na nÓg and Tír Tairngire, that's a hint about the otherworld as a whole. It has its heavenly features, but it is hardly a place of endless bliss and uncomplicated joy. It is, rather, a place of both light and shadow.

THE PATH OF THE OTHERWORLD

Located as it is on the westernmost edge of northern Europe, with only the vast waters of the Atlantic to its west, it's not only understandable that Ireland would see the spiritual world as existing "out there, over the water," but also that a sub-genre of mythic tales would develop, all of which told the story of intrepid travelers who sailed to the west, into the uncharted waters—only to find one or more islands of the otherworld. These stories depict a wide variety of lands peopled by a vast assortment of denizens: some are heavenly, others horrifying. Some otherworldly islands are filled with endless laughter and joy, while others are the realms of endless tears and sorrow; some are silent and mysterious; more than one simply cannot be penetrated at all. Interpreters have suggested that these mythic tales of voyaging into the islands of the otherworld might represent a sort of Celtic *bardo*, or "book of the dead"—initiatory manuals of instruction on what happens to a soul after death. If so, then the tradition depicts the soul's postmortem voyage as a colorful and mysterious journey indeed.

THE PATH OF THE OTHERWORLD

One singularly fascinating otherworldly island, that appears in both the story of the adventures of Bran and the most complex of Celtic otherworldly voyages, that of Máel Dúin, is Tír na mBan—the land of women. It's the heterosexual man's ultimate fantasy: a paradise of friendly, gorgeous, and sexually precocious women, where the food is good and the living is delightful (fans of British humor will recognize how Tír na mBan was spoofed as "Castle Anthrax" in the movie *Monty Python and the Holy Grail*). On the surface, what could be wrong with such a place? Only that it symbolizes the core problem of addiction: allowing a pleasure (in this case, sex) to control life rather than enhance it. This realm serves as a giant distraction—those who journey to the otherworld often have a different destination in mind other than the land of women, but find that its seductive pleasures are just a little too difficult to leave. One version of the story of Máel Dúin has him severing his hand in order to escape the addictive pleasures of this island. Tír na mBan is not about women (or men) so much as it is a metaphor for any addiction: sweet and beguiling on the surface, yet deep within it is a place that lacks any real ability to sustain the soul.

THE PATH OF THE OTHERWORLD

Eventually the pagan underworld undergoes Christianization, and begins to appear in later folklore and in Celtic ballads as an ambiguous place: on the one hand, "fair elfland," a fairy realm that evokes the pleasures of Tír na nÓg; but on the other hand, it's an ominous place, where tithes are paid to hell and certain rules must be obeyed by any mortal daring (or foolish) enough to enter. Typically, mortals don't wander into the underworld on their own initiative—the tales that do talk of such proactive exploration almost always end badly (or at least with the mortal never being seen again in our world). But they often do end up in the otherworld after having been seduced by a randy fairy or invited there to share a skill or talent. Warriors like Cúchulainn might be drafted to help fight an otherworldly battle, while musicians and midwives often find their skills are highly in demand. But as time goes by and myth becomes folklore, it is the realm of fairies, those mischievous spirits who are neither gods nor demons, who do the summoning and the inviting; and a musician might find himself playing endlessly for a frenzied fairy dance, or a midwife pressed into helping deliver a fairy babe. Such stories are almost always told with an ominous edge, with a clear underlying message: to be invited to provide your services to the fairies is hardly a desirable turn of events!

THE PATH OF THE OTHERWORLD

Contemporary Irish priest and mystic John O'Donohue speaks of "the inner landscape" as part of the Celtic tradition. And so here we find where the otherworld has come to rest in the skeptical, nihilistic postmodern world—it is the magical realm within. No longer located over the waves, above the clouds, or beneath the soil, it is an "underworld" in the sense that it lies "under" ordinary consciousness, in the hidden shadowy places of the human soul. All it takes is a willingness to suspend disbelief in Jung's theory of the collective unconscious, and suddenly the link between the inner otherworld and the mythic realms of spirit from time immemorial seems both plausible and sensible. We can find the otherworld by opening a gate to it, not in a cave or at a holy well, but simply by pausing at the threshold of the imagination. Truly, herein we will find a land not dissimilar to the external world, where pleasures and sorrows, addictions and liberations, all may be given to the mindful explorer. But remember: like the fabled Tír na mBan, this inner universe can seem to be a place of endless delights (or wisdom or healing), but do not tarry there too long, or else it may not be so easy to leave.

THE PATH OF THE SHAMAN

A number of contemporary writers and teachers of Celtic spirituality—John and Caitlín Matthews, Tom Cowan, Francesca De Grandis, Frank MacEowen, among others—have collectively articulated an entirely new dimension to the Celtic mysteries. I call it new, but that's not entirely fair, for these seeker/teachers are drawing on the rich traditions of Celtic myth and lore, along with surviving practices found in the more remote areas of the British Isles, to present their unique vision of how Celtic spirituality can make a difference in the lives of seekers today. What's truly new about their work is the name they have given it: "Celtic shamanism."

It could be easy to say there's no such thing as Celtic shamanism. Strictly speaking, shamanism is a Siberian spiritual practice, and so talking about Celtic shamanism makes about as much sense as saying that Irish Catholics who meditate are practicing Celtic Zen. So the purists who criticize the very concept of Celtic shamanism do have a point. To that we could just as easily say, so what? Christianity is no more inherently Celtic than Zen or shamanism, and yet few would deny that there is a 1500-year Christian presence in the Celtic world, or that when the Celts encountered Christianity, they shaped it to create a unique (and beautiful) expression of that faith. If there is such a thing as Celtic Christian spirituality, then it's just as valid to explore the concept of Celtic shamanism.

THE PATH OF THE SHAMAN

Purists might insist that Celtic shamanism is really just a misnomer applied to druidism or to the seer tradition in the Celtic world. And maybe that's true. But it's a misnomer where the metaphorical cat has been let out of the bag of limitation, and so the concept of Celtic shamanism is making sense to increasing numbers of people today, both in the Celtic lands and beyond. If an Irish or Scottish healer chooses to describe what he or she does as shamanism, who am I, a fourth-generation American, to criticize their choice of words? Likewise, the small but growing genre of books on Celtic shamanism reflects a popular trend in Celtic wisdom that marries old practices with new interpretations. The purists, I'm afraid, have lost this round. Celtic shamanism is here to stay. But what exactly *is* it?

Here's a portal of entry: Celtic shamanism refers to a cluster of magical and spiritual practices grounded in Celtic traditions but similar to, or inspired by, explicitly shamanic practices from around the world.

You see, it's not about Celts pretending they're Siberian medicine men or Native American healers. It's about discovering the similarities between those and other spiritual paths and what's been in the Celtic tradition all along.

THE PATH OF THE SHAMAN

The story is told of how the great epic poem *The Tain* had been lost, but was rediscovered in the seventh or eighth century when a bard named Senchán Torpéist made spirit contact with Fergus mac Róich, a royal figure who appears in the epic. Elsewhere, I've told this story as a celebration of the enduring spirit of the bard's craft. But here let's look at it in the context of shamanism.

For shamanism often is concerned with making spiritual contact with the otherworld. Sure, many modern "shamans" interpret this metaphorically, regarding the "spirits" as archetypes or aspects of the unconscious mind. But in the old days, the shaman would probably have taken such work much more literally (and yes, some modern shamans are equally literalist in their thinking). But no matter whether you approach this as a true believer or sophisticated skeptic, shamanism is a spiritual system that traffics in spirit contact—usually with a specific purpose in mind. A spirit might be contacted to bring wisdom back to the tribe, or to find a healing practice, or a specific cure for a mysterious fever. Maybe the spirits are contacted for guidance in securing a bountiful harvest or a successful hunt. The shaman, like the priests of many later and more complex cultures, is the one responsible for mediating with the world of the spirits.

THE PATH OF THE SHAMAN

Many stories in the Celtic tradition tell of mortals who travel to the land of fairy, or to otherworldly lands such as Annwn or Tír na nÓg. Sometimes these travelers are gone for a weekend, sometimes for seven years, sometimes for three centuries. A few, like the Scottish minister Robert Kirk, are said never to have returned. Then there is the equally likely possibility of spirits roaming the earth, particularly on sacred nights such as Samhain or Beltane. Compare this to the Christian view of the cosmos, where heaven is "up there" and earth is "down here," and never the twain shall meet, at least not on this side of Doomsday. Clearly, the ease with which Celtic tradition speaks of passage between the human and spirit worlds comes from deep within the Celtic tradition—and is, for lack of a better name, evidence of the shamanistic nature of primal Celtic mysticism.

THE PATH OF THE SHAMAN

When the Celts journey to the otherworld—in shaman-speak, to the spirit realm—they go for more than just their jollies. Their journeys often have involved some sort of quest. In the bizarre Welsh poem *Preiddeu Annwn*, Arthur and his companions raid the otherworld to bring back valuable treasures, including the great cauldron of rebirth. Thomas the Rhymer, without particularly realizing it, follows the Elfin Queen into her land because he's entranced with her beauty, but he returns with the dubious gift of a tongue that cannot lie. Pwyll makes the first of several trips into Annwn as a way to repay a debt he owes to the king of that land.

So not only can the Celtic shaman travel between the worlds, but he or she does so for specific reasons. Shamanism is not a hobby, not some sort of vivid game of inner exploration like a spiritualized version of *Dungeons and Dragons*. It is meant to convey benefits to the practitioner and his or her clients: wisdom, healing, knowledge, spiritual growth, and enlightenment. The otherworld contains many treasures; it is the shaman's job to find and enjoy them.

THE PATH OF THE SHAMAN

I've mentioned healing as a key element of the shaman's craft. And so it is in the Celtic tradition: druids and seers alike functioned as healers within their societies. Healers like Brigit or Dian Cécht played pivotal roles in Celtic myth, and ancient writers speak of the druids having knowledge of herbs and other natural remedies for physical ailments. Wisdom, by itself, was meaningless—only in its application was it beneficial to the community. And not surprisingly, the most fundamental way a wise person could be of service was in the healing arts.

Dian Cécht, the Irish healing god, had a jealous streak; and when his son proved to be a better physician than him, Dian Cécht killed him. From his gravesite 365 healing herbs grew, and Dian Cécht's daughter attempted to gather them. But the jealous father scattered the herbs to the four winds, and so their healing knowledge was lost. Here we have a myth not only of patriarchal jealousy, but also of the secret nature of healing—it involves knowledge that has been lost, or is so widely scattered that only a gifted healer can access its mysteries. And so, the druid/shamans of old used their wisdom and knowledge to heal others—but guarded their secrets carefully, passing them on only to worthy students.

THE PATH OF THE SHAMAN

Cows are sacred to Brigid and Boand. Ravens are associated with the Mórrígan. Pigs play a part in the myths of several Celtic gods and heroes, including Gwydion, Culhwch and Manannán. The salmon is significant in the story of Fionn, just as the dog plays a pivotal role in the life of Cúchulainn. It's clear that animals play a meaningful role in the magical world of Celtic spirituality; however, can we infer that the Celts ever approached these animals as "power animals"— in other words, as helpful spiritual guides who provide information, knowledge and power?

Just a cursory reading of the myths would suggest that, yes, the animals play a significant, spiritual role. The Mórrígan's raven was considered an omen, often of death in battle; indeed, it was not until a raven landed on Cúchulainn's dead body that anyone would approach it. Speaking of Cúchulainn, he was under a *geas* or sacred vow not to eat dog meat, suggesting that his strength was tied to his respectful relationship with dogs (not unlike Samson's strength being linked to his vow never to cut his hair). Perhaps the most obvious link between a mythic animal and spiritual ability involves the story of Fionn, who received his knowledge and prophetic gifts after eating of the salmon of wisdom.

THE PATH OF THE SHAMAN

Shamans in cultures around the world use trance and ecstatic rituals and practices (such as drumming and dancing) to enter altered states of consciousness, where they can more easily communicate with the spirit realm or connect with their power animals. Hints of similar practices may be found in the Celtic world as well. Druids, bards and seers would seek to connect with the *imbas forosnai*—the inspired knowledge—said to come through supernatural means. Similarly, the *awen* (poetic inspiration) called to Welsh bards in a similar fashion. When possessed of the *imbas* or the *awen*, the poet or seer could channel information directly from otherworldly sources. And such shamanic states of consciousness were not only used for spiritual purposes—Cúchulainn's *ríastrad* (battle frenzy) involved an altered state where he physically transformed into a deadly foe capable of slaughtering forty enemies with a single blow. So, like many other elements of shamanic spirituality, the Celts' use of altered states of consciousness appears to at least be similar to practices of shamans from many different cultures.

THE PATH OF THE SHAMAN

So what's the point behind Celtic shamanism? Just the fact that the concept of shamanism can be used to help us understand the wisdom and spirituality of the ancient Celts may be point enough. Folklorists have also explored how more recent practices among rural Celtic healers, fairy doctors, and wise women can be interpreted as living shamanic practices. Just as Celtic music has been invigorated by cross-fertilization with rock and roll, jazz, and other genres, so the multi-cultural dialogue between "Celtic shamans" and other explorers of shamanic spirituality from other parts of the world can only be a positive development for the ongoing survival of traditional Celtic wisdom.

For the individual person interested in integrating shamanism and Celtic wisdom, I'd suggest keeping an open mind and remembering to explore the Celtic path as fully as possible. Sadly, many books written on "Celtic spirituality" reflect a minimal knowledge of the mythic or living traditions in the Celtic lands. Making the effort to read scholarly as well as popular surveys of the Celtic world can only help anyone interested in finding a Celtic form of shamanism for our time.

THE PATH OF THE NIGHT

The ancient Celts reckoned time in terms of darkness coming before light. A day began at sundown and consisted of the nighttime, followed by the day. There's nothing uniquely Celtic about this—in Judaism, the Sabbath begins at sundown on Friday evening. In a similar way, Gaelic holidays began at sundown and ran through to the following day (such as Samhain which began at dusk on October 31). In fact, Samhain (which means "summer's end") marked the beginning of a new year—which began by entering the "nighttime" of the year, or winter, before leading to the summer or light half of the year.

So light comes out of darkness; day issues forth from night. The night is feminine, like the goddess, and gives birth to the more masculine energies of the day. And so it is that magic most readily flows at night—midnight is, after all, "the witching hour." In the ballad *Tam Lin*, young Janet rescues her lover from the fairies at a crossroads at midnight. In the matrix of the dark, at a place marking the four directions, she can see into the otherworld and snatch her treasure from it.

THE PATH OF THE NIGHT

One of the most fearsome qualities of the night is the Wild Hunt. Celtic tradition (along with folklore from other lands with similar earth-based mythologies) tells of a supernatural host that sweeps across the landscape at night, consisting of otherworldly dogs, horses and riders, and fairies (or demons), searching for evildoers or sometimes for less culpable victims. Some traditions maintained that the Wild Hunt was a force of utter chaos, destroying or kidnapping anyone unfortunate enough to be in their path. The spectral hounds of the Hunt were said to be huge, black, and fiery-eyed; they would emit fearsome, heart-stopping sounds as they barked and bayed for their prey. Depending on the region, the Hunt's leader was said to be a fairy king like Gwynn ap Nudd, or a folkloric hunter such as Herne (who may have been a modern version of the ancient horned god, Cernunnos). When Janet rescued Tam Lin from the clutches of the fairy queen, it may have been with this kind of supernatural hunting party that he rode.

THE PATH OF THE NIGHT

What are we to make of the Wild Hunt? Could it be just some sort of psychological metaphor for the forces of chaos that roam freely within the darkness of the mind's shadow? Certainly that's the comfortable explanation. Like a recurring dream in which the baying of hounds and wolves causes a supernatural shudder to flow through the mind, the Wild Hunt invites us to acknowledge (if not befriend) our inner wildness, usually kept firmly under control—at least until nighttime. For the night is the time of wildness, both in the world "out there" and in the even less untamed regions within. No matter how tamed we may be by the demands of society, church, and career, the call of the wild will always have some sort of a claim on us. This is not to suggest that Celtic wisdom calls for us to reject the niceties of life just to go run naked in the woods—at least, not necessarily. But perhaps it does call for us to gaze without fear into our inner wildness, and to listen to the baying of the hounds as they come closer to swooping down upon the conscious mind with their chaotic energies. Listen, and then strive to hear the link between our wildness, our creativity, and our passion. That's where the treasure is buried.

THE PATH OF THE NIGHT

Some stories in the Celtic tradition speak of perils in the night. At one time the monstrous being known as the burner, Aillén mac Midgna, terrorized the royal site of Tara every year at Samhain. During the night, all the warriors and guards heard a mysterious music that would lull them to sleep; they would wake only to find that the burner had struck again and razed the compound to the ground. The next year would see Tara rebuilt, only to be destroyed again on Samhain. This went on for over twenty years.

It was to this tense situation that the young Fionn mac Cumhaill came on his first visit to Tara. Finding the greatest warriors of the land at a loss as to how to defeat Aillén mac Midgna, the young hero devised a plan. When Samhain arrived, he ingested a small amount of poison from his poison-tipped spear—just enough that it prevented him from falling asleep. Aillén appeared and played his music, lulling all the other warriors into their stupor, and the fairy monster began to spew molten rocks from his mouth. But before he could cause any damage, young Fionn thrust his spear at the enemy, handily killing him. And so Tara was safe once again, and the young hero had proven himself to the warriors of the land.

THE PATH OF THE NIGHT

Fionn mac Cumhaill defeated a monster associated with two levels of darkness—the darkness of the night and the darkness of Samhain. He did this by staying awake, and staying alert through the power of his own weapon. So mindfulness and self-confidence prove to be the portals by which the terror of the night is vanquished. The story of Fionn and Aillén is a David and Goliath tale—a young boy taking on a fairy demon who spews burning rocks out of his mouth, potent enough to burn a royal site to the ground. A hero challenges forces that appear to be well beyond him. And yet Fionn triumphs simply by staying awake where others were lulled to sleep.

Keeping your eyes open can take you a long way toward achieving your goals and overcoming your obstacles. The ability to pay attention forms the heart of meditation, and it's a key to common-sense living. Letting go of the distractions of the past and future, and simply being present, can enable you to find the path to fulfillment. Even, sometimes, in the dark.

THE PATH OF THE NIGHT

A Welsh legend tells of the disappearance of the goddess Rhiannon's baby one night shortly after his birth. Rhiannon is falsely accused of killing the child and forced to endure public humiliation as her punishment. Several years pass by; meanwhile, a lord named Teyrnon has a mare that gives birth every year on Beltane night, but the foal promptly disappears. So Teyrnon keeps a vigil and discovers that a beast with a giant claw has been stealing the foals. He fends off the monster, only to find that the foal magically transforms into a child—who turns out to be Rhiannon's missing son.

It's a mysterious story with more puzzles than answered questions. But it's a curious counterweight to the tale of Fionn and Aillén. Instead of a tragedy every Samhain, the clawed beast attacks at the opposite side of the year, on the first of May. And somehow, the attacks on Teyrnon's foals are linked with the kidnapping of Rhiannon's son (as Rhiannon is clearly a horse goddess, this is not so far-fetched). What both Teyrnon and Fionn achieve is protecting their world against the chaos of the two most otherworldly nights of the year. Chaos, of course, can be creative—Fionn earns the respect of his comrades and Teyrnon emerges as a hero after each vanquishes their respective adversaries. So while the stories don't exactly celebrate the anarchy of the magical night, they do affirm that grace may emerge from the darkness when faced with courage and valor.

THE PATH OF THE NIGHT

It's not a particularly Celtic image, but central to the Christian mystical tradition is a concept that comes from Saint John of the Cross—the Dark Night of the Soul. If spiritual growth represents a process of learning to orient ourselves to spiritual values rather than focusing exclusively on the transitory pleasures of the material world, then there comes a time when even spiritual "goodies" may need to be surrendered, particularly if they stand between us and our total liberation. This process of releasing spiritual pleasures is the dark night of the soul—a process often described as terrifying and disorienting, as one learns to rely on faith, rather than experience, as the compass of the spiritual life. But like all other night metaphors, it is meant to be understood as just a beginning—beyond the dark night of the soul is the glorious light of Divine Union. Birth only comes out of the womb. Initiation emerges out of darkness. Truly, the night is our friend.

THE PATH OF THE NIGHT

The most powerful and gripping passage in the Irish epic *The Tain* comes when the hero Cúchulainn faces his dearest friend and soul brother, Ferdiad, in one-on-one combat. The two men had studied martial arts under the same mentor, but the fortunes of their lives led them to fight on opposite sides of the great war between Connacht and Ulster. For three days the mighty warriors engaged in combat; in the end, Cúchulainn won, and his lament for the death of his friend may well be the most poignant moment in Celtic myth. But what is equally fascinating is how, when night fell, the two men put aside their weapons and embraced one another, looking after each other's wounds before retiring for the night. Even though the story goes on to its tragic conclusion, it is only after the men find at the end of the day a momentary respite from their battles and a chance to reaffirm, albeit briefly, their bonds of friendship.

So here we see night not as a source of chaos, but as a respite from it. The day is given over to battle, but the restful energies of dusk allow for an alternative to conflict to be possible. Perhaps every twilight time could function like this— as a time for reflection, for reconsideration, for entertaining possibilities that seem impossible in the light of day which, if embraced, could literally change the course of our lives.

THE PATH OF THE NIGHT

Sometimes a child can be afraid of the dark. But such fear is only real in the dark itself. In the light of day, the child plays and enjoys life with no worry for the coming of nightfall. Eventually the child learns that the same confidence which sustains her in the light can empower her to trust in the safety of the dark. The Celtic tradition offers us contradictory images about the place of darkness and the mysteries of nighttime in our lives. But consistently, the dark is the time when mysteries are revealed. The fairies and other spirits roam the land, chaos threatens, and yet alternatives become possible.

Folk traditions from the Gaelic lands concerning the Festival of Brigid (Imbolc) suggest that night before Brigid's day is a time of blessings. A cloth dedicated to Brigid and left outside on the eve of Imbolc will receive her blessing. It is said that she travels throughout the land on this night, offering her prayers and protection to the faithful. In some communities, a doll symbolizing Brigid is made and placed in a crib by the hearth fire on this night, a metaphor for inviting Brigid's energies into the house. Perhaps this is the final word on the Celtic view of the night: it's a time from which blessings and healing may emerge into the light of a new day.

THE PATH OF MEDITATION

Meditation is a word that means many different things. Each entry in this book can be thought of as a "meditation"—but they take many different forms. One way to meditate is by thinking reflectively; considering information related to the topic you're exploring. But just as important is the type of meditation more commonly associated with the word—an intentional inner journeying, either with or without mental images as a form of guidance or structure for the experience.

Meditation is not a topic explored as such in the Celtic tradition—pagan myth tends to be much more extraverted and dramatic, focusing on conflict and action rather than on inner process, while the Celtic Christians generally spoke of the inner life in terms of prayer. But there is a lovely Irish word for meditation—*dercad*—and historian Peter Berresford Ellis suggests in his book *The Druids* that Gaelic spirituality may have included a meditation practice designed to achieve inner peace (*sitcháin*). But regardless of meditation's place in Celtic tradition, it is a universal spiritual tool that can serve as a beneficial application within Celtic mysticism.

THE PATH OF MEDITATION

Christian monks have long practiced a spiritual discipline called *lectio divina*, or "sacred reading." It consists of reading a passage from the Bible or some other holy text, slowly and deliberately, allowing the words to sink gradually into consciousness. The point is to read the section slowly, deliberately, reflectively, with all due regard toward allowing the words to reveal their meaning in subtle ways. The period of *lectio* would then be followed by meditation on the words, prayer, and finally, silent contemplation. For a Celtic devotional practice, consider using the *lectio* technique with the stories of Celtic saints, or even the tales of the old gods and goddesses and heroes. Such tales may not be considered sacred in any kind of a scriptural or canonical sense, but they are certainly windows into the world of Celtic wisdom, and can be a meaningful springboard into prayer and meditation according to the dictates of your overall religious practice. Be sure to follow up the sacred reading with time for meditative reflection, prayer, and silence.

THE PATH OF MEDITATION

Identifying a meaningful figure from Celtic myth, legend, or lore can be another valuable doorway into meditation. Such a figure could be drawn from either Christian or pagan sources, and could be historical or mythical; such a person might be a saint or a scholar, a god or a goddess, a bard or a warrior or a seer. The point is to find a figure who speaks to you, either because of their achievements, or the stories told about them, or perhaps even just because you like their name! Trust your heart, and see who in the world of Celtic spirituality you are drawn to. Then, approach this person as a soul friend, or companion to accompany you on your spiritual path. Read and learn all you can about your chosen guide, discovering what stories were told about them, what values they embody, what spiritual powers they might have possessed, and what animals, plants, colors, or places are most associated with them. Basically, get to know your meditation partner inside and out. But don't just stop at mental knowledge—reflect on this mythic or historical figure as part of your spiritual practice. Invite his or her spiritual energies into your life. If you find you have a strong emotional or spiritual reaction, write it down and reflect on it (many figures in Celtic myth are scary or unsettling. It's useful to understand just what qualities you admire, and which ones frighten you).

THE PATH OF MEDITATION

In the theatre of your imagination, you may find that your inner soul friend takes on a life of his or her own. Allow this process to unfold, for you may find that the process of meditating on such a figure can help you to feel much more deeply connected to the Celtic tradition. You may see this figure as a spirit guide, or you may feel he/she is just a metaphor functioning within your mind. Either approach is fine—just go with what works for you. As you meditate, you may wish to visualize yourself interacting with your inner soul friend. Ask him or her a question that has been burning within you. See what kind of response you get. When you are done meditating, write it down.

In your inner journeys, you may find that your chosen inner guide is not particularly interested in you. Don't take it personally! Instead, remain open to allowing the right figure from the Celtic tradition to connect with you. You may make this connection during meditation, or you may feel drawn to another mythic figure, who turns out to be "right" for you. Trust the process.

THE PATH OF MEDITATION

If your interests run toward shamanism, you might also try meditating on an animal or tree connected with the Celtic tradition. Consider working with a divination deck, like *The Celtic Tree Oracle* or *The Druid Animal Oracle.* Try to learn about elements of nature that have a long-standing connection with the Celtic world—species native to (or long ago imported into) the British Isles, or ones that appear in the mythology and lore. One or more of the Ogham trees can be valuable objects of meditation, as can animals like the salmon, raven, or pig.

To a student of shamanism, an animal or plant that makes a powerful impression during times of meditation or visualization might be a power animal—a helping spirit that can bring wisdom, knowledge, or healing power to the seeker. If you find a particular tree or plant is continually holding a vivid place in your meditation, speak to it—perhaps it has a gift for you.

THE PATH OF MEDITATION

Another great source of meditation is Celtic art. Go to the library or search online for a collection of images from *The Book of Kells* or any of the other great Celtic masterpieces. For that matter, look for modern designs by artists like Courtney Davis, Jen Delyth, Cari Buziak, or Jim Fitzpatrick. Celtic art is colorful, organic, fluid, repetitive, geometric, filled with spirals and knotwork designs and fanciful depictions of animals—all powerful images for inner reflection. Think of *lectio divina* as an approach to Celtic art—it doesn't have to be used just for written texts. Think of illustrations as a different kind of "text"—after all, images weave together *text*-ures of meaning and spiritual reflection as surely as do words on a page.

Gaze into Celtic art and let it be for you an icon—that is to say, a window onto heaven or the spiritual world. Turn off your mind, let thinking take a holiday. Simply be present to the colors and the designs. Allow them to speak to your soul at a level deeper than words.

THE PATH OF MEDITATION

Another great tool for Celtic meditation is Celtic music. Whether it's the modal frenzy of high-energy Irish or Scottish dance music, or the contemplative introspection of a Welsh choral group, or the dreamy soundscapes created by the pipes or harp, plenty of sonic textures can be found in the Celtic world. Many forms of Celtic music lend themselves well to introspection, either because the music itself is slow and meditative (it's no accident that Enya has been the bestselling Celtic musician over the past decade), or because in its energy and vibrancy it can inspire a state of self-forgetful reverie. Both strategies work for cultivating a deepened inner life. Music may not teach us anything in a heady, philosophical sense—but that's because it's too busy transforming us where it really matters, in the heart and the belly. Of course, much Celtic music is dance music, and the "meditation" you may be inspired to explore involves movement and dance. Go with it. Meditate with your entire body. Remember: Celtic spirituality is about the goodness and beauty of nature, and your body is about as natural as you can get it. Be joyful, and dance!

THE PATH OF MEDITATION

Nature, indeed, is the ultimate window through which Celtic meditation may be accessed. Some secularists love to proclaim, "It's easier to find God in nature than in church!" Of course, the devout Celt would reply, "Open your eyes, and you'll find him in both places." But naturally, the wilderness is to the Celt nothing less than an epiphany of divine radiance, the stage on which the eternal movements of spiritual love and presence are continually enacted and reenacted. Look carefully and listen closely, and you can find Spirit in nature and through nature. Don't worry about whether or not you are worshipping nature—any reverence you give to the creation is naturally bestowed upon the creator. Besides, to the Celtic mind the line that separates creator from creature is joyfully ambiguous and fuzzy. Don't worry too much about getting it right—simply follow your heart and allow the devotion to flow.

How can we meditate in nature? It can be as extreme as climbing Mount Everest or as lowly as tending to a potted African violet in your office. Take walks. Go to the mountains or the beach. Work in your lawn or garden—and if you don't have one, find someone who does. Remember, you are a part of nature—but you're only as close to it as you allow yourself to be.

THE PATH OF MEDITATION

Whether your style of meditation is to visualize or to sit in austere silence; to connect with guiding spirits or to prefer the flight of the alone to the alone; whether you are particularly inspired by art, or myth, or music, or nature—give yourself the gift of a regular meditation practice. Think of meditation as the equivalent of brushing your teeth or taking a shower. Cleanliness may be next to Godliness, but it also requires daily attention. It doesn't take long for your breath or underarms to smell unpleasant! Now, think of meditation as a cleansing for the mind and soul. Not that your mind and soul are "dirty" in some sort of sinful or evil sense, but simply that it's lovelier to bask in the spirituality of relaxation and reverie, than to be continually troubled by the turmoil and distractions of a harried mind trying to maintain control over a frenzied life. Meditation offers us many benefits. Sure, it can be a way of deepening our conscious sense of connection with spirituality; but some of meditation's best gifts to us come purely on the physical level: reduced blood pressure; relaxed heart rate, general sense of well-being, even reduced cholesterol levels. And since your body is part of nature, meditation is not only a psychic wash-up, but it's also a tool for taking care of your natural environment—an environment that begins at home, within your very skin. So meditate daily—and feel the love.

THE PATH OF THE GODS

We have no reason to believe the ancient Celts were matriarchal, or even matrifocal. Irish law and ideas found both in classical writings and Celtic myths suggest that women probably enjoyed higher status in Celtic culture than in the Mediterranean societies of ancient Europe—but that does not mean the Celts practiced true gender equality or embodied any kind of a pre-feminist paradise where patriarchy was unknown. That being said, it's remarkable how Celtic mythology gives so much more color and excitement to the goddesses than to the gods. See how John Milton's poem *Paradise Lost* makes Satan a far more attractive figure than the God Milton worshipped. In a similar way, one would think that a heroic warrior culture like the Celts of old would revere dramatic and powerful manly gods. But the gods of Celtic tradition seem to be little more than superhuman warriors— handy with a sword, or else sexy studs, available to give the goddesses pleasure when they so desire it.

Different theories have been put forth to explain why the goddesses are so much more colorful than the gods. Perhaps the gods were censored more thoroughly by Christian scribes. Perhaps the Celtic understanding of the goddess as the land and the god as the tribe reflected a bias toward feminine depictions of spirit. Whatever it may be, Celtic myth does have its gods—they're just for the most part not star material.

THE PATH OF THE GODS

The most impressive of the gods, at least from the Irish tradition, is Lugh—a radiant figure who has been seen as a god of the sky, of light, or perhaps of the sun. Like most of his fellow deities, Lugh is a champion and a warrior, but also a poet, harper, gamesman, diplomat, statesman, and craftsman. Indeed, he is the one skilled at all the arts, and gained his entry to the sacred hall of Tara because of precisely that multi-skilled talent. He's also courageous, not afraid of a fight even when it involves standing up to the deadly and threatening armies of the Fomorians, the beings of chaos led by Lugh's own grandfather. Lugh charmed the king of the Tuatha Dé Danann, Nuadu, into surrendering the throne and allowing Lugh full authority to take on their feared enemies. Lugh assumed power and immediately organized his army according to the skills of each of the gods, goddesses and heroes who pledged to fight with him. It's a strategy that paid off—and Lugh did what few Celts since him have been able to manage: he organized his people into a functioning and powerful army, leading the Tribe of Dana to victory and personally killing his own grandfather. That's Lugh for you: radiant and luminous, yet not above killing a family member if they march on the wrong side.

THE PATH OF THE GODS

Given the number of warrior heroes in the Celtic tradition, it should be no surprise that many of the gods are remarkable chiefly for their courage, ferocity, and might in battle. Just as many of the goddesses embody sovereignty—the spirit of freedom itself, arising from the land—so do many of the gods embody guardianship, or the sacred trust of the warrior who vows to protect the land (and the people she nurtures). One larger-than-life example of this divine function in the Welsh tradition is Bran the Blessed, a son of the sea god Llyr. Bran was a giant, too large to live in conventional buildings; his sister, Branwen, married the king of Ireland, but because of several unfortunate events she was stripped of her rank and forced to be a servant in the royal kitchen. When news of this indignity reached Bran, he literally waded across the Irish Sea to avenge his sister's honor. In the battle that inevitably ensued, he was shot by a poisoned arrow, and instructed his comrades to sever his head from his rapidly dying body. The head lived on for an enchanted period of time, and Bran instructed his men that eventually his head should be buried in London—on what is now the site of the Tower of London. There he could remain ever vigilant, protecting the land from foreign invasion.

THE PATH OF THE GODS

Perhaps the most comical of Celtic gods is the Irish father-deity known as the Dagda, which means "the good god"—good not in a moralistic sense, but rather like Lugh in the sense of possessing many skills and talents. But where Lugh is a gorgeous, radiant warrior, concerned with issues of justice and leadership, the Dagda is clownish and fat, known for overindulgence in sensual pleasures, both culinary and erotic. But he is no slouch in battle: the Dagda possesses a club that is mighty enough to kill nine foes with a single blow—and yet just as one end of the club is a force for such destruction, touching a dead warrior with the opposite (handle) end will restore his to life. The Dagda also possesses the great cauldron, so abundant that an entire army can be fed from within it.

The Dagda represents abundance in the most grossly physical of ways—he's big: a big god, a big eater, and a vigorous lover. He does nothing halfway. But where Lugh's largeness is writ upon the sky in light and orderliness, the Dagda is earthy and not a little bit chaotic. Unseemly perhaps—but out of his messy earthiness he serves as a father to the gods, siring many children, the most famous being Brigit and Angus Óg.

THE PATH OF THE GODS

If Lugh is the sky and the Dagda the earth, then the god who symbolizes the third great realm in the Celtic cosmos is Manannán (in Welsh, Manawydan), the son of the mysterious and shadowy sea god Lir (Llyr). Manannán is often thought to be one of the oldest of Celtic deities; in Irish tradition he appears to be independent of the Tuatha Dé Danann. He is a trickster and a magician, and his skills include the ability to appear and disappear at will, and to travel long distances over both land and water. Like Poseidon, he is able to command the waves of the ocean like great horses fashioned of water. He is said to wear a bag fashioned of the skin of a crane, in which he keeps a number of magical treasures; some scholars have suggested that this is similar to a spirit-bag worn by shamans, indicating a possible link between Manannán and primal Celtic shamanism. More evidence for this link comes out of his recurring function in mythology as a guardian of the gates between the physical world and the otherworld, or indeed as one who escorts mortals into the fairy realms. Indeed, modern druids sometimes invoke Manannán as the spirit who guards the entry into the spiritual dimension.

THE PATH OF THE GODS

One of the great comic figures in Welsh myth is Pwyll, the Prince of Dyfed. The poor guy just can't get anything right, it seems. One time he unwittingly insulted the Lord of the Underworld; on another occasion he made a blunder that nearly lost him the woman of his dreams (who just happens to be the great queen-goddess, Rhiannon). Indeed, when he met Rhiannon he displayed just how (un)clever he was. Seeing Rhiannon ride her otherworldly steed in what appeared to be a gentle trot, Pwyll chased after her; but no matter how hard he rode his horse, he could not catch her. Finally, in desperation, he called out to her to wait for him. This she willingly did, commenting that if he had only had the brains to ask her to wait to begin with, he would have saved his horse quite some effort.

The moral of this story is so obviously simple: if you want something, ask for it. If you don't state your needs as clearly as possible, you are just about guaranteed that they will go unmet. Spiritually speaking, asking for what we want or need is not for the benefit of the Spirit, but for *our own* benefit. To ask for what you want requires not only that you make the effort to be clear-minded about your desires; it also calls for good old-fashioned humility.

THE PATH OF THE GODS

The goddess Brigit is known as a goddess of blacksmiths. This has led some to speculate that she was a warrior goddess; after all, wasn't it the blacksmith who forged swords, and spearheads, or other military equipment? But Brigit's role at the forge may have been mostly peaceful, consistent with her role as a goddess of the land and of livestock. Horseshoes may have been more important to her than shields or helmets. Meanwhile, the Celts had their smith gods, similar to Vulcan or Hephaestus, who presided over the forge and governed all technology—including military might. The Irish smith-god is Goibniu, and may be related to a similar figure in Welsh tradition called Gofannon, or a folkloric smith known as the Gobbán Saor. He is the ultimate defense contractor. When Lugh requested aid from all the gods and heroes of the Tuatha Dé Danann, Goibniu offered his technical skill—to forge weapons that would not break or miss their target. While Lugh and the Dagda symbolize skill in the sense of personal mastery, Goibniu's skill is more of the artisan or craftsman—he can work with the mighty energies of nature to shape elements of the physical world into useful, desired ends.

THE PATH OF THE GODS

A number of deities, both gods and goddesses, have varying skills as healers, but the most famous in this category is probably Dian Cécht, physician to the Tuatha Dé Danann. His name means "swift power," and the power he possesses is the ability to mend wounds and foster health. He is the father of Cian, who in turn fathered Lugh. Dian Cécht's other children included Miach and Airmid, both gifted healers in their own right who inspired jealousy in the father—perhaps the closest the Celtic tradition comes to "original sin" is the story in which Dian Cécht kills Miach because of his superior healing skills, and then scatters the herbs Airmid gathers from Miach's grave (thereby scattering the knowledge of plants that could heal every conceivable form of illness). But when he wasn't playing rival to his children, Dian Cécht served the greater community of gods well enough; during battle not only did he work feverishly to heal the wounded, but he also presided over a holy well that could cure anyone except for those decapitated. He also created a prosthetic arm, made of silver, for Nuadu after he lost his limb during one battle.

THE PATH OF THE GODS

Finally, let us consider one of the most mysterious of Celtic deities, who appears not in the myths of either Ireland or Wales, but comes to us through the largely mute world of archaeology—Cernunnos, whose name means "Horned One." This god (or godlike figure) is often depicted with antlers on his head, seated in what appears to be a yogic pose, with animals attending to him (most notably the mysterious ram-headed snake). He appears to be a god of wilderness and forest, perhaps a totem figure of the stag or the serpent, and possibly a representation of a helpful shamanic spirit. Various figures from myth and folklore have been the object of speculation concerning Cernunnos, including the Dagda and the great hunter of British folklore, Herne. Cernunnos is also seen as a form of the popular "Green Man" figure who appears carved in many old churches and who may represent a vestigial image of an ancient forest god. Of all the Celtic gods, Cernunnos is the one most widely embraced by modern neopagans, probably due to the fact that several scholars of witchcraft and folklore have suggested that European witchcraft is traditionally oriented toward the worship of a mother goddess and a horned god. Although that theory is no longer seen as anything other than modern speculation, its legacy is the ongoing popularity of what may well be the Celtic world's most mysterious male figure.

THE PATH OF HOSPITALITY

Recently I was heading, with Celtic harpist Gwen Knighton, to Saint Petersburg, Florida, to present a workshop. In Valdosta, Georgia, Gwen's van overheated. Fearing a cracked head gasket, we looked for a mechanic, and found Earl Copeland's Garage. Earl was a soft-spoken gentleman who took time out of a busy day to look at the engine, assess the problem, discuss the options with us, and—when it became obvious that we would need to rent a vehicle to make it to our gig—drove me 8 miles to the car rental office at the local airport. All this, and he refused a penny for his time and effort, even though we made arrangements to dispose of the van rather than pay for repairs (that would cost more than the vehicle was worth). We tried to pay him, but he refused with a modest shrug. "You folks have enough to worry about," he said simply.

We don't know if Earl has Celtic blood, but we do know that "southern hospitality" has its roots in the Scots-Irish immigrants who populated the region. So we responded to his generosity as best we could: Gwen gave him two of her CDs— and now I'm offering him—and his hospitality—due honor. If Earl ever reads this, he'd probably wonder what the fuss was about. That's because one of the characteristics of hospitality is that it's not about reward or recognition. It's just a simple and sacred way of living.

THE PATH OF HOSPITALITY

Celtic lore is clear about the importance of hospitality as a core value holding society together. The reigns of mythic kings were judged on their hospitality (or lack thereof). In fact, when a Fomorian warrior became king of the Tuatha Dé Danann, he soon became renowned for his parsimony. The Fomorians, after all, were the "bad guys" of Irish myth, alternatively seen as pirates, tyrants, forces of chaos, and just plain demons. This particular king, Bres, raised inhospitality to a fine art. Bards complained that those who visited his house could count on leaving with no smell of beer on their breath! Finally, a bard named Cairbre was fed up enough to write a satire about the ungenerous king—the first satire ever composed in Ireland. Its effect was blistering—literally—as it caused sores to burst forth on Bres' face, blemishing him and making him unfit to rule.

I don't think the message here is about taking revenge on those we encounter who lack hospitality. For like charity, hospitality begins at home, and so the story of Bres is a reminder that if we want to live in a world of hospitality, we begin by opening our own doors (and hearts).

THE PATH OF HOSPITALITY

A few years back I attended a workshop featuring the Celtic author Caitlín Matthews. At one point during the workshop, which was attended mostly by neopagans, the question of religious tolerance came up. Caitlín spoke for a minute or two about the many Christians who attend her workshops, and even the Christian centers who host her events. She finished this little discussion with the sentence I found the most memorable of the entire weekend: "I'm willing to speak anywhere where a spirituality of hospitality is practiced, whether Christian, Pagan, or whatever." Those words electrified me, and gave me a clear sense of how Celtic wisdom transcends religious boundaries. After all, in the consciousness of hospitality, religious (or any other) differences are not erased or eliminated. But they cease to become the defining factor of who we are. If I am focusing on how you and I are so different from one another, community becomes strained if not impossible. But when we choose to place our attention instead on our hospitality and the spirituality of shared resources and open hearts, then our differences are reduced to the simple ways in which we embody diversity and distinctiveness—lovely qualities, after all, for they have their roots in nature.

THE PATH OF HOSPITALITY

Celtic tradition sometimes employs sly humor when considering the place that hospitality holds in the social order. On the eve of the great battle between the Tuatha Dé Danann and the Fomorians, the great god of the Dana tribe known as the Dagda went to pay a visit on the camp of his foes. Now the Dagda was a god of abundance, and as such was known for the abundance of his waistline. The Fomorians decided to have some fun at their guest's expense. They dug a gigantic pit in the ground and filled it, not only with porridge, but also with huge cuts of meat and entire bushels of produce. Wanting to humiliate the Dagda, they insisted that he eat the meal they prepared for him—to the last bite. It would have been rude for him to refuse their hospitality, after all.

As it turns out, the joke was on the Fomorians, for the Dagda had an appetite to match all his other abundances. He asked for a shovel and used it as a makeshift spoon, cleaning out the entire pit and even scraping the gravel at the bottom!

Of course, the moral of the story is that the Fomorians really *weren't* hospitable at all, since their aim was to humiliate rather than to honor their guest. But the Dagda met their mean-spiritedness with his own generosity, happily eating all that was offered him.

THE PATH OF HOSPITALITY

As the story of the Dagda and the Fomorians so clearly demonstrates, it's a commonplace idea in the Celtic myths that refusing hospitality is itself an act lacking in hospitality. In fact, the great hero of Ulster, Cúchulainn, was under a sacred vow, or *geas*, never to refuse hospitality. Many of the mythic heroes had one or more *geasa* imposed on them, prohibiting them from certain acts lest tragedy ensue if the *geas* were broken. Alas for Cúchulainn, he had another *geas*, never to eat the meat of a dog. The moment of truth came when he encountered an impoverished old woman who offered him a bowl of stew. The gruel contained hound meat. Faced with an impossible dilemma, Cúchulainn finally accepted the food and ate the meat, even though this violation of his *geas* set into motion the events that would claim his life. Disregarding for a moment the larger themes of tragedy in that story, consider how Cúchulainn, knowing that he would break his vow no matter what he did, chose to preserve his commitment to hospitality before he maintained his dietary taboo. I'm not trying to suggest that a diabetic should eat a candy bar just because someone offers it; but simply that the Celtic path regards hospitality with such honor that even a warrior as mighty as Cúchulainn couldn't bear to refuse it.

THE PATH OF HOSPITALITY

Celtic hospitality is not just a matter of myth and legend. Indeed, when Gwen and I talk about our experiences at Earl's Garage, we compare it to the kind of treatment we've received in the British Isles. One time I was in Banbridge, County Down, and was having difficulty finding lodging; I mentioned this to the owner of a pub and he spent the next half hour driving me around until I found a room for the night. An even better tale comes from a former student of mine, who had a flat tire once while traveling in rural Ireland. Stopping in front of a farmhouse and hoping to use the phone, he met the farmer who insisted on fixing the tire himself—and then the farmer's wife invited my student and his family in for dinner! And of course, talk of payment was quickly squelched. "No need for that," the farmer said simply.

Maybe in some parts of the world these stories would be unremarkable. But to an American used to living in a rapid-paced urban environment where too few people really reach out to others, I find such examples of hospitality to be inspiring even if sadly unfamiliar. And I live in Atlanta, Georgia, the heart of the region in America renowned for its hospitality! And yes, southern hospitality does exist—but the student must not presume to be better than the master.

THE PATH OF HOSPITALITY

I've already talked about the link between generosity and sovereignty, a link that underscores the place that hospitality holds in the Celtic consciousness. For true hospitality can only be given freely—implying a certain self-autonomy that the word "sovereignty" implies, whether applied to an individual or an entire society. Of course, hospitality extends beyond material generosity. A corporation will give away tremendous resources in its promotional campaigns, but it's always done with an eye to future sales and profits. Meanwhile, true hospitality can be found in a moment of attention or a simple glass of water on a sweltering day. Perhaps the single most important quality in hospitality is freedom. If I give, in order to receive later, it's not a free gift, nor does it come out of my sovereignty. For I am a slave to my own need for self-protection. Only when I am truly liberated from all bondage, standing proud and free in relation to the land and my community, am I in a position to open up to receive the stranger and support those who come to me with a need. That's when hospitality happens.

THE PATH OF HOSPITALITY

Those of us who live far away from the Celtic lands, or whose lives are immersed in the competitive, guarded, alienated world of modern urban society, may be at a loss as to how hospitality can be applied today. Sure, maybe a mechanic in a small Georgia town can afford to devote an hour of his time to a non-paying customer in need (although, in fact, he really was too busy for such generosity), but for most of us, that kind of grand gesture could lead to disciplinary action from our profit-minded supervisors. How can hospitality be nurtured today?

Perhaps two principles apply here: letting things be imperfect, and letting miracles unfold slowly. In other words, be hospitable toward yourself as you seek ways to cultivate hospitality in your world. None of us has to go from being Bres the Fomorian to becoming Mother Teresa overnight. But we all can find small ways to offer grace to others. Drive a little less aggressively. Invite the neighbors over for dinner. Take time to comfort an upset coworker. Visit your great aunt in the nursing home, and take her to church. And of course, be available to host guests in your home—if not total strangers, then at least out-of-town friends when they're passing through. Remember, hospitality doesn't demand that your house feels like an elegant New York hotel. It just needs to be warm, clean, and most of all, loving.

THE PATH OF HOSPITALITY

"I can't afford to offer hospitality to others. Think of all the psychos and nutcases out there! Once I open my home to one of them, I'm vulnerable." Okay, so there's a difference between offering hospitality and being stupid. Cúchulainn hardly showed hospitality to the army that invaded Ulster. Like anything else, the virtue of hospitality requires discernment and common sense; it is not meant to be a rule so rigidly applied that the role of host becomes a prison. Remember the relationship between hospitality and sovereignty: it's only true hospitality when it is given out of utter freedom. The minute we feel obligated to be generous, what we are doing is something different from hospitality. Maybe it's saving face, or keeping up appearances, or trying to please mom or God or someone. Such behavior may not be bad—but it's not true hospitality. So don't check your brain at the door. You're only free to say yes when you are simultaneously free to say no. (This applies to many things, not just hospitality).

THE PATH OF DEVOTION

Just two miles south of the Cliffs of Moher in County Clare, Ireland, is a small and beautifully landscaped park situated between the highway and a cemetery at the top of a hill. This park features a lovely statue of Saint Brigid (encased in a glass booth for protection from the salty ocean air) and a small building which houses a holy well—a natural water source that has been venerated for generations. As the statue suggests, the well (like many others in Ireland) is dedicated to Saint Brigid. But what is most remarkable about this humble site is the interior of the well-building: for it contains literally hundreds of religious statues, rosaries, mass cards, and other items, both sacred and secular, that represent and symbolize the prayers of countless supplicants who have visited the well over the years. Saint Brigid's Well is a site of prayer and devotion. It is also a site where votive offerings are made—a practice that has its roots in the pagan water worship of the ancient Celts, but is now performed by most devotees in a strictly Christian manner. It seems that while religious forms may change, the essential practice of devotion has remained more or less consistent. If the practice at this holy well (and countless others) is any indication, devotion is a central feature of Celtic spirituality.

THE PATH OF DEVOTION

No one knows exactly how many holy wells are still venerated in the Celtic lands. Maybe hundreds, maybe even thousands. Many are dedicated to Saint Brigid, others to Saint Patrick, and still others to the Virgin Mary or some other saint. A few wells, like Tobernault near Sligo, have no official connection with a saint, but still are places of prayer, pilgrimage and devotion. Many wells are particularly visited on "Pattern days" which local devotees observe, often on the saint's feast day or some other day significant for each well. Large crowds will visit the well on such days to perform the patterns—ceremonial acts of prayer and devotion that may include specific prayers as well as ritual movements such as walking clockwise around the well a specified number of times. Other common practices at holy wells include leaving money or other offerings (such as the paraphernalia found at Saint Brigid's Well in County Clare), tying prayer rags or clooties on a tree near the well, and drinking the water or immersing an ailing limb into the well. It's not easy to describe customary acts of veneration at holy wells, for the traditions and practices vary from well to well. Local customs dictate the nature of the devotions that take place at such sacred spots.

THE PATH OF DEVOTION

Holy wells have always been somewhat controversial, because their critics see in them too strong a vestige of pagan practice. But other acts of devotion within the Celtic world have a purely Christian orientation. The village of Knock in County Sligo is a major site for pilgrimage and devotion to the Virgin Mary, thanks to a miraculous apparition of the Virgin and other saints that occurred there in August of 1879. It may not be as famous as Lourdes or Guadalupe, but Knock has still become well known enough as a site for spiritual yearning to entirely transform the town, including the construction of a large basilica where the faithful may offer their prayers. Just as some may be put off by the apparent paganism within the holy-well tradition, others might find at Knock a type of religious spirituality that is more sectarian than universal. But Knock and holy wells have in common a profound sensibility of devotion. They are disparate examples of just how important this quality is to the Celtic path. This is not a path of dry theological speculation or restrained, formalistic worship. It is a path of the heart, and of heartfelt love and yearning for authentic spiritual experience.

THE PATH OF DEVOTION

What is devotion? What is the role that it plays in the spiritual life? It is often thought of in emotional terms, as if spiritual devotion means expressing love or heartfelt worship to God or some other divine source. But the word's meaning actually has more to do with the will. "Devotion" literally means "of the expression of a vow." Vow, meanwhile, has to do with making a promise. This begs the question, of course: just what exactly is it that the promise is expressed *towards*? So devotion always has an object, whether human (as in a lover) or divine (as in God or Mary or Brigid). Furthermore, a promise involves a commitment—a focusing of the will. Such a focusing might naturally include an element of profound feeling, but it's important to remember that it's first and foremost about a choice, a vow. Devotional spirituality involves the act of making a deep commitment—to honor or worship or venerate the object of faith. Therefore, what makes the holy wells (or the shrine at Knock) so special is not how they make people feel, but rather how they inspire people to a committed expression of their spiritual life.

THE PATH OF DEVOTION

Celtic devotion has implications far beyond sacred waters or the sites of visions. Consider the traditional practice of leaving food or milk for the fairies. This could be dismissed as mere superstition, but strictly speaking, it is a simple devotional (willfully chosen) act with roots in ancient beliefs. If the land is filled with the presence of supernatural beings, then offering nourishment to those entities is a sensible way to try to ensure future prosperity and lack of trouble. It may not be devotion in the kind of emotional sense that we have come to associate with the word; after all, offerings to the fairies were often made as a way of buying them off, since they were seen as amoral and potentially dangerous. But it is devotion in the sense of a commitment to actions designed to foster positive relations between humanity and the spirit world—or humanity and nature (since, metaphorically speaking, the fairies symbolize the personification of the natural world).

THE PATH OF DEVOTION

Consider the pre-Celtic burial grounds such as Newgrange or Carrowmore in Ireland; or the various cairns and dolmens found throughout western Europe. On top of that, consider the folk practices of offering food for deceased relatives on the night of Samhain, when the spirits of the ancestors were believed to walk the earth. Such evidence points to devotion to the ancestors as an important element of Celtic wisdom. This does not necessarily mean ancestor worship, although the ancients may have done so; we can express devotion to an object without necessarily expressing worship. We can see in ancestral devotion the Celtic concern with place and tradition; the place where our forebears lived, died and are buried is an important clue to understanding who we are; and the spirits of the ancestors represent the traditions and histories and similarly define who we are. It is from our ancestors that we get our lives, for it is their DNA that lives in us; so devotion to the ancestors is a way of expressing love for ourselves.

THE PATH OF DEVOTION

Devotion to the land and devotion to the ancestors (which is a way of expressing devotion to the tribe, or the collective human family to which we belong) can be seen as two thirds of a sacred trinity. The final part, of course, is the ultimate form of devotion—devotion to the Divine. For Christians, naturally, this means devotion to God; although the Catholic devotion to Mary can also be seen as an expression of committed faith toward the Divine. Pagans, however, would direct this kind of devotion to one or many different divinities, including the various gods and goddesses of Celtic myth. Although religious beliefs will shape how we understand the Divine, our acts of devotion offered in this direction could be the same regardless. Remember, both pagan and Christian Celts have made offerings at sacred water sources. It is just how they understood the Spirit who received such devotions that separated the two practices. No matter what one's religious persuasion, devotion to the Divine means a commitment to express faith to that Source, however it is understood. This, indeed, is the heart of the most profound dimension of Celtic spirituality.

THE PATH OF DEVOTION

What is the point of devotion? Why bother leaving offerings at wells, or making a pilgrimage to Knock, or remembering the spirit of a deceased relative? How does spilling an ounce or two of milk on the ground for the fairies make a difference in the world? There are two ways of approaching such questions, depending on how seriously one takes the expression of faith. For the true believer, devotion is clearly important because it expresses a committed, ongoing relationship between the devotee and the spiritual being(s) receiving such veneration. If I'm a devotee of Brigid or Mary or whomever, I don't just think about them when my thoughts randomly land on them. Rather, I make a choice to make them part of my life. And therefore, I can trust in their goodwill and favor.

But devotion is beneficial in a way that even a skeptic can appreciate. For making the commitment to be devoted spiritually is making an inner commitment to growth and development. Just as any commitment (marriage, work, and so forth) can make us better people, so a spiritual commitment can support psychological growth.

THE PATH OF DEVOTION

Devotion, like so many aspects of spirituality, is important not only in itself, but also in terms of where it takes us. There is more to the spiritual life than merely expressing committed love toward the god, goddess, or fairy spirit of our choosing. Devotion matters not only for itself, but also for how it helps us grow and expand spiritually (but in practical ways). The true devotee to the fairies does not just leave out the occasional spot of milk, but also begins to think about how to take care of the land in a way that honors the spirits. The devotee to Brigid or Mary seeks not only to say the right prayers, but also to live life in a manner that honors the one receiving the veneration. And a devotee to the spirits of the ancestors will sooner or later consider how living a noble and ethical life is a particularly meaningful way to express love for those who have gone before.

Service. Care for others. Sanctity. Ethical living. These virtues are not caused by devotion, but rather rise out of a devotee's behaviors and beliefs. If you make the choice to be devoted (by reading this book, perhaps you have already chosen to be devoted to the realm of Celtic wisdom), know that your choice/commitment will change you. How or when may be up for negotiation. But the change will come.

THE PATH OF THE ANAMCHARA

One of the loveliest of Celtic words is *anamchara* (also spelled *anam cara*), a Gaelic term that means "soul friend." In a world where we tend to rely on licensed professionals to nurture our mental and emotional well-being, the homely and unassuming idea of a friend who tends to the soul—not a therapist, not a psychiatrist, not a pastoral counselor, just a friend—seems almost subversive, if not revolutionary. It is reminiscent of the subtitle of one of psychiatrist and spiritual guide Gerald May's books: *Stop Fixing Yourself and Start Living*. Ours is a world of striving and competition, where consumerism defines reality and dying with the most toys really is what "wins." But none of this is the Celtic way, where a quiet afternoon sipping tea with an old friend means far more than the latest Hollywood blockbuster or the newest must-have technological doodad. A soul friend is important because friendship is essential to the soul—what makes an anamchara special is not the fact that he or she attends to the soul, but simply that the friendship is based on the conscious awareness and recognition that a relationship like this not only nourishes life, but is essential to it. So many of us go through life with one or more "accidental" soul friends— people who nourish our souls because it is their nature to do so. Identifying them as our soul friends simply acknowledges their gift, as well as our need.

THE PATH OF THE ANAMCHARA

Among the earliest Celtic Christians, it was said that "Anyone without a soul friend is like a body without a head." It's an extreme notion, and yet exemplifies how serious this concept of intimate, personal spiritual nurture has been to walkers on the Celtic path. In other words, a soul friend—someone with whom you might share the most intimate details of your spiritual journey—is not some sort of luxury that bored socialites can indulge in between their garden club meetings. It's an essential for living an authentic spiritual life. The ancients realized that truly engaging with the demands of spirituality meant being able to share the dynamics of the inner world with a trusted companion. Why would it be any different for us today?

Of course, many of us rely on professionals to provide our "soul friend" experience. Others are fortunate enough to have someone who functions as an anamchara by default. Perhaps we need to make it a priority to be intentional about having (or finding) a relationship that extends beyond the weather or the daily drama of our feelings—and take the contemplative time necessary to truly befriend the hidden depths that lie within each of us, but that we so rarely allow a voice.

THE PATH OF THE ANAMCHARA

What does a soul friend do? It's not a therapeutic relationship, so there's no agenda based on achieving a goal or managing an emotional or mental dysfunction. Nor is it a pastoral relationship, where a mentor provides theological and moral guidance. Then again, a soul friend relationship might include a therapeutic or pastoral dimension—but it's a different focus. The soul friend is a spiritual companion—sort of like the best friend we turned to for advice and insight when we first fell in love as teenagers. It's not the job of a friend like this to provide answers, or to fix problems—but rather, simply to be present, to offer an opinion when it's appropriate to do so, but just as often to refrain from spewing unneeded advice. The ideal soul friend is one who takes his or her own spiritual life seriously enough that there can be a shared language or vocabulary of experience when discussing the landscape of the inner journey. Often a soul friend will share your religious or spiritual persuasion, but even this is not absolutely essential. Far better that your soul friend shares the yearning of your heart rather than the duties of your faith. In Christian terms, a soul friend will be your companion in prayer. Neopagans might prefer to see such a person as a partner in living the magical life. Use the language that works for you—listen to your heart, and seek someone who speaks to it.

THE PATH OF THE ANAMCHARA

Who can be a soul friend? Almost anyone, really. I've heard it said that a husband or wife or lover is not the best choice, but that shouldn't be an inflexible rule—even though there's wisdom in befriending a person with a bit of distance. If necessary, a minister or counselor can do the job, but that makes for a blurring of roles that might not always work out very well. Ideally, a soul friend is just exactly that: a friend with soul. Someone with whom the most natural and appropriate style of relating is friendly—equal, intimate without being sexually charged, relaxed. Like all friends, this is a person with whom it's easy to feel you're "on the same side." The soul aspect has to do with the indefinable quality of interior depth and awareness that reaches out from your friend's inner landscape to your own, and back again. That quality cannot be adequately described in a book. It can only be yearned for, searched for, and ultimately experienced. Sadly, therefore, a soul friend cannot just be ordered through a website or found in a phonebook. A true soul friend may take weeks, months, even years to find. But such a connection is worth the wait—and the search.

THE PATH OF THE ANAMCHARA

What is it like to spend time with a soul friend? Well, that's up to you and your anamchara, isn't it? Some such friends may enjoy praying or meditating or doing ritual together, or sharing ideas and discussing interesting books you're both reading; such friends may be the active sort who love to go hiking or the contemplative sort who prefer long moments of silence while the tea is brewing. Although some soul friends might spend nearly all their time talking about "spiritual stuff" and others only bring it up occasionally, there will be on some level a conscious sense of shared spirituality. But this can take many forms. Likewise, soul friends might be very structured in their relationship, meeting for ninety minutes once a month, with a new appointment set up before the old one is finished. But it might just as easily be the sort of comfortable companionship that connects on a strictly "as-needed" basis. Conceivably, soul friends might live in the same building or on the other side of the world (thus communicating by mail, phone or online). If there's a shared religious orientation, presumably friends will enjoy the opportunity to do the work of their faith as part of their companionship, whether that means going to church together, participating in a service-oriented project, or reciting a shared prayer or sacred poem.

THE PATH OF THE ANAMCHARA

The paradox of a soul friend lies in this: to be a true soul friend, one should have a sense that this is what's going on; as I've said before, while most of us have or have had "accidental" soul friends, the true riches of this kind of relationship only reveal themselves when it is entered into consciously. And yet, the biggest threat to the soul friend connection (aside from our culture's hell-bent desire to turn spirituality into just another consumer commodity, which could threaten to turn soul friendship into a fashionable "must-have" spiritual accessory) is self-consciousness. So the key to making this relationship work is humility, in the best sense of the word: that is to say, self-forgetfulness. I know I'm a friend of your soul, and so now I forget all about it—it's no big deal, really (and yet, it *is* a sacred big deal). This is a paradox, and I'm back to the old trick of the druids, talking in oblique and mysterious ways. Yet it's a paradox worth keeping in mind. We need to value soul friendship enough to make it a priority—and then, having found a soul friend, we need to value the uniqueness and potential of the relationship itself by making it as unstructured, and unbeholden to an agenda, as possible.

THE PATH OF THE ANAMCHARA

Earlier today I saw my soul friend. He talked about the difficulties he faced in relating to his grown son, and so we talked a bit about the challenges of parenting in the postmodern world. At one point I said, "I know it's not my place to tell you how to be a parent," and my friend smiled— because I kept asking the hard questions and he kept responding as best he could. Next time we get together, it might be *my* parenting style, or career, or troubled relationship with institutional religion, that provides the raw material for our soul-sharing connection.

Soul friends are accountable to one another. No, not in any sort of formalized way—when I see him next month, my friend will not have to report back to me about how things are going with his son. But I will be interested in his soul (as he will be in mine). So we will probably talk about declarations we've made, promises to ourselves or to God or to others, where the integrity (and where the BS) can be found in our lives.

Spirituality can be a terribly narcissistic thing, as we get all cozy and comfy with God or the Goddess in our precious inner universes. Soul friendship breathes space and light into that tightly bound dynamic, allowing the spiritual feedback-loop to be integrated into the eyes and ears and discerning mind of another soul.

THE PATH OF THE ANAMCHARA

What makes the soul friend relationship "Celtic"? Sure, the word anamchara is Gaelic enough, but the value and quality of a soul friendship is universal—it can provide meaning in any cultural, religious or spiritual context. This is something good to keep in mind. Celtic wisdom and spirituality are ultimately only valuable insofar as they help us not to be more purely or securely "Celtic," but rather provide insight and guidance into finding greater depth, joy, and connection in being *human*. Still, the soul friend comes to us specifically from the Celtic world, so it's fair to ask how Celtic symbolism and ideas shape this meaningful relationship.

I think the key lies in the virtues: hospitality, earthiness, honor, courage, and peacemaking—these are the qualities that shape a deep friendship with a conscious spiritual dimension. Once again, you could argue that these are not just Celtic values; they are universal values. No argument there, actually. And yet, it is in the context of the Celtic tradition—the context of our interest in the druids of old, or the early saints—that we can find a meaningful way to be such soul friends to one another. So here we have a lovely example of Celtic spirituality inspiring us simply to be more truly alive, more deeply connected with wisdom—in whatever form it might take.

THE PATH OF THE ANAMCHARA

One more thought about the anamchara—it's a way of relating to others that encompasses the best qualities of the ancient druids, bards, and seers, woven together into a single approach toward spiritual intimacy. Like a druid, a soul friend can help us create rituals and ceremonies, or ask challenging questions, or learn powerful insights from psychology or science or history—in short, to help us to stay alert and mindful of our souls' needs. Like a bard, a soul friend can tell us meaningful stories, and invite us to become the bard of the most important story we'll ever know—the unique and powerful story of our own soul's journey. And like a seer, a soul friend takes us beyond the dance of psychology into the ineffable realm of spiritual experience and meaning, discovering the thin places within our hearts and souls, and traversing those gateways to encounter the eternal places that shape who we truly are.

So not every soul friend will do all of these things, or some friendships may be more druidic or more bardic in their orientation. That's okay. Remember—the anamchara is a gentle, homely, okay-to-be-imperfect kind of friend. And within that earthiness and simplicity, there's plenty of room for miracles to occur.

THE PATH OF THE GODDESSES

Celtic spirituality is goddess spirituality. Celtic mythology and ancient sacred art reveal a vibrant pagan spirituality, complete with many different goddesses (and gods), many of whom were only revered in particular locations. Many of the pagan deities were linked to nature, and had associations with a specific river, or mountain, or other feature of the landscape.

In recent years many spiritual seekers have become devoted to "the Goddess"—in other words a great, overarching feminine deity, sort of a womanly counterpart to the father God of Christian and other monotheistic faiths. There's no evidence, however, that the ancient Celts ever venerated such a universal deity (of either gender). Before the coming of Christianity, the Celts appear to be either animists (worshippers of nature) or polytheists (worshippers of many different gods and goddesses). Indeed, the closest they seem to come to a great goddess would be the various figures of sovereignty venerated in different parts of the Celtic world. Often these sovereignty goddesses were linked to the land, or to the king and the seat of power.

When the Celts arrived in Ireland, they met three goddesses: Banba, Fódla and Ériu. Each one offered to support the Celts in their quest to settle there, and each asked in turn that the land be named after her. Since Ériu offered the best help and was encountered near the center of the land, her name became the primary name for Ireland.

THE PATH OF THE GODDESSES

Áine is a mysterious figure in Celtic lore; she is an Irish fairy queen, and may well be the vestigial form of the mother goddess Dana, for whom the mythological Tuatha Dé Danann are named. Two hills in Kerry are known as the Paps of Anu, and some scholars believe Anu, Áine, and Dana are the same figure. But there's little fact and much speculation in trying to piece together the loose ends of ancient Celtic lore. A few tales here and there, or a place or two named after this god or that heroine, often leave an unsatisfying sense of the role that any one spiritual personage might have played in the lore of the people. Áine is one such mysterious figure.

She's associated with a hill called Knockainy in County Limerick, and it is said that this hill was her home and that even until modern times she was venerated as a powerful fairy presence there. According to tradition, the local people would process by torchlight to the top of the hill and invoke Áine's aid and protection of the crops and livestock. Some tales were even told of young girls who could see the fairy queen and her retinue at the top of Knockainy. Áine has strong fertility associations, and so she appears in folklore as a sexy, lusty figure, who enjoys the pleasures of many lovers both mortal and immortal.

THE PATH OF THE GODDESSES

Long before it was referred to in the hit song by Fleetwood Mac, the lovely name Rhiannon belonged to one of the most elegant and memorable of Celtic goddesses. This Welsh name means "great queen," and refers to one of the major figures in the cycle of Welsh myths called the Mabinogi. Rhiannon appears riding on her magical horse, accepts the bumbling romantic overtures of the mortal prince Pwyll, and helps him salvage their romance when he unwittingly allows another suitor to claim her hand. After their marriage she gives birth to Pryderi, and immediately suffers great loss when the baby disappears and her ladies in waiting accuse her of killing and eating the child. She is forced to suffer a humiliating punishment for several years until the baby (now a small child) is magically rescued and restored to her. Other stories in the Mabinogi link Rhiannon to the sea-god Manawydan. In addition to her powerful horse associations, three lovely white birds are associated with her.

Rhiannon is said to be the patroness of sorrowful mothers, offering hope just as she eventually received hers in the restoration of her son. She may be equivalent to several other deities in the Celtic world, including the Gaulish horse goddess Epona, the mysterious British goddess Rigantona, and perhaps the Irish goddesses Macha and the Mórrígan.

THE PATH OF THE GODDESSES

The Mórrígan may be Ireland's answer to Rhiannon. Not only do both have names that mean "queen," but both have horse associations—Rhiannon obviously so, and the Mórrígan through her aspect as Macha. But while Rhiannon is generally seen as regal, elegant, a symbol of refinement or luxury, the phantom queen of Irish tradition has a darker, edgier, bolder persona. She is a battle goddess, and under her guise as a raven could strike fear in the hearts of warriors who feared for their lives (according to legend, she last appeared at the Battle of Clontarf in 1014, when Brian Boru was killed). But she also had a frankly sexual, erotic side; she mated with the burly god known as the Dagda at Samhain, and attempted to seduce Cúchulainn—unsuccessfully, since he was so dedicated to his craft as a warrior that he single-mindedly rejected her, to her undying wrath.

The Mórrígan was also a prophet; she would appear, as an old hag washing her clothes at the ford, to warriors who were about to fall in battle; and at the end of one major fight, she solemnly predicted chaos, disorder and the end of all good things. One can only hope that such a prophecy is meant as a warning, and that in heeding the warning (and in learning to relate properly to such primal qualities as fear and rage and violence) the human family can avoid her vision of an ominous future.

THE PATH OF THE GODDESSES

Many Celtic goddesses are tragic figures, and it's debatable whether this is just because the Celts are so fond of sad stories. It might also be a subconscious effort to memorialize the loss of goddess energies with the one-two punch of Roman occupation in much of the Celtic lands, and the subsequent arrival of Christianity with its image of a single masculine deity. For whatever reason, it is remarkable how the stories of the Celtic goddesses are often profoundly poignant. The fairy goddess Macha dies after being forced to run in a race when her mortal husband brags about her speed. Rhiannon spends years in a humiliating public punishment for a crime she didn't commit. And then there's Branwen, daughter of the Welsh sea god Llyr, who marries the king of Ireland but is reduced to the status of a servant girl when the king blames her for the insulting actions of her half-brother. This indignity sets into motion a horrific battle between the people of Ireland and Britain, which leads to terrible carnage on both sides and ultimately to Branwen dying from a broken heart.

What can we learn from the tragedies of the goddesses? Clearly, they are a call to honor the feminine face of the Divine more carefully and clearly. But they are also a somber reminder that the goddess is not just about sweetness and light. She invites us into the wisdom and power of darkness and loss, even when it's a painful journey.

THE PATH OF THE GODDESSES

The goddess of the River Boyne in Ireland, Boand is not a major figure in the mythology, although she is the mother of an important god, Angus Óg. Yet one story about her, which explains the origin of the river that she personifies, is worth pondering. She is forbidden to gaze into a well that belongs to her husband, Nechtan; but she couldn't bear simply to obey such a rule, and so would steal away to the well when he was traveling. The waters, however, did not tolerate her transgression and so rose up after her. Frightened, she ran away, and the waters rushed after her, overtaking and drowning the hapless goddess. And so the river was born which preserves her spirit.

Is this an innocent folktale? Or could it be a metaphor for the submersion of goddess energies under the control of male-oriented religion? The Celts have never been very good at following orders, and while Boand paid for her disobedience with her life, she also gave of herself in the creation of one of the largest and most important of Irish rivers. She is a sacrificial figure—in her death, countless others are given life.

THE PATH OF THE GODDESSES

Many neopagans have adopted the Welsh figure Cerridwen as a moon goddess, although in the tradition she doesn't appear as a divine figure, but rather as a witch or a crone. She was certainly an accomplished magician, shapeshifter and herbalist, best known for the spell of wisdom she concocted for her son Morfran, who was ugly and misshapen. Hoping to give him an advantage to offset his hideous countenance, Cerridwen set about the yearlong task of brewing the potion, with the help of Gwion Bach, a servant boy whose job it was to stir the cauldron for a year and a day. But as the potion neared completion, the boy tasted it, and so gained the wisdom meant for Morfran. Enraged, Cerridwen set after him, leading to a great tale of shapeshifting, as greyhound chased hare, then otter chased salmon, hawk chased starling, and finally a hen pecked at an ear of corn—and so Cerridwen ate Gwion Bach, only to become pregnant; his spirit now reincarnated as her baby. And so she gave birth to Taliesin, the greatest of the British bards.

Perhaps what's most important about Cerridwen is her love for her son. Overlooking his physical deformities, she did what she could to give him a chance at life. Her rage at Gwion Bach is a symbol of a mother's ferocity in protecting her own. Indeed, when she finally gave birth to Taliesin, her maternal instincts overpowered her wrath, and she could not kill him.

THE PATH OF THE GODDESSES

Queen Meadbh of Connacht is one of the great fireballs of Celtic myth. She is proud, fierce, uncompromising, beautiful, lusty, polyamorous, and won't take no for an answer. She comes across rather badly in the great epic *The Cattle-Raid of Cooley*, where she seems to be a petty and avaricious monarch; but even when she is portrayed as scheming and manipulative, enough dignity shines through that it's apparent there's more to Meadbh than meets the eye.

Start with her name. The Gaelic spelling reveals its etymological ties with mead; and indeed, her name literally means "she who intoxicates." But Meadbh is more than just a sexy queen who can promise the worthy warrior a night he'll never forget. Her original self was a goddess of sovereignty who offered her intoxicating mead to the man who would be king. The king, as the leader and therefore symbolic representative of the entire tribe, was seen as the goddess's lover. Ancient coronation ceremonies included a priestess offering a cup of mead to the new king, ritually symbolizing the offering of the goddess' body (the land) to her new lover.

When Queen Meadbh brags in *The Cattle-Raid of Cooley* about her many lovers, it's a mistake to see this as some sort of indictment against an immoral woman. Rather, it's a clue to a time when the goddess of the land really was seen as enjoying the pleasure of many lovers, as kings in royal succession each took their turn as her favored one.

THE PATH OF THE GODDESSES

Is there room for a single "great Goddess" in the world of Celtic spirituality? It may not be an ancient part of Celtic wisdom, but some modern mystics are devising interesting ways to incorporate the Celtic path into the modern spiritual landscape. Mara Freeman hints that Brigit could be seen as a great mother goddess, while Frank MacEowen makes a similar case for Dana. Others have seen in Rhiannon's relationship with her son Pryderi, a fundamental pattern of the Divine Feminine that is recognizable to anyone who's ever seen a statue of the Virgin Mary: the sacred mother with her divine child.

Spirituality is a living, organic thing, and since there is no such thing as Celtic dogma, there's no reason why the universal goddess cannot be incorporated into the Celtic world-view. After all, Christianity came to the Celtic lands as an exotic faith from the Middle East, and the Celts truly made it their own. There's no reason that today's Celts can't do the same with the great Goddess. But my guess is, if the great Goddess learns to speak with an Irish or Welsh accent, she'll be very concerned with the sacredness of nature—and her name, or nickname, will have something to do with Sovereignty.

THE PATH OF DREAMS

The word for dream in Irish is *aisling*, a lovely word that means not only "dream" in the nocturnal sense, but also "vision." In the world of Celtic wisdom, a dream is far more than just the subconscious discharge of emotions and thoughts expressed in vivid imaginative scenarios. It is a gateway to the otherworld, a meaningful venue where spiritual guidance or divine knowledge might be transmitted to the dreamer. It is the psychic stage on which new possibilities for the present and the future could be discerned. Of course, this is not unique to the Celtic world—consider how prominent a role dreams play in the Bible, as a means to spiritual guidance—but it shows up often enough to send a clear message: Celtic spirituality calls us to follow our dreams. Which also means being faithful to our vision—being faithful to the innate, intuitive capacity to see the world as it *could* be, and to allow such a dream to guide us into the best of possible futures.

THE PATH OF DREAMS

Angus Óg (Angus the Young) is more or less the Irish answer to Cupid. He lived at Brugh na Bóinne ("the hostel on the Boyne River"), now known as Newgrange, the great prehistoric monument. Angus appears in many stories, often as a divine figure who helps lovers to get (or stay) together. But in the loveliest of stories concerning him, *Aislinge Óenguso*, it is his own heart that is on the line. As its name implies, the story begins with a dream—Angus' dream of a beautiful (but unknown) woman, so lovely that he awoke heartsick with longing for her. His father and others helped him search throughout Ireland; he eventually discovered her, a woman named Cáer, who was enchanted so that she spent one year as a human and the next as a swan. Angus proved his love for Cáer first by correctly identifying her among 150 swans, and then by changing himself into a swan so that they might fly off together. As they flew to Brugh na Bóinne, they sang a song of such otherworldly sweetness that anyone who heard it fell asleep for three days. One can only wonder if those who slept after hearing Angus and Cáer's songs, dreamt dreams of their own—in which their own true love appeared.

THE PATH OF DREAMS

The Dream of Macsen Wledig is a pseudo-historical, twelfth-century tale about a fourth-century Roman emperor, with some interesting parallels to the story of Angus's dream. The emperor had a dream about a lovely maiden in a far-off land, and sent out men to search throughout the empire to find her. She was eventually found in Britain, and Macsen traveled there to meet her, seeing things exactly as they appeared in his vision. He rewarded the lady's father with dominion over the land of Britain, and eventually the favor was returned when Macsen's authority was challenged in Rome, and his British ally sent troops to help him regain power. The politics of the story may have more to do with a desire to depict Britain as rather important to the Romans, but the mystical heart of the story—the vision of the beloved through the dream, and then making the effort to find this love in the real world—is Celtic through and through. Dreams, it seems, can convey the deepest desires of the heart, and when listened to, can lead to one's true and sovereign destiny.

THE PATH OF DREAMS

A mysterious medieval tale called *The Dream of Rhonabwy* recounts how a Welsh warrior had a detailed and intricate dream in which he encountered King Arthur and his men. What makes this event so startling is the relative size of the men: compared to the king and his companions, Rhonabwy and his party were small, puny men. The heroes of old were giants in every sense of the word, matching the height of their virtue and courage with a similar hugeness of stature. In the dream, Arthur's behavior seemed odd, when he appeared to be more concerned about playing a board game with Owain, the legendary patron of the bard Taliesin. Like many dreams, this vision ended with no real resolution or climax, leaving the hapless Rhonabwy to discover that he had slept for three days!

Could this dream be said to have a prophetic function? Perhaps, although the only truly useful information Rhonabwy gleaned from his vision was that the heroes of old were truly larger (that is to say, greater) than the people of his own age. And so it is that dreams can give startling insights into ourselves and our relationships. Rhonabwy won no battle, seduced no lover, and enjoyed no enlightenment because of his dream. Instead, he was simply humbled by the greatness he encountered. And that humility, perhaps, is what the dream was truly about.

THE PATH OF DREAMS

Dreams played an important role in the life of Patrick. As a young boy, Patrick was captured by Irish raiders from his home in Britain and spent seven years as a slave in the Emerald Isle. This was a powerful time in his life, for it was during his enslavement that his profound faith in God was honed. Soon this faith paid off, for Patrick received guidance to run away from his master through a dream. And run away he did, eventually finding passage on a ship to mainland Europe, from where he made his way back to his homeland. But God wasn't done with Patrick—nor was he done using dreams to reach the young man. Another dream revealed "the voice of the Irish" to Patrick, begging him to return to the land of his captivity and preach the message of Christianity. Patrick followed the dictates of his nocturnal vision, and thereby ensured his place in Irish history.

THE PATH OF DREAMS

Dreams play an interesting role in the selection of mythical Irish kings. According to legend, when a new king needed to be selected (in ancient times kingship was not necessarily passed down family lines), the seers would perform a ritual known as the *Tarbfheis*, or "bull feast." The ceremony involved sacrificing a bull for the purpose of divining the new king; the chosen seer would feast on meat from the slain animal and drink the broth in which the beef was cooked. Basically, he would engorge himself until fatigue set in; as he fell asleep four druids would chant incantations over him that would enable the seer to discern in his dreams who the next king would be. This ritual was quite possibly related to a Scottish practice called *taghairm*, in which a seer would wrap himself in the warm, steaming(!) hide of a freshly-killed bull, enter into a trance state, and then receive divinatory visions. While the totemic power of the bull was clearly an important factor in having divine knowledge revealed through these rituals, the seers put great faith in dreams as a portal for receiving spiritual guidance.

THE PATH OF DREAMS

So dreams can be portals for spiritual guidance, or for prophetic information, or for keen psychological insight. They can be repositories of bardic poetry or meaningless reviews of the energies of the day. What, then, can we finally say about how dreams fit in with Celtic wisdom?

The ancient druids spoke often in riddles and taught their students obliquely. Perhaps as we approach dreams we can see in them a bit of the old druidic style of pedagogy. In her book *Creating Form From the Mist*, Lynne Sinclair-Wood suggests, "The Otherworld can be accessed in dreams, visions, meditation or within ritual at special times of the year, particularly at sacred places." So perhaps the ultimate function of dreams is to open us up entirely to the otherworld and its mysteries and demands. And that, it seems, encompasses all the differing types of dreams. For the otherworld (the fairy realm) can reveal profound truths not accessible any other way, but can also be a source of silliness and merriment. Understanding dreams is therefore a lot like understanding the spiritual world—it means being willing to flow with ambiguity and not always having things figured out.

THE PATH OF DREAMS

"History is a nightmare from which I am trying to awake." Or so says Stephen Daedalus early in James Joyce's *Ulysses*. The question Joyce never ponders is, what would await Stephen if the desired awakening ever occurred? Whether or not Stephen ever shook off his nightmare, Joyce went on to write what is arguably the greatest representation of a dream from the inside—*Finnegans Wake*, that murky, mysterious, luminously incomprehensible novelization of a Dublin publican's puzzling and earthy dream. In Joyce's hands the barkeep's dream transcends itself to become an enigmatic meditation on the march of western civilization (and the power of Celtic myth). Dreams, therefore, are composed of nested layers of meaning, each layer signifying something different, whether personal, social, or transpersonal. We can enter a dream and be quickly bored silly by its apparent absurdity, or we can suddenly be ushered into an as-yet undiscovered pattern that handily reveals the meaning of life. Apparently, it's all in how you look at it.

THE PATH OF DREAMS

The Irish writer and mystic George Russell, who went by the name of AE, once pondered on the possible hidden meanings of dreams. "The moment we close our eyes and are alone with our thoughts and the pictures of dream, we are alone with mystery and miracle. Or are we alone?" he writes in *The Candle of Vision.* After all, the neoplatonic "flight of the alone to the alone" makes no sense in a polytheistic cosmology. Perhaps one is never alone, whether one is attempting to obey the traffic laws or is busy creating the universe. Another way of looking at this would be to ponder: are our dreams really our own? Do we truly "own" our consciousness? Or is it perhaps on loan from a more transcendent source? Perhaps we are not the dreamer, but merely that which is dreamed. In the words of the Irish author John O'Donohue, "If we take Nature as the great artist of longing then all presences in the world have emerged from her mind and imagination. We are children of the earth's dreaming." In the end, perhaps what matters most is not to figure out what our dreams mean, or what is symbolized within their mysterious worlds. Perhaps the key is simply to let the dreams flow, seeing in them not a cipher to decode life's meaning, but simply a doorway through which life's richness may be encountered in a new and different way.

THE PATH OF SACRED SITES

Celtic spirituality is a spirituality of place. The lore of the Celts takes seriously the history of sacred sites, the stories behind how hills or rivers or other features of nature came to be named, the legends of where great battles were fought, great heroes buried, or where gods and goddesses made love. To fully enter into the world of Celtic wisdom, we must embrace a way of seeing the world where every place is meaningful and every location has its own part to play in the grand story of the cosmos.

Nowhere is this more clearly realized than Tara, the legendary seat of the high kings in eastern Ireland. Today Tara is simply a gentle hill in the middle of fertile farmland, visited by pilgrims and dreamers and thankfully unspoiled by the more commercial interests of the tourist trade. The site is full of archaeological treasures, including burial mounds, ceremonial earthworks, a holy well, and a standing stone once said to be the key to identifying the high king of all the land.

Tara is associated with Meadbh—not the scheming warrior-queen of later mythology and folklore, but the primal goddess of sovereignty, who by her sacred marriage to the king conferred upon him his royal status. This goddess lives on today, in the green land, named in Gaelic after another sovereignty figure, Ériu. From the crest of Tara, nearly thirty percent of all Ireland is visible. It is truly a site worthy of a king—and of his lady.

THE PATH OF SACRED SITES

One of the most mysterious sites in the Celtic world is the awe-inspiring 5000-year-old passage tomb called Newgrange. Located about an hour's drive north of Dublin in the lush Boyne valley (and not far at all from the Hill of Tara), Newgrange is today a popular tourist attraction with a state-of-the-art interpretive center. But thousands of years ago, this site was a major religious center where funerals and other ceremonies were held—especially on the winter solstice.

From a distance, Newgrange appears to be just a large man-made hill with an attractive white granite façade. But in the center of the granite wall is a small doorway leading to a small, 65-foot corridor that opens up into a magnificent subterranean chamber with three alcoves, where cremated remains were once interred. Mysterious decorative carvings decorate both the interior of the tomb and the large kerbstones that ring the structure on the outside. But the most remarkable feature of Newgrange is its orientation to the Winter Solstice sunrise, so that for seventeen minutes on the morning of the year's shortest day, brilliant sunlight illuminates the heart of the tomb.

We'll never know exactly what the ancients believed when they built this magnificent structure. But the powerful symbolism of light bursting into darkness, when darkness is at its height, is obvious enough. This ancient monument testifies to that most human of yearning—for inextinguishable light that will triumph over the most formidable darkness.

THE PATH OF SACRED SITES

Nestled in a valley in the Wicklow Mountains south of Dublin, the sixth-century Christian monastery of Glendalough sits at the base of two lakes in a scene of utter loveliness. The ruins feature several well-preserved buildings that have stood for approximately a thousand years, including a splendid round tower, the gates into the old enclosed community, and a small church with a miniature tower.

Saint Kevin, the founder of Glendalough, came to this remote mountain location to be a hermit. Tales of his humble piety spread, and others who desired the life of prayer in the wilderness soon formed a community around the reluctant saint. He eventually retreated from the monastery village to a small beehive hut near the upper lake; he would also withdraw into a cave on the edge of the lake where he could finally find some much desired solitude.

After Kevin's death, the community continued to prosper; other renowned figures associated with it included the twelfth-century archbishop Laurence O'Toole. But it will always be known as the home of Kevin, echoing his reputation as a sort of Irish Saint Francis by the sheer natural beauty of this mystical valley.

THE PATH OF SACRED SITES

If it weren't for the solemn statue of Ireland's most loved female saint on the town square, and the fact that both the Protestant cathedral and the Catholic church within a short walk's distance are named for that same saint, a visitor could easily miss Kildare Town's claim as the home of Brigid (and the once powerful monastery she founded). And unless you walked around the Cathedral and stopped to wonder at the mysterious "Fire Temple" foundation located in its shadow, you might never know that before Saint Brigid, Kildare was in all likelihood the site where the great Goddess Brigit was honored with a perpetual flame tended in her honor—a practice that the Christian nuns kept alive after the coming of the new religion and is even today preserved by two sisters of the Brighidine order.

There's very little to be found about Brigit or Brigid in Kildare; a couple of holy wells not far from the center of town are dedicated to the saint, and the Brighidine sisters have written a lovely book that invites visitors to make a meditative pilgrimage in honor of their patroness. But that's about it. There's nothing flashy or polished, no postcards to send home or souvenirs to buy in the local shop. The message of Kildare is simple: sometimes spiritual greatness thrives best when we take a "nothing special" approach to it.

THE PATH OF SACRED SITES

Probably the best-known sacred site popularly thought to be associated with the Celts, Stonehenge was built in stages over a period of approximately 1700 years—long before Celtic culture arrived in Britain. The earliest Stonehenge, built before 2100 BCE, consisted of a large circular earthwork enclosure, with only a few standing stones (and several wooden posts). A ring of pits, some of which were used for burial, also date from that period. Later came the addition of an avenue leading from the circle to the sunrise point of the midsummer sun, along with the addition of two incomplete, concentric circles of bluestones. These stones, of Welsh origin, came from approximately 135 miles away. The years 2000 BCE–1500 BCE marked the "golden age" of Stonehenge, when it began to assume the awesome look it has today, even in ruins. The builders of this age erected an outer circle of 30 upright stones, which supported a ring of lintel stones. Within this circle stood a horseshoe of five trilithons—two standing stones each supporting a horizontal lintel. Not only were these stones huge (weighing up to fifty tons), but they were shaped—using hammers—to fit the specifications of the henge architecture. The labor force necessary to complete this massive project has been estimated at 1500 men. Finally, around 1100 BC, the avenue built a thousand years earlier was lengthened. Thus, Stonehenge reached its present, mysterious form five hundred years before the arrival of the Celts.

THE PATH OF SACRED SITES

Avebury, eighteen miles from Stonehenge, lacks the more famous circle's awesome trilithons and the dramatic setting of the lonely Salisbury plain—indeed, the town of Avebury has grown up right in the middle of the prehistoric site, with houses and roads and megaliths sharing the same land. This may make the site less appealing to the casual tourist—but Avebury also lacks the "commercialized" feel of Stonehenge.

Like Stonehenge, this prehistoric site is now in ruins. In its original grandeur, however, Avebury was the far more elaborate of the two sites. The main part of the site consisted of a huge circular earthwork—a ditch with a bank outside it. Within the earthwork stood a large circle of approximately 100 standing stones, and within that, two smaller circles. To the east and west existed two avenues made of long rows of standing stones, making the entire length of the site approximately three miles long. Today, most of the stones have been removed—for various reasons, including overzealous Christians attempting to destroy "the devil's handiwork," to more practical-minded farmers trying to clear lands and use stones for masonry.

Avebury most likely dates from the late Neolithic period, making it contemporary with the earliest periods of Stonehenge. Could ancient Celtic druids or priestesses have ever used it? Only the mute stones know for sure.

THE PATH OF SACRED SITES

The small island of Iona, located near the larger Hebridean isle of Mull off the west coast of Scotland, is geographically tiny but looms large in the history of the Celtic tradition. For it was here that Columcille of Ireland established his monastery in exile in the year 563 CE. It became the center of Celtic Christianity in Scotland, and the mother abbey to the equally famous foundation at Lindisfarne, on the Northumbrian coast of northeast England. Here Scottish kings were buried, and the legendary *Book of Kells* was likely the product of monks of Iona. Eventually the monastery was abandoned, but in 1938 a Scottish visionary named George Macleod founded a new intentional Christian Community that renovated the ancient abbey and revived the spirit of Celtic Christianity, through a ministry of service and hospitality, not only on Iona, but also in other locations such as urban Glasgow.

Iona is an austere place, a windswept island where the powerful elements of sea and sky touch all who live or visit. Yes, of course, it is a thin place. And that sense of closeness to the sacred otherworld calls countless pilgrims, today just like a millennium and a half ago.

THE PATH OF SACRED SITES

The village of Glastonbury in Somerset, England is full of Celtic, Christian, and Arthurian romance. Once the site of a powerful monastery, it is today a charming town with a curious blend of traditional British and hippie/new age culture. The heart of the town remains the ruins of the abbey, legendary because it is the traditional burial site of King Arthur and Queen Guinevere (Camelot is widely believed to be an Iron Age hill fort located several miles to the south of town). An imposing and beautiful tor dominates Glastonbury's skyline. Many stories told about the tor hint that it is a magical site—an entrance to the fairy-world, a power center, or the "heart chakra" of the earth. Meanwhile, near the foot of the hill is a gorgeous Holy Well, called Chalice Well because of legends that the Holy Grail is hidden here. Grail or no grail, today the Chalice Well is surrounded by beautiful gardens where a deep sense of peace prevails.

Glastonbury is said to have been at one time a druid college; it is also believed to be the "Avalon" that figures so prominently in Arthurian myth. All the legends related to this town point to its being a place where history and myth, legend and lore, are woven together in a union of sense and spirit.

THE PATH OF SACRED SITES

The Celtic world is full of sacred sites. There is Emain Macha, the legendary seat of the King of Ulster, made famous in the great Irish epic called *The Tain*...Tintagel, Cornwall's castle by the sea, famous as the legendary birthplace of King Arthur...the Standing Stones of Callanish, located in a remote island setting in the north of Scotland...Anglesey, the ancient island of Mona in Wales where Roman soldiers once massacred a community of druids...Chartres Cathedral in France, built on a site widely believed to be an ancient *nemeton*, or druidic sanctuary...countless holy wells where prayers and supplications have been made for thousands of years. This list could go on and on. But one final point I feel needs to be made: in a way, the greatest sacred site is wherever your feet happen to be planted. What makes a site sacred, ultimately, is not how many Neolithic graves or mythological associations are located there, but rather the extent to which it is a place where humankind and nature may come together in harmony and mutual care. And that, to someone who is conscious of Celtic wisdom, is something that can occur anywhere. Indeed, that ought to occur anywhere. So if the place where your feet are currently rested is not, in your mind, a "sacred site," consider this question: what can you do to make it one?

THE PATH OF COMMUNITY

One important concept that is essential to understanding Celtic wisdom is the *tuath*. According to MacLennan's Gaelic dictionary, this word means both "the country" and "country people." In other words, it is a word that refers both to a community of people and to the land that community dwells upon.

Community is a buzzword that gets thrown about a lot in the modern world, often because so many people seem to be hungry for it or seeking it. Nearly all religious groups talk about community; but so do businesses and educational institutions. Neopagans often will speak of "the community" to describe all neopagans, in much the same way that Christians will talk about "the church." In Buddhism, community (*sangha*) is considered one of the three sacred refuges for the follower of the Buddha's path.

With so much interest in community, it is significant that the Gaelic word *tuath* signifies not only a community of people, but also the land on which the people live. It's as if the Celts have long realized that members of a true community lives not only in relation to one another, but collectively in relation to their natural environment.

THE PATH OF COMMUNITY

In *The Druid Animal Oracle*, Philip and Stephanie Carr-Gomm wrote, "When we let go of believing we are superior, we open ourselves to the experience of living in the community of Nature—being a part of it, not separate from it." Truer words were never spoken. One reason why the Celtic concept of the *tuath* may be so unusual is that for most people, community has nothing to do with nature. Think of a "planned community"—a collection of homes and streets, carefully designed and built by contractors and then sold to individuals who may have no professional or personal interests in common whatsoever. The only thing they have in common, in fact, is their land, but since every parcel is privately owned, no one really has much of a reason to form significant relationships with their neighbors. So a planned community is really just an economic scheme—about as unlike a *tuath* as you can get. By contrast, an authentic Celtic-style community would be more like a Native American tribe, where people not only live in proximity to one another, but work together and support one another in their common goal to survive and thrive—a group of people, relating to their environment together.

THE PATH OF COMMUNITY

The word community literally means "shared tasks or goals." Which suggests that a true community exists for the mutual benefit of its members. Pardon me for sounding utilitarian, but "what's in it for me?" is a valid question to ask a community. Unless your community promises spiritual happiness, financial prosperity, environmental responsibility, psychological comfort, personal security, or some additional goal that others can share in common with you, it's not really much of a community. If it benefits you without also benefiting others (or vice versa), it's not a community at all. And then, it's worth asking just how powerful a force community plays in our lives. Many communities offer fellowship or the comfort of spending time with people of similar values and interests. But as soon as someone experiences real tragedy or loss in their life, the community seems to disappear. Perhaps there never really was a true (or at least, meaningful) community to begin with.

THE PATH OF COMMUNITY

The great mythic race of Irish gods and goddesses and heroes and heroines was known as the Tuatha Dé Danann—literally, the tribe (community) of the goddess Dana. Although it was their relationship to Dana that named the community, it didn't really define them. As Irish mythology makes clear, what truly held this community together was its shared commitment to settle in Ireland, to defeat their enemies, and to live in harmony with the land on which they settled. Of course, the fact that they shared a common heritage—as people of the same goddess, Dana, who is a shadowy figure in the myths but could be understood as a goddess of the land—enabled them to form the bonds of community ever so tightly. And so, it is important for us to seek common ground with those in our community—whether that means shared spiritual values, shared heritage or ancestry, or that most Celtic of qualities, a shared relationship with the same place in the natural world. Even so, having shared identity to help form a community is only part of the process; there still must be shared goals and objectives for a community to truly thrive.

THE PATH OF COMMUNITY

When the god Lugh appeared at the hall of the king of the Tuatha Dé Danann, he offered his many-skilled services to help the tribe of Dana defeat their enemy, the Fomorians. At first, it looked as if Lugh, who had many different talents, would try to defeat the foe single-handedly. But that is not what the god did. Instead, he convened a meeting where he asked each member of the tribe how they could contribute to the cause of defeating the enemy. One by one, each god, goddess, hero and heroine present offered their services: the ability to forge superior weapons...the ability to heal the wounded ... the ability to fight with courage and valor. After everyone had spoken, it was clear what Lugh had truly brought to the Tuatha Dé Danann—hope. As they found ways to work together, they could at last hope to truly triumph over their adversaries.

Lugh's visionary leadership helped the tribe to coalesce into a genuine community. No one person became responsible for doing it all, but rather each individual discovered how he or she had an important part to play. And together, their skills merged to form a community truly dedicated to making their goals come to fruition—together.

THE PATH OF COMMUNITY

At one point in history, the Celts were in a position to establish the first European empire. They controlled most of the best lands in Europe, and were feared by their more "civilized" neighbors in Greece and Rome. But as a rural people who showed little interest in bureaucracy or hierarchy, the various Celtic tribes chose not to band together but rather remain a loose network of free, sovereign peoples. And then along came the Romans, and in little more than a century, nearly all the free Celtic lands fell under the control of Rome. Why did this great civilization fall so easily? The answer appears to be related to the question of community. The Celts loved their decentralized, small-scale way of life; but were unable to unite when it came to defeating a common threat. Here we see an important lesson of community: it needs to come in all shapes and sizes. We may think the ideal community has ten members, or a hundred—but if we are unable to deal with problems that call for the resources of a larger community, then the purity of our small community means nothing. When we think about applying Celtic wisdom to the demands of the twenty-first century, we need to be careful not to over-romanticize the idealized Celtic world. Sure a tribe is a great concept. But what is needed today is a truly global *tuath*, a shared humanity living in a nurturing and healing relationship with our common natural habitat.

THE PATH OF COMMUNITY

When Christianity came to the Celtic lands, it brought a new model of community: the monastery. Into the rural lands of the British Isles beyond the influence of the Roman Empire, the earliest Christians brought the ideal of a new form of community: gathered together to praise God and strive for each individual's spiritual salvation. The monastery became a prominent feature in the Celtic world, and since there were no cities where bishops could rise to prominence (great cities in the Celtic lands like Dublin or Galway would be settled centuries later, by the Vikings or the Normans), the monasteries and their abbots became the heart and soul of Celtic Christianity.

Celtic monasteries were different in many ways from the typical Christian monastery of the time. Often men and women lived in monastic communities together, and the settlements often included families as well as celibates. The abbots and priests often were married, and passed down their office to their own descendents. Although piety and devotion to God were stressed, the Celtic monastery was a place not so much removed from the world, as intended to inject a sense of heaven into the world.

THE PATH OF COMMUNITY

Even in the deeply religious setting of the monastery, the Celtic notion of community still included a sense of humanity living a common life in relation to the land. This is often expressed in charming stories about the earliest Celtic monks and saints. Saint Kevin of Glendalough once held his arms aloft in prayer long enough for a bird to build a nest, lay her eggs, and raise her babies until they flew off. Saint Columba of Iona, meanwhile, would swim out into the frigid Irish Sea to pray where seals would accompany him. Although these stories are mythic, they are meant to convey an important truth: that a Celtic community, even when dedicated to the Christian concept of heaven, is still intimately involved with its natural environment. A Celtic community is located in a specific place. Out of that place comes not only the community's self-identity, but also the natural resources needed to support the community—and the inspiration for the community to give of its resources to take care of the environment, which provides so much support.

THE PATH OF COMMUNITY

Trying to form an authentic Celtic-style community today might seem like a daunting task. After all, few of us who live in the postmodern, postindustrial world of western Europe, America and Australia have much of a sense of who our neighbors are, let alone a clear sense of caring for our land or having it directly care for us. So how can a genuine, deep community emerge in our alienated world?

The only workable answer is, "one step at a time." If we cannot find a group of people to support one another in living close to the land, then at least we can take steps to deepen our own personal ties to nature. If no one in our lives seems to share a deep sense of common mission or purpose, think of how transformational it would be to find just one person with a harmonious vision. And even if that is not possible, writing poetry or keeping an online journal can be a meaningful (and potentially life-changing) way to put our longing for community "out there." Just one person reading your work can open the door to making a real community happen. Of course, forming authentic community means more than just finding people with similar or shared interests. It also means forging a commitment within those harmonious relationships—and a commitment that extends to a deep, caring relationship with the natural environment.

THE PATH OF SACRED DAYS

The Celtic tradition is so oriented toward the sacredness of place—of the land and of holy sites—that it's easy to forget that time has just as strong a claim on the rhythm of wisdom in our lives. Calendars dating to the first century CE have been discovered in Celtic lands, revealing an awareness not only of the passage of time, but of some days as being more auspicious than others. The druids were said to harvest mistletoe on the sixth day after the new moon; and in Ireland four days were seen as especially sacred: Samhain, Imbolc, Beltane, and Lughnasa, originally holidays linked to seasonal agricultural events, but eventually established as the first days of November, February, May, and August. These days, rather than the solstices and equinoxes, marked the beginning of the seasons. A day was seen as beginning at sundown, while the year began at "summerdown"—the end of the harvest season and the beginning of the wintertime. Out of darkness came light, both in the sunrise of a new day as well as in the new spring at the midpoint of the year.

THE PATH OF SACRED DAYS

Samhain means "summer's end" and signifies that poignant moment when harvesting is done and the agricultural work of the community largely ceases until the time of plowing and sowing arrives the following spring. Any crops left in the fields after Samhain belonged to the fairies; it would be most unlucky to eat what belonged to them. As the time when summer (and the old year) dies, it is indeed a festival of death: livestock thought incapable of surviving the impending winter would be slaughtered, perhaps leading to a harvest feast. The death theme extended to the folklore of the season, for Samhain is a thin time—a time when the veil separating the worlds is thin or even drawn aside, making it an auspicious time to honor the ancestors (but also a dangerous time when the living needed to protect themselves from the "tricks" of the dead). The children's customs associated with Halloween— wearing masks and offering hospitality to trick-or-treaters— originates in the Celtic lands where spirits were believed to roam the earth on this sacred night. Another custom involves setting a "dumb supper," or a meal in which the favorite foods of a dead ancestor would be served on a plate set specifically for that person's visiting spirit. Samhain is also a wonderful time for prophecy and divination—looking through the thin veil to see what the future year might bring.

THE PATH OF SACRED DAYS

The astronomical dates for the changing of the seasons—the solstices and equinoxes—do not have significance in the old pagan myths, probably because the seasonal changes were marked by the agricultural festivals. But the winter solstice was certainly a date well known to the early Celts, for at least one dramatic site has a strong link to the shortest day of the year: the passage tomb at Newgrange. On the morning of the winter solstice, the rising sun would shine for a few short minutes directly into the chambers at the heart of the subterranean monument. As the sun rose, darkness would again descend on the remains of the ancestors buried in the structure, a darkness that would not be lifted (save by torchlight) for another year. That our forebears from five thousand years ago would build a massive tomb (that probably took over a century to construct) oriented toward the solstice is spectacular, and speaks to the critical role that the sun's pilgrimage to its most southerly point—and back again—must have had in their spiritual consciousness. Was the sun seen as a link to the otherworld? Or were the ancestral spirits believed to command the sun to reverse its day-shortening course? We can only speculate on just how the solstice-spirit connection was understood.

THE PATH OF SACRED DAYS

Imbolc marks the coming of spring; it begins at sundown on January 31, an odd time perhaps to mark the end of winter but it makes sense when you consider that this is the time in the British Isles when crocuses are first in bloom and pregnant ewes are heavy with milk for the soon-to-be-born lambs. Imbolc is a mysterious word that has been translated as both "ewe's milk" and "in the belly," both ideas pointing to the idea of pregnancy and new birth as the key themes of this time of year.

On Imbolc night in Ireland, Saint Brigid is said to travel around the land, bestowing her blessings on the homes of those dedicated to her. Some families leave a special cloth outdoors: a "Brigid's mantle," said to be blessed by the dew of the morning, and thereby imbued with Brigid's healing powers. If such a cloth is left outside on seven consecutive Imbolc nights, it achieves a maximum potency as a healing object.

Scholars have identified possible links between this springtime Festival of Brigid with other ancient pagan rituals, such as a Scandinavian ceremony for hunting a hibernating bear, which may be the origin of the modern Groundhog Day custom still observed on February 2.

THE PATH OF SACRED DAYS

The equinoxes, both spring and fall, have become popular holidays among neopagans, balancing out the solstices and the agricultural holidays to create what has become known as "the wheel of the year"—a sequence of eight sacred days, roughly occurring at six- to seven-week intervals. The spring equinox celebrations are more rooted in Norse rather than Celtic traditions—a Germanic goddess named Ostara is associated with the spring and the dawn, and is symbolized by rabbits and eggs—all themes that have survived as elements of the Christian holiday of Easter. Perhaps more authentically Celtic is a day close to the Equinox, Irish in origin but now celebrated around the world: Saint Patrick's Day. The religious origins of the holiday have long been swallowed up in its overall celebration of anything and everything Irish. Americans especially love Saint Paddy's Day, reveling in parades, green beer, and "Kiss me I'm Irish" buttons. The overall feel is of festive merriment—not at all inappropriate for welcoming in the promise of light and warmth and a new year's crops.

THE PATH OF SACRED DAYS

Halfway around the great wheel of the year from Samhain comes Beltane, signifying the beginning of the "light" half of the year just as the final harvest signified the summer's end. Beltane means either "fortunate fire" or "the fire of Bel," referring to a continental Celtic god who may have been associated with agriculture and fecundity. Marked by the blossoming of the Hawthorn, it was a thin time when fairy mischief needed to be guarded against—May I was a particularly unlucky time for sharing butter or milk with strangers, who the folklore suggests could often be the good people in disguise. But the overall energy of this sacred day was, and is, one of hope and celebration. Great fires were lit in traditional observances of the holiday, and livestock were driven between the bonfires as a symbolic ritual of purification and protection. Modern neopagans have given Beltane a fun and flirty reputation, derived from the explicitly phallic English traditions of Maypole dancing. Meanwhile, movies like *The Wicker Man* have suggested a more sinister side to Beltane—as a time of human sacrifice to appease the demands of the old gods.

THE PATH OF SACRED DAYS

If the winter solstice belongs to Newgrange, then the summer's longest day goes to Stonehenge, that mysterious pre-Celtic monument that has become the spiritual Mecca of druid revivalist groups over the past few centuries. Although not as dramatic as the shaft of light piercing the heart of Newgrange each December, the sunrise on the Midsummer's Day anchors the great stone circle of England as a marker of the progression of the seasons. Stonehenge has been called a mighty sundial, and it is calibrated to the year's longest day.

Modern druid groups that have performed ceremonies at Stonehenge are in all likelihood doing little if anything that would have been recognized as spiritual practice by the ancient Celts or their pre-Celtic forebears. But such ceremonies still have meaning, for they embody our modern desire to be more fully connected to our natural environment. We no longer need to cajole the sun into "returning" from the south (or the north, to those of the southern hemisphere) at wintertime, nor do we need to bring any anxiety to bear on the turning of the summer. But when we are mindful of such days, we are just a little bit closer to the harmonious connection to the earth that the Celtic tradition represents.

THE PATH OF SACRED DAYS

The last of the old Gaelic holidays is Lughnasa, marking the beginning of harvest just as Samhain marks its end. The name means "Lugh's assembly" and probably refers to a link between the luminous god of skill and the harvest. Neopagans see this as a time of sacrifice, when the "corn king" was killed (harvested) so that we mortals might live. The myths of the Irish tradition depict a slightly different interpretation: this was a time when Lugh defeated his oppressive grandfather, Balor, whose "evil eye" (perhaps a metaphor for the late summer sun) killed all in its path. And so the harvest was a time of some urgency, when crops needed to be gathered in before being spoiled or lost to the ensuing autumn.

Traditionally, Lughnasa was a time of fairs and feasts, when youths would engage in contests of skill and couples would announce their intention to wed. Apparently as a harvest fair, it once lasted an entire month. But as a spiritual holiday, it survived the coming of Christianity as a time of pilgrimage, particularly to the tops of sacred hills or mountains—the most famous being Croagh Patrick, now sacred to Saint Patrick but originally dedicated to Lugh, where pilgrims climb to the summit every year at the end of July.

THE PATH OF SACRED DAYS

The wheel of the year is completed with the fall equinox, another day without a strong Celtic mythic or folkloric tradition. It became linked to the Welsh god/hero Mabon, but like its spring counterpart may be best understood in the light of a Christian festival: the feast of Saint Michael on September 29. Michaelmas, like its older counterpart Lughnasa, became a favorite time for fairs and harvest celebrations. Michael, as an archangel, was regarded as the escort who conveyed souls from their deathbed to their eternal reward; he is known as a protector who is God's chief agent in defeating the energies of chaos of death. Many churches dedicated to Michael are built at the top of hills or other elevated sites (a tower dedicated to Michael still stands in hollow ruin at the summit of Glastonbury Tor), which some observers have seen as implying that Michael has a particular role in competing with the old pre-Christian religion—in that churches sacred to him were built on established pagan sites. On the other hand, Michael could be another Brigid—a Christian figure who did not fight, but merely subsumed and replaced, a prior mythic figure (most likely Lugh). This makes sense, for the Michaelmas celebrations of September represent in the main a simple continuation of the initial harvest celebrations of Lughnasa.

Six weeks after Michaelmas, Samhain and the final harvest return. Another year ends, and a new cycle begins.

THE PATH OF VIRTUE

Several modern druid organizations and others who are working to revive ancient Celtic spirituality for our time have put together lists of virtues to represent the good life according to Celtic wisdom. These virtues are drawn from the values preserved in myth and folklore, as well as values associated with key figures (such as Brigit or Lugh). While there is no universally held set of "Celtic virtues," some—such as hospitality, honor, and sovereignty (freedom)—are so prominent in the tradition that it's easy to imagine they are values that have been espoused since the days of the earliest druids.

Pursuing virtue is an essential part of wisdom, so it seems appropriate to consider wisdom itself as a key Celtic virtue. Wisdom is more than just the acquisition of knowledge; rather, it is the ability to apply knowledge, through the considered merit of virtue and values. One can amass endless amounts of information and never be truly wise, but when the knowledge at one's disposal is considered in light of what is true, beautiful, and good, then knowledge has been placed in service of a nobler and higher end: wisdom.

Think of the virtues to come in the following eight days as keys to unlocking true wisdom. Consider how these keys can make a difference in your own life.

THE PATH OF VIRTUE

Hospitality is an important enough Celtic virtue that I've considered it at length earlier in this book. But it's so crucial that it deserves mention also here in this consideration of virtues in general. Virtue is about choice, and what more fundamental choice can there be than to welcome the stranger, to offer help to the person in need, to share of your abundance with another? For each of these qualities is encompassed in the glory of hospitality. Indeed, of all the virtues, of hospitality it can most truly be said: to embody this virtue is to embody virtue itself. One need not be wise, or courageous, or sovereign, or even honorable to practice hospitality; and yet the person who lacks hospitality cannot truly express any other virtue in its fullness. Sure, in our world it may not be feasible to simply open one's door to any and all strangers (sadly, in the modern city such behavior could be dangerous rather than virtuous), but the future of Celtic wisdom may well depend on our ability to evolve new ways of practicing hospitality that make a difference and truly make the world a better place.

THE PATH OF VIRTUE

On *Star Trek*, the alien Klingons were warlike, aggressive, heroic, brutal—and utterly bound by the highest code of honor. The similarities between this futuristic race of aliens and the Celts of ancient myth are hardly accidental. For even a cursory reading of Irish or Welsh myth reveals the degree to which the ideals of the warrior defined and described the virtues of the Celtic world—including the demands of honor. Simply put, this meant a warrior fought fair, was a person of his or her word, and always lived according to the highest principles of the tribe. If a warrior behaved dishonorably, it reflected badly on the entire tribe, so of course the pressure (both social and internal) to live up to one's honor was enormous.

What implication does this have for us today? Dishonorable behavior still reflects not only on those misbehaving, but also on their entire community. So even those of us who have little or nothing to do with the warriors of our society (i.e. the military or law enforcement), still have a role to play in upholding not only our own esteem in the eyes of others, but the honor of any group with which we are affiliated. If the word "honor" seems a bit too—well, Klingon-ish—for our taste, consider these equivalent concepts: integrity, self-respect, pride. To be a person of honor means to be one who is faithful to the demands of each of these.

THE PATH OF VIRTUE

Courage simply means, "having a heart." The man or woman of courage is one with the heart to stand up to whatever situations may come his or her way. It's not just about having the guts to fight—although certainly that's a key aspect of courage. But true courage also means knowing when *not* to fight, knowing when to let go of the ego's need to be in control or be right all the time. Courage, ultimately, is applied honor—taking the principles which guide our personal or collective pride and self-respect, and having the strength of will to live by those principles and values, each and every day. But as its definition suggests, courage involves more than sheer willpower—it's the virtue of emotion and relationship as well, for courage means both standing with (others who share the same values), standing for (those who need protection or support), and standing against (those with whom we are in conflict). Each of these relationships is important in defining our courage—and therefore, who we ultimately are. The person of courage understands this, and respects all those who shape his or her courage—even those who, by fate or chance, are the "enemy."

THE PATH OF VIRTUE

With all this talk about courage and honor, it's easy to see the Celtic tradition as one-dimensionally pugilistic. But that would be a great mistake. Sure, the tradition is dominated by great heroes like Cúchulainn, Lugh, and Fionn mac Cumhaill—but it is also the tradition of Brigit, the goddess who tried to find a diplomatic solution to the conflict between her people and the Fomorians; and her Christian namesake, Saint Brigid, well known as a peacemaker and champion of the poor. Brigid's commitment to peace, set alongside the tragic nature of Cúchulainn's excessive warriorship, helps to define the "hidden agenda" of the Celtic wisdom—as a tradition in service to peacemaking. This lives on today especially in devotees to Brigid/Brigit, both Christian and neopagan, who gather in Kildare for a peacemaking conference each year at the time of Imbolc, the festival of Brigid. Being a peacemaker, for most of us, may have little or nothing to do with conflict resolution between nations—but it may well have everything to do with fostering stronger relationships in our families and work environments. Being a peacemaker doesn't mean being a pushover, and running from conflicts. On the contrary, it means having enough honor—and courage—to make resolving conflicts the highest of priorities.

THE PATH OF VIRTUE

Peacemaking is a form of healing. And healing, clearly enough, is another important virtue in the Celtic world. In addition to being a peacemaker, Brigit is a healer, a midwife and a herbalist. Other figures in the myths have strong healing powers, such as Dian Cécht the physician and his children. The Dagda could raise the dead with his magic club, and several cauldrons in both Irish and Celtic lore have healing powers. Probably the greatest symbol of healing is the Holy Grail. Druids were said by classical writers to be accomplished healers.

If you work in healthcare, the healing tradition of the Celts is something you can directly apply in terms of your vocation. For others, a bit of creativity may be required in order to walk the path of the healer. But it's like the path of the peacemaker—it can be applied in simple, down-to-earth ways. Healing, like charity (or for that matter, peacemaking) begins at home. What needs to happen for you to heal broken relationships in your life? To mend bad habits in yourself—and offer support for similar healing changes in others? Healing not only means caring for yourself and others, but in a very real way it also applies to the earth. How are the choices we make in service to healing the earth? Questions like these invite us into the heart of Celtic virtue.

THE PATH OF VIRTUE

At Saint Brigid's Holy Well near Kildare, five standing stones represent five qualities (virtues) traditionally associated with the Saint. One of these qualities is meditation—Brigid as a woman of prayer. For the purpose of celebrating the virtues of Celtic tradition as a whole, I'd like to expand meditation to include the notion of contemplation.

Celtic virtue is linked to mindful attention to our spiritual well being. This can take many different forms for different people, and to a great extent is shaped by our unique religious and cultural needs. Meditation can include prayer, or Zen-style silent attention, or shamanic trance states, or the repetitive mantra-prayers of the rosary. All are valid and meaningful ways to cross the threshold between the worlds. Speaking in terms of virtue, the important thing here is not how we put our spirituality into practice, but simply that we do it. And like any other virtue it thrives best when it is nurtured. Thus, the life of meditation and contemplation ought not be just a when-I-feel-like-it commitment, but truly reflect a routine effort to deepen the inner life. Daily meditation/prayer/contemplation is not too much to ask for, in terms of cultivating a powerful and meaningful spiritual life.

THE PATH OF VIRTUE

Another value associated with Saint Brigid at her holy well is earthiness—or being a guardian of the natural world. The guardian energy is closely related to sovereignty, another virtue explored at length elsewhere in this book. For now, let's look at the humbler concept of "earthiness." And calling it humble is a clever pun, for humility truly means "of the earth." So practicing the virtue of earthiness means several things: it means cultivating true humility (not humility as inverted pride, but humility as self-forgetfulness), living in harmony with nature, doing what is necessary to protect nature, and honoring the goddess energy found in nature. In other words, humility and nature are not important just because it's a nice liberal thing to be good custodians of the environment. On the contrary, this virtue is derived from the old custom of the king symbolically marrying the goddess at his coronation. Care for the earth—whether it's the earth of the environment or the "earth" of our own bodies—is ultimately a way of loving and revering the goddess herself.

THE PATH OF VIRTUE

Out of the goddess/earth energies comes the last virtue to be discussed here in this section of this book—but hardly the last word on Celtic virtue—that being "eros." Sure, it's a Greek word referring to a Mediterranean pagan god, but it's helpful in understanding the Celtic tradition in that it implies not merely sexuality, but the entire experience of living enfleshed, embodied lives. The king/goddess liaison shows that Celtic wisdom is, or at least was originally, sex-positive and affirming toward the physical dimension of life. Written evidence suggests that the ancient Celtic societies were (relatively speaking) organized in ways that were favorable to women, and that multi-partner marriage relationships may have been common for both men and women. But to say that eros is a Celtic virtue is not just a matter of lauding the ancient Celts as the original polyamorists—but rather, seeing in this tradition a positive and honoring relationship between the soul and the body, not only in terms of sex but in terms of all aspects of life. Celtic virtue values the erotic dimensions of life, and seeks to express those dimensions in positive and appropriate ways.

THE PATH OF SACRED ANIMALS

Students of shamanism and magic have long understood that animals can be powerful symbols of spirits or of helpful energies from the otherworld. Since Celtic spirituality and wisdom are so intricately interwoven with respect for and honoring of the natural world, it is not surprising how animals figure in the mythology and folklore of the tradition. Modern skeptics may dismiss the druids as "tree-huggers," but in truth the horse or the bull played as significant a role in their religious landscape as did the oak or the hawthorn. Celtic myth links certain animals with different gods and heroes, while the helmets of ancient Celtic warriors are often decorated with stylized representations of different beasts. In the great illuminated manuscripts like *The Book of Kells*, animals dance across the pages, adding color and whimsy to the majestic medieval calligraphy. Nor is the role of animals in the Celtic world strictly a question of ancient ideas: modern Celtic Christianity has embraced the wild goose as a symbol of the Holy Spirit, a correspondence unknown to the saints of old but meaningful to many in our day.

THE PATH OF SACRED ANIMALS

If there were one animal most firmly linked in the consciousness and mysticism of the Celtic world, it would be the horse. To the ancient Celts the horse represented the ability to travel long distances, the ability to plow, and the ability to fight in battle, both for cavalry and for charioteers. Visit the Irish National Stud in County Kildare, Ireland, and you'll see majestic racehorses, lovingly reared and tended, the latest generation of a long and valiant tradition of royal beasts who have been storied in Celtic legend as long as there have been such tales. Several deities have strong links to the horse, most notably the goddesses Epona (from Gaul), Rhiannon (from Wales) and Macha (from Ireland). Indeed, Epona was one of the most widely revered of Celtic goddesses, who became a favorite of Roman soldiers as well as of Celts. Cúchulainn's majestic horse, the "Grey of Macha" was not only named for the goddess, but shared his master's heroic status— the horse was called the "king of horses." In folklore, horses appear as the hobby horses that figure in Beltane revels, and at least one Irish king was said to have ritually "mated" with a horse as part of his coronation ceremony—suggesting a further link between the horse and the goddess of sovereignty.

THE PATH OF SACRED ANIMALS

Pigs and boars have a mysterious place in the Celtic world, often appearing as symbols of abundance, magic, the otherworld, or of sheer force and determination. One of the most dramatic scenes in all of Celtic mythology involves the hero Culhwch chasing two supersized boars, Ysgithrwyn and Twrch Trwyth, as part of his quest to prove himself worthy of wedding the lovely Olwen. Culhwch's name means "pig-run," suggesting that this function of hunting the wild boars may have been an essential part of this mythic hero's identity, even though in the myth that has come down to us he hunts the boars only to retrieve Ysgithrwyn's tusk and a comb and razor embedded in Twrch Trwyth's bristles between his ears. The hunt for Twrch Trwyth is particularly amazing—Culhwch chases the boar from Ireland to Brittany, and back to Cornwall, where with the help of King Arthur and his knights the hero can finally capture the comb and razor.

Other pigs that appear in the tradition aren't quite as colorful, but often have a magical quality. Arawn, king of the underworld, gives a gift of magical pigs to his mortal friend Pwyll. Gods such as Manannán or the Dagda are seen as owning magical pigs that can be killed and eaten, only to be alive and fatted for the feast the very next day. Clearly, these animals transcend their biology to symbolize abundance in a universal way.

THE PATH OF SACRED ANIMALS

Dogs are universally known as man's best friend; in Celtic lore they appear also as protectors and companions in the hunt.

The most remarkable story concerning a dog in the Celtic tradition involves how the hero Cúchulainn got his name. As a boy he was called Setanta, and even as a small child he was renowned for his superhuman strength. One time the warriors of Emain Macha were invited to a feast at the home of Culann the blacksmith; because he was playing a game, Setanta (who was only about 6 at the time) was late in arriving, and reached the smith's home to find that the doors had been shut. Culann's property was protected by a huge hound, which proceeded to attack the boy. When the men inside the hall heard the commotion outside, they remembered that Setanta had not yet arrived and so hurried outside, fearing they would find the boy mauled by the guard dog. Instead, they found him standing over the dog's carcass. Setanta had bested the beast—to Culann's grief, for such a fine watchdog could not easily be replaced. Seeing his unhappiness, Setanta offered to train a puppy to be Culann's new hound—and furthermore, to function as the "hound" himself until the puppy were old enough and trained enough to take on the guard dog's responsibilities. For this the boy received much acclaim, and forever after was known as the Hound of Culann—or "Cúchulainn."

THE PATH OF SACRED ANIMALS

Cows and bulls have played a pivotal role in the Celtic world since ancient times. The cattle-raid is its own genre of Celtic story, with the great *Cattle-Raid of Cooley* culminating in an earth-shattering fight between two larger-than-life bulls, a brown bull from Ulster and a white bull from Connacht. As these animals fought, they may well have symbolized a long-standing rivalry between their respective homelands; the story ends with the brown bull defeating the white, but so mortally wounded that after one final rampage he himself expires. So much for the glory of battle.

More peaceful, perhaps, are the cows. A common theme in folklore is the cow with great abundance of milk; one such story tells of a cow in Donegal that gave milk endlessly, enough for the entire village to share in the wealth. But when one greedy man tried to take more than his share, the cow dried up, and everyone lost the benefit. Meanwhile, many mysterious cow-stories are related to Saint Brigid. As a girl, she would only consume milk from one particular white cow with red ears (the colors symbolizing an otherworldly pedigree), and in folklore Saint Brigid is still said to travel around Ireland on the eve of her festival, accompanied by her cow (not unlike Santa Claus who travels, accompanied by his reindeer).

THE PATH OF SACRED ANIMALS

"I am the stag of seven tines," recounts Amairghin in some versions of his visionary poem, which he uttered upon first setting foot in Ireland. Perhaps by calling the spirit of the stag into himself, he was also invoking Cernunnos—the horned one, the mysterious god/shaman who is depicted in Celtic art wearing a stag's antlers. Proud and tall and one of the most vivid symbols of masculine energy, the stag embodies the spirit of the year through the rhythm of antlers grown and shed. Folklore suggests the stag can be a guide to the otherworld; indeed, it is a stag that Pwyll hunts on the fateful day when he first encounters Arawn, lord of Annwn. A variety of Celtic deities both famous and lesser known have connections to the stag, including the Mórrígan (who transforms into a stag) and Flidais, a goddess of wild things who has the epithet "Mistress of Stags."

THE PATH OF SACRED ANIMALS

Many birds appear in Celtic lore. These range from the graceful swans that appear in the romantic story of Angus' dream, to the ominous ravens, symbol of the war goddesses, that appear in the midst of battlegrounds as harbingers of death and misfortune. Rhiannon is one of several goddesses who are accompanied by birds that would fly about her, singing heavenly and heartbreaking melodies. Manannán wore the skin of a crane as his shamanic spirit bag. When Blodeuedd arranged for the murder of her husband Lleu, he transformed into an eagle to escape his death; later she was transformed into an owl as punishment for her sin. Perhaps the most poignant of bird myths involves the children of Lir, Irish demigods transformed into swans by their jealous stepmother, and cursed to spend nine hundred years imprisoned in their animal form before finally regaining their aged, infirm, dying human forms.

THE PATH OF SACRED ANIMALS

Regarding fish in the Celtic tradition, much of the lore revolves around magical or lucky fish that appear in holy wells or sacred springs, and by so appearing confer good luck or healing power onto those fortunate enough to see them. The legendary Well of Connla featured hazel trees with branches overhanging the well; nuts would fall into the water where the salmon would eat, gaining the wisdom from the tree in the process. It was a salmon that Culhwch consulted as the oldest of living beings in his quest to win Olwen's hand, and it was a salmon of wisdom that Fionn consumed to gain his magical powers. Cúchulainn has his own connection to this sacred fish: one of his mysterious, unexplained military maneuvers is called the "salmon leap"—perhaps simply referring to the aggressive way a salmon returning to its birthplace can leap upstream. Presumably the great warrior demonstrated similar prowess in battle.

THE PATH OF SACRED ANIMALS

Patrick is renowned for chasing the snakes out of Ireland (in reality, they never made it to Eire, having failed to cross into the Emerald Isle before the rising waters after the last ice age cut it off from the mainland); and some have suggested that the "snakes" symbolized the druids whose priesthood and religious leadership Patrick supposedly eclipsed. This idea may have a bit of merit, especially given the snake's prominence in Celtic iconography. The Gundestrup Cauldron, one of the great treasures of Celtic archaeology, shows the horned Cernunnos holding a similarly horned snake—which in itself is a magical archetype that appears in a number of different ancient carvings. Like Cernunnos, the horned snake may have had a shamanic function in the ancient spirituality— suggesting that the snake was an important symbol to the earliest practitioners of Celtic magic. Today, it's easy to project our own biases about the snake: a symbol of femininity, of the goddess, of sin and evil—that we need to be mindful that the original iconography of the snake may have meant something entirely unfamiliar to our modern minds. Like Cernunnos himself, the snake that is his most reliable companion comes to us shrouded in mystery.

THE PATH OF FAITH

In 1911 a young American scholar named W.Y. Evans-Wentz published a book on the folk beliefs of the Celtic world, called *The Fairy-Faith in Celtic Countries.* This book examined the *Creadeamh Si*, or "Fairy Faith," throughout the various Celtic nations, considering the stories told in rural locations about belief in the existence of fairies, insights into how fairies behaved, the different kinds of spirits, and so forth. Although the Fairy Faith is in no way an organized or systematic belief system, what emerges in Evans-Wentz's book is not a study of superstition but rather a sympathetic look at the profound faith of the Celtic people—a faith which not only extended to "authorized" beliefs such as in the Christian God or Jesus Christ, but also included a worldview that made sense to the inhabitants of the rural landscape. So walking the Celtic path includes opening our hearts to the experience of faith. This is not the same thing as fanaticism, but it is a deep and profound commitment to belief in that which cannot be proven. Such a faith goes deeper than merely choosing to believe in spiritual beings that cannot be scientifically measured. It also entails choosing to orient our entire life toward the values of faith: hope, belief, trust, and love. Indeed, these values mean more, ultimately, than whether or not we think fairies are real (which of course they are).

THE PATH OF FAITH

On March 15, 1895 her husband and several other men burned a woman named Bridget Cleary to death. They were holding her over the hearth fire in her own home, trying to reclaim her from the fairies. You see, Bridget Cleary had been sick, and her husband believed that she had been taken by the fairies. The sickly creature left in her place was not the "real" Bridget Cleary. So he and several of his friends and relatives held Bridget over the fire, trying to force the fairies to give the real Bridget back. When this horror was over, only a charred body remained.

A century later, it can be easy to dismiss the Cleary tragedy as only so much superstition, which sadly took a deadly turn. But if we accept that Michael Cleary and his associates genuinely believed that an evil spirit had possessed his wife, then we must face the fact that faith has a dangerous dark side. Indeed, it's not unlike the faith that inspired Al-Qaida terrorists to fly planes into buildings, or anti-abortion extremists to take the law into their own hands and murder family-planning doctors. Celtic mysticism and belief in the fairies is a lovely thing, but it is as susceptible to fanaticism as any other spiritual path. Opening ourselves to the wonders of the inner world does not excuse us from taking responsibility for the real-world consequences of our actions (or beliefs).

THE PATH OF FAITH

The classical historian Diodorus Siculus offers a fascinating insight into the Celtic mind in his *Library of History*: "Brennus, the king of the Gauls, on entering a temple found no dedications of gold or silver, and when he came only upon images of stone and wood he laughed at them, to think that men, believing that gods have human form, should set up their images in wood and stone." Brennus' laughter has echoed for the past twenty-three centuries and still can be heard today. For we live in a world where it's all too easy to give our worship to "images in wood and stone." No, I'm not talking about idols. The images that Brennus would snort at today include our love for technology, our trust in the stock market, and our tendency to hold on tightly to our beliefs, to the point that our ideologies actually enslave us. In his book *Out of the House of Slavery*, Brian Haggerty suggests that the Hebrew commandment "You shall have no other gods before me" actually calls us to resist any belief, dogma, or ideology that threatens to become an "idol"—that is to say, that we worship and revere to the point that it diminishes our freedom.

The Celtic path to Spirit is a path of the wildness of nature, the sovereignty of the human heart, and the incessant whispers of the mysteries at the edges of life. Those are all things that can never be put into images—or words.

THE PATH OF FAITH

Pagan Celtic myht is undeniably polytheistic, but not every modern druid or neopagan believes in the gods and goddesses as literal deities. For many, the mythic spirits are seen as archetypes or metaphorical symbols. Some would argue the Celtic gods and goddesses are like the saints of the Catholic tradition—not supreme in any sense, but nevertheless friendly and powerful spiritual entities to which we can turn for help and assistance. Still others may not assign any "belief" to the Celtic pantheon at all, but enjoy the old myths because they're entertaining stories and help to strengthen our collective sense of Celtic identity.

So people may think about, or experience, Celtic spirituality in a variety of different ways. This is to be expected, for human beings are rich and multi-faceted creatures. The Celtic way is not to impose our beliefs in any sort of dogmatic sense, but rather to share the stories of what is spiritually meaningful for us in a spirit of optimism, love for the diversity of nature, and trust in the healing, loving ways of Spirit. Then, in this setting of free inquiry, we each may come to our own conclusions about what we find—and believe—in our spiritual lives.

THE PATH OF FAITH

*D*ia non Dùl is Scots Gaelic for "God of nature." Literally it is "God of the elements" or "God of creatures." This phrase encapsulates the heart of the Celtic mysteries. Celtic wisdom begins and ends with the spirituality of the natural world. All of the elements are held intimately and lovingly in the hand of Spirit. This is a truth not just of Celtic spirituality, but of all earth-positive religions; yet it is in the Celtic world where so often we find the expression of this nature mysticism expressed so poetically and beautifully.

We sometimes think of nature as something found on farms or in national forests. For people living in urban or suburban settings, nature seems like something that is far away, only accessible on weekends or holidays. The rest of the time we labor in our encased worlds defined by technology and consumerism.

Ah, but what is *not* of nature? Even the most inorganic of manmade items comes originally out of the elements. Our concrete and steel cities are simply the beehives and ant colonies of our species. Sure, our modern culture may not be as lovely or bucolic as the nature of the wildlife conservatory, but the *Dia non Dùl* is every bit as present here as there. It's a good spiritual practice to begin to look for the presence of the Sacred even in the most artificial corners of our lives. When we find God in the plastic places, we will be inspired to see nature there as well.

THE PATH OF FAITH

In 664 CE, Celtic Christianity changed forever with the Synod of Whitby. This event considered such weighty matters as calculating the date of Easter and the proper tonsure (haircut) of the Celtic monks. The conflict was between the Celtic Christians and the growing influence of Roman-style Christianity in England. The king sided with the Romans, and even though Irish Christianity persisted in its Celtic ways for some time, this event marks the triumph of Roman authority in England.

Today, Whitby appears quaint if not downright silly. But it is a stark reminder of the power of dogma in people's lives. To the priests and monks who argued their case at the Synod, questions such as the dating of Easter were of central importance to their understanding of spirituality.

It's tempting to dismiss dogma as a useless relic of ultraconservative models of authority. But it's not really that simple. Any community, of any size—from a married couple to the Catholic Church—requires commitments, agreements, and shared values. In our modern world, we often live with unspoken values and beliefs that have been created for us by business, government, and media. Celtic spirituality calls us to be mindful of the "dogmas" (shared beliefs) in our lives—even when that means we have to negotiate with others over something as seemingly minor as a haircut.

THE PATH OF FAITH

Faith is related to hope. It is a spiritual declaration, linked with an ongoing choice not to give up. All great wisdom traditions invite us to hope, and the Celtic path is no exception. In Irish tradition, we see the hope of Lugh who inspired the Tuatha Dé Danann to fight against the oppressive Fomorians; we see the hope of Cúchulainn who single-handedly defended the province of Ulster against an invading army; we see the faith of Brendan the Navigator, who set forth in a tiny boat to traverse the vast Atlantic ocean, seeking the blessed isles to the west. Likewise, in the Welsh tradition the faith of Rhiannon preserved her dignity when she is unfairly accused of killing her own son, and the faith of Gwydion saved Lleu after he was almost slain by his unfaithful wife's lover. Faith and hope are woven into the very heart of the Celtic soul, whether expressed in a religious sense (faith in God) or a less directed spiritual sense (hope that, in the words of the medieval English mystic Julian of Norwich, all shall be well).

THE PATH OF FAITH

In his book *The Music of What Happens*, Irish priest John J. Ó Ríordain muses on how faith is linked with praise. He considers the custom, still found among the more devout members of Irish society, of weaving into everyday language the poetry of praise, *Deo Gratias* ("thanks be to God") and *Kyrie Eleison* ("Lord have mercy"). I've heard Irish speakers say the reason they prefer their native language to English is because in Irish, every sentence contains a prayer. What comes first—the faith, or the praise? This is probably a chicken-and-egg question. Choosing to approach life from a perspective of praise may in fact help to foster a deeper faith, which in turn supports the choice to praise and bless, rather than curse and condemn.

THE PATH OF FAITH

John J. Ó Ríordain sees faith as not only linked with praise, but also with wonder. This reminds me of the Irish musician Van Morrison, whose song "A Sense of Wonder" simply and beautifully expresses the mystical experience of regarding life and the world with the open eyes of faith. Wonder is a lovely word, for it is related to the word *wound*—indeed, in Middle English wonder is spelled "wounder." Opening ourselves to spiritual enlightenment is a process of vulnerability, which means "capable of being wounded." But the wounding of wonder comes not from a knife or a bullet, but from the luminous glories of supernal light, from the profound beauties of graced nature, from the inspiring sense of divine presence that can propel us into a state of ecstasy—"out of the body" and into the heart of the Divine. One need not believe anything to experience wonder—only an open mind, heart, and soul are necessary. And yet that openness can, once the blessings are received and acknowledged, serve only to foster a faith that will carry us forward in hope, even when our experiences may not transport us into the ecstasies we desire. Wonder, like any other experience, comes and goes. But the faith that it inspires and supports (and that in turn inspires and supports all luminous experience) anchors within the soul at a level deeper than experience, a level where the choice is made to say "Yes" to God.

THE PATH OF BRIGIT

One of the most fascinating figures in Celtic tradition is Brigit (also spelled Brigid, Brighid, Bride, among other variants). She is profound and intriguing precisely because she stands at the crossroads between the pagan Celts and the Christian tradition. For in many places of the Celtic world, goddesses were venerated with names that began with Brig-: Brigit, Brigantia, Brigindo, and simply Bríg. Some commentators believe these various names refer to the same goddess (or at least, the same type of goddess); the name itself is actually a title, "the exalted one." But as anyone familiar with Ireland today can attest, the name Brigid is indelibly linked with the piety of the Christian faith, for the second most popular Irish saint after Patrick is Brigid of Kildare. Let's muddy the waters further: Brigit may well have been worshiped as a goddess in Kildare before the coming of Christianity, and some commentators have suggested that the saint is nothing more than a Christianization of the old pagan goddess. Indeed, the goddess and the saint share many qualities in common, and today they both stand as powerful symbols of the feminine spirit within the Celtic world. I think that Brigit's most significant contribution to the Celtic path may ultimately be in opening a doorway between these two religious expressions. Indeed, tradition holds that Saint Brigid was born in a doorway—so even this is a perfectly appropriate image to ponder.

THE PATH OF BRIGIT

A tenth-century Irish manuscript describes Brigit as a triple goddess. She is actually three sisters, all bearing the name/title of the Exalted One: the first a goddess of poetry, the second of healing, the third of smithcraft. If you consider that a blacksmith's art is practiced using the fires of a forge, that healing often requires salves and potions prepared over the fire of the hearth, and that poetry is linked to the "fires" of inspiration, it is easy to see Brigit as a fire deity. And fire is an element that purifies and transforms and releases energy that rises, all appropriate characteristics for a goddess of exaltation. Some observers think of Brigit as a battle goddess, for after all wouldn't she use the forge to create weapons of war? But it's not a distinction that fits her well. Other Celtic goddesses have a much stronger warrior connection, and Brigit's role as a healer implies a different set of priorities. In Irish mythology, Brigit is even shown marrying a member of the Fomorians, her tribe's greatest adversaries. She is said to have attempted to broker peace between the warring factions, in an unsuccessful bid to prevent hostilities.

THE PATH OF BRIGIT

The goddess Brigit was the daughter of the Dagda, the great father god of the Tuatha Dé Danann. But some scholars have speculated that she (as "the Exalted One") may have been Dana herself, the goddess for whom the tribe was named. Like so many elements of ancient Celtic tradition, the story has come down to us in garbled and incomplete ways. Whatever Brigit's place in the genealogy of the gods, she married Bres the Fomorian, and gave birth to a son, Rúadán. When open hostilities broke out between his father's and mother's peoples, Rúadán sided with the Fomorians, only to be killed in battle. At his death his mother lamented with a chant of grief and mourning that became known as the *caoineadh*, or "keening." This eventually entered Irish folklore as the wail of the banshee, the female fairy said to mourn the death of a member of the Gaelic nobility.

THE PATH OF BRIGIT

Brigit of Irish tradition may be an equivalent goddess to Brigantia, a goddess who was venerated in Britain. She was the patroness of the Brigantes, a Celtic tribe from the time of the Roman occupation. Evidence points to her being regarded as a deity connected with the veneration of water—the River Brent takes its name from this goddess. What's fascinating about this is the prevalence of holy wells now sacred to Saint Brigid. Perhaps these wells were originally dedicated to Brigit/Brigantia in her guise as a water goddess.

Of course, how could Brigit be both a fire goddess and a water goddess? It's not a hard question to answer: consider especially holy wells, where water rises from under the earth to the surface. Compare this movement to fire, where energy in the form of heat rises. As the Exalted One, Brigit would naturally be concerned with energy that rises—whether in the form of fiery heat, or water surging up from the underworld.

THE PATH OF BRIGIT

Water seems to be important to both Saint Brigid and her pagan counterpart, but can the same be said of fire? Brigit the goddess is linked to three fires: the hearth, the forge, and inspiration. In a similar way, fire plays a prominent role in the story of Saint Brigid: A twelfth-century writer, Gerald of Wales, describes how the nuns of Saint Brigid's monastery in Kildare kept an eternal fire burning; indeed, Gerald describes it as "inextinguishable." Nineteen nuns tended the flame, and on the twentieth day it was left alone, to be watched over by Brigid herself; Gerald reports that the flame never faltered under Brigid's watch, and furthermore that the fire miraculously produced no ash. Needless to say, this practice with its clear pagan roots was not always met with ecclesiastical approval; and when the monasteries were suppressed in the days of Henry VIII, the fire was put out, apparently for good. But not so fast; in the closing years of the twentieth century, nuns of the Catholic Brighidine order established a house in Kildare and relit the flame, where it burns even now—a beacon of light and hope from the Celtic Spirit of the Sacred Feminine.

THE PATH OF BRIGIT

Saint Brigid is described in medieval biographies as a pious young woman, the daughter of a pagan man and his Christian slave-woman; from her childhood she displayed a penchant for generosity, hospitality, charity for the poor, and the occasional working of a miracle. When a suitor arrived to marry her, to the horror of all she gouged out her eye. The shaken man left abruptly, whereupon Brigid promptly healed herself! In another story, she gave away her father's sword to a beggar (perhaps implying not only her commitment to charity, but also to peace, not unlike the spirit of the goddess whose name she bore). Legend holds that Brigid was "accidentally" consecrated a bishop when she took her monastic vows. She eventually founded a monastery in Kildare that for many years was a prominent and powerful site for Irish Christianity; it may well have been a preexisting pagan sanctuary, since Kildare in Irish means "the Cell of the Oak," referring to a great oak tree that once stood where the Anglican Cathedral of Saint Brigid now stands. Incidentally, it was said that no weapon could be set against the trunk of this tree—yet another connection between Brigid and peace.

THE PATH OF BRIGIT

Saint Brigid is called the "Mary of the Gael," implying that she has a special role to the Celts similar to the part that Mary plays within Christendom as a whole. Brigid is also called the "foster-mother of Christ," and a charming Scottish legend suggests that angels escorted Brigid to the stable in Bethlehem, traversing space (and time!) in a miraculous fashion. All this points to the special place Brigid holds in the Celtic heart. Among the miracles attributed to her was the changing of water into beer (predating the Guinness brewery by over a thousand years) and blessing a cow so that she gave enough milk to fill an entire lake. Indeed, milk and cows have a particularly strong place in the story of Brigid: her mother was carrying milk when she gave birth to the saint; as a child Brigid had a habit of giving away milk and butter to beggars, and on the eve of her feast day she visits the houses of her devotees accompanied by her cow. One folk tradition called for leaving straw before the front door of a house that evening—so that Brigid would have a comfortable place to kneel when she offered her blessing, and so that her cow would have something to munch on.

THE PATH OF BRIGIT

The First of February is known in many parts of the Celtic world as the Festival of Brigid. It corresponds with the Catholic feast of Saint Brigid, but also corresponds with the pagan festival of Imbolc. This ancient agricultural festival marked the beginning of spring; in all likelihood Imbolc was a time when the goddess Brigit was particularly venerated, and so it was transferred to the saint after the coming of Christianity. Of course, tradition holds that Saint Brigid died on February I (hence it being her day), but that could be a later insertion, just as fixing the birth date of Christ on December 25 was an arbitrary matter. The Festival of Brigid featured a variety of charming folk traditions, including the making of Brigid's crosses out of rushes, using braided straw to make a large hoop (called a Crios Bríde or "Bride's Girdle") through which people would step to receive a blessing from the saint, and fashioning a doll to symbolize the saint (a Brídeog, or "young Brigid") which would be ceremoniously carried throughout the village and then ritually welcomed back into the home where it was made. And thus the themes of healing, holiness, and hospitality are reaffirmed for another year.

THE PATH OF BRIGIT

How can we honor Brigit/Brigid today? Naturally, becoming familiar with her stories, as elusive and fragmentary though they may be, is a good place to start. While Christians may wish to focus upon her as a saint and neopagans prefer to stress her divinity, I think much can be gained from befriending both the goddess and the holy woman. Along these lines, don't worry too much about whether the saint is really just the goddess in Christian disguise, or if she truly represents a historical figure who broke from paganism to embrace the new faith. At this point in time, we can only speculate over what truly happened in Kildare fifteen hundred years ago. So it's better to follow Brigid's example and extend charity and hospitality to both the goddess and the saint, marveling at their similarities and giving thanks for how Celtic spirituality continues to be the place where paganism and Christianity can meet on friendly terms.

THE PATH OF THE STORYTELLER

One of the loveliest days in my life came in the summer of 2002. I was in Ireland, researching for *The Complete Idiot's Guide to Celtic Wisdom*. At the suggestion of Patricia Monaghan, I contacted a retired farmer in County Galway named Tom Hannon. Patricia described Tom as one of the finest storytellers she knew, and "the world authority on Saint Colman." Since I'm a McColman, he seemed like an auspicious fellow to meet. So on a Saturday night that June, I drove into the smallish town of Gort, famous for being the home of Lady Gregory and also a summer home for William Butler Yeats. After dinner I called Tom, having written and introduced myself to him a month before. We made arrangements to meet at a local pub the following afternoon. This was during the World Cup, and Ireland had a match with Spain at the time. So Tom and I had to find a little nook where we could have a bit of quiet, away from the crowd gathered to watch the game on the pub's big screen TV. It seemed an unlikely setting for an encounter with a genuine Irish *shanachie*, or storyteller. But when Tom started to tell his stories, our noisy environment suddenly didn't matter. For like all great storytellers, my new friend did not merely entertain me with his tales—he transported me to a magical world. For this is what storytelling can do: it can bring magic and mystery into our lives.

THE PATH OF THE STORYTELLER

I spent a good eight or ten hours with Tom Hannon on that magical Sunday in County Galway. He told me tales about the fairies (whom he described as fallen angels loyal neither to God nor the devil), about the mythic community of magical beings called the Tuatha Dé Danann ("perhaps one of the twelve lost tribes of Israel, although no one knows for sure" he speculated), about various local saints and heroes, including my namesake, Saint Colman. Woven into many of Tom's stories was a profound sense of place, in which he talked about such-and-such a standing stone or holy well. Finally, he suggested that we needed to actually go visit some of the local sites that had appeared in his tales, and so off we went on that rainy day, to visit the ruins of churches and monasteries and a charming, still active holy well dedicated to Saint Colman, located in someone's back yard. Finally we returned to the pub where we had started for one final cup of tea, Tom all the while still saying things like, "And that reminds me of when…" or, "And did I tell you about…" before launching into another tale. When the day ended, I felt a sense of amazement most unusual for an urban American. For in the eyes and words of this unassuming farmer, I had gazed into centuries of Celtic wisdom.

THE PATH OF THE STORYTELLER

Why would something as simple as storytelling be a doorway into Celtic wisdom? Consider this. In the old days (and in some remote parts of northwest Europe where Celtic languages are spoken, those old days weren't so very long ago), people would gather at a neighbor's home after a day's work in the fields or on the water. A roaring fire would be built on the hearth, and all would gather around, cheerful and thankful for the warming. Children would be cuddled up with their mums and dads, and before long one of the young ones would ask one of the elders—perhaps a grandchild speaking to her grandfather, to "tell us a story." And then the tale would be told, perhaps not very different from some of the tales that old Tom told me, in which fairies play tricks on unwitting or unpleasant farmers, or Fionn mac Cumhaill defeats the terrible monster that comes out at Samhain (Halloween), or Saint Patrick triumphs over the sea serpent in Lough Derg. Or it might be a very simple local story, of how the nearby holy well came to be blessed, or the local river got its name. In the telling of the stories, the people found or reaffirmed their identity, as well as the identity of the world in which they lived. The stories not only entertained, but they wove the blessings of the past into those of the present.

THE PATH OF THE STORYTELLER

Folklorists in the Celtic lands began collecting traditional stories in the nineteenth century. Ireland has been especially dedicated to archiving its folk traditions, with the Irish Folklore Commission recording tens of thousands of tales, many of which have never yet been translated out of Irish. These stories cover a wide terrain, from vestigial legends of the old gods and goddesses, to fairy tales and other supernatural yarns, to pious stories of Christian saints. As is so often the case with Celtic wisdom, many traditional stories have significance mostly for the local area in which they were told, often linked to a place name or a figure of regional renown. After all, the Bible was the book that provided a sense of place for the cosmos as a whole; so the old stories of fairies and local legends provided a meaningful counterpoint, a sense of connection to the local and the particular, in balance with the religious sense of connection to the cosmic and the universal.

THE PATH OF THE STORYTELLER

Storytelling, as it has evolved into a folk tradition (which, alas, has been a dying art for some time now, endangered both because of the decline of the Celtic languages but also because of the encroaching "corporate storytelling" of mass media entertainment) may have roots that extend all the way back to the pre-Christian days, when bards were the keepers of history and genealogy. In the days before the coming of Christianity (and of the written word), the bards were the guardians of the past, the keepers of the tribal memory and the archivists whose knowledge preserved the identity of the people. All of these functions remained, if in shadowy and vestigial ways, as part of the charm of the folk storyteller. Sometimes a storyteller would begin a tale with, "Do you know how the first plow was invented in Ireland?" and then launch off on a tale of a man's misfortune arising from his bad dealings with the fairies. The story ends with the building of the first plow, but more than a plow has been created in the telling of the tale—a deepened sense of the interwoven mysteries of the human and supernatural worlds has been passed down from teller to listener.

THE PATH OF THE STORYTELLER

What makes a traditional Celtic story? Naturally, if it has to do with a place or a person out of Celtic history, it most certainly is a tale worth telling. And so most of the stories you'll hear if you have the good fortune to meet a *shanachie* today will have some sort of link to the tribe or to the land. But the power of these stories comes from something more than just their local color. A story conveys wisdom when it reinforces, even if in a subtle way, the ideals, values, or customs of a community. It conveys wisdom when it reminds the listener, even if in indirect or oblique ways, that the cosmos often extends far beyond what meets the eye. And if the story has a "moral"—a point worth remembering and applying to one's life—then it most certainly is a conduit of wisdom as well as of pleasure. In short, Celtic stories may be "magical" because they are peopled with fairies and saints and otherworldly voyagers—but they are "wise" because they create and recreate a tapestry of language that supports the ongoing existence of the Celtic way of thinking about, and living in, the world.

THE PATH OF THE STORYTELLER

I've lamented that traditional Celtic storytelling appears to be a dying art. Television, the Internet, the loss of the Celtic languages, and the modern mobility that disrupts the stability of rural life, have all contributed to the decline of this tradition. Fortunately, many of the old stories have been recorded or written down; and a few dedicated folks are committed to keeping the tradition alive, even if now many (like my friend Tom) tell their tales in English. But storytelling is not just for Celts, nor is Celtic storytelling just for the rural places in the British Isles. Anyone, anywhere, who cares about Celtic wisdom, should seek ways to incorporate stories into their lives. If you live in New Jersey, find stories about your local land and history. If your great-great grandparents emigrated to Australia because of the Great Hunger or the Highland Clearances, find some way to preserve their memory and make their stories known. Of course, taking the time to learn about Irish or Welsh mythology, or the lives of the Celtic saints, would provide the aspiring storyteller with an arsenal of tales. Storytelling is rarely if ever done on a stage in front of thousands—it's best done in a living room or a pub, with a small circle of friends and associates. Tell your stories. And then look for wisdom in the words.

THE PATH OF THE STORYTELLER

I have suggested that the power of Celtic storytelling has to do with how local and particular and specific it is: the traditional tales generally do not bother themselves with the great events of world history or the awesome dynamics of God in heaven; rather they are more homely tales of family history, local color, and regional legend. Even so, to delve into the magical world of the story is to discover, sooner or later, how all stories, no matter how unique or idiosyncratic, function on one level as elements in the "Great Story" of our shared and common lives as members of the human family. Every little tale told in Cornwall or the Isle of Man concerning a local legend or feature in the landscape is a part of the great story of the Celtic world. And so it is with all of our individual stories. Which is why we all need to do what we can to keep telling our own stories; the stories of our families and our homelands. Our voices must be heard if the Great Story is to be told in full.

THE PATH OF THE STORYTELLER

Storytelling keeps the past alive. But it can also beckon us into the future. Each person who lives is, in a sense, an unfinished story. J.R.R. Tolkien said, the "tale grew in the telling," to explain how *The Lord of the Rings* turned out to be such a long novel. Each one of us has the opportunity to grow our own tale as it is being told. Think of your life as a story. Maybe you think the plot is pretty dull so far (or perhaps you think it has had more than its share of drama or tragedy!). How, then, can you shape your story from here on out? What can you do to design a story that is noble, or funny, or touching, or entertaining? Perhaps you'd like your story to be calm or peaceful, or extreme (as in extreme sports). As a walker of Celtic wisdom, tell stories to remain related to the past. But also be mindful of how you live your life, for with each passing day you are designing a story for the future.

THE PATH OF MAGIC

The Gaelic word for druid is also the word for magician. In addition to being the philosophers and priests of the Celts, the druids (then as well as now) have at least the reputation of being adepts in magic. But what does that mean?

Magic is one of the most spectacularly misunderstood of spiritual concepts. To some it implies an unsavory dalliance with dark and manipulative energies. To others it is a psychic birthright, a doorway into the self-fulfillment and happiness we all deserve. Still others dismiss it as a topic fit only for myths, legends, and children's stories.

Well, everyone seems to have it partially right. Those who reject magic as evil (often because it is a topic that religious authorities have rarely condoned), should remember that the line separating magic from miracle is often nothing more than ecclesiastical approval. Meanwhile, those who hunger after magic's purported ability to sculpt the life of one's dreams should take a hard and critical look at the lives of people who practice magic. It may be a tool for spiritual happiness or mystical insight, but it confers no more happiness or power than any other strategy for living. Finally, those who reject magic as nonsense may simply be reacting to the caricatures of magic found in Hollywood, but they could also be biased against any form of spiritual endeavor. Magic cannot replace science, but as a tool for inner growth and meaning, it sure beats a slide rule.

THE PATH OF MAGIC

So how can we think of magic in a way that makes sense for the twenty-first century? Perhaps the first point to consider is the role that spirituality plays in our lives. If faith or religious practice is only about "getting right with God," then there is little room for personal fulfillment. But if we believe that God loves us enough to desire our happiness and joy, then perhaps the spiritual life has an additional function— to support that quest for self-actualization. Here's where the druids come in. No one can say for sure what kind of magic the ancient druids performed, and most modern druids engage in practices that are unapologetically borrowed from shamanism, Wicca, or fraternal occult organizations like the Golden Dawn. So the question is not so much *how* druids do magic, but *why*. And the best answer in my mind is to balance personal fulfillment with spiritual growth. Which handily describes the function of the two traditional categories of magic: thaumaturgy and theurgy. If you don't like the word *magic* because of religious or philosophical conviction, then don't use it. But consider the role that spiritual growth and personal fulfillment play in your life. And consider what spiritual resources may be available to you for achieving such goals. A rose by any other name: those resources (prayer, meditation, ritual, affirmations, visualizations, and so forth) are the raw material of magic—whether Celtic or otherwise.

THE PATH OF MAGIC

Thaumaturgy is a fancy word that means "the working of wonders" and involves using magic to make something out of nothing, or to make enough of an impact on the world "out there" that one's goals are achieved. It can cover anything from making it rain to causing an angry ex-husband to see reason. You want more love or money in your life? Thaumaturgy is the way to go.

Sure, there are ethical issues involved in performing magic that, at least in theory, could impact someone else's free will. Thus, many magicians insist that they will only work magic on themselves—instead of whipping up a spell to cause someone to fall in love with you, do magic to make yourself more attractive to the right person.

Decide for yourself if thaumaturgy is "real" or not— suffice to say, many people believe in it and report that spiritual efforts make a real difference in their quest for happiness. In balance, it's good for people to take responsibility for their well-being (spiritual and otherwise), and if thaumaturgy is a spiritual tool for such self-reliance, then it is a concept worth exploring. Meanwhile, spiritual strategies for fulfillment should never stand in the way of the old-fashioned hard work of taking care of one's self. Using magic to make money is pointless unless you're willing to start a business or find a new job!

THE PATH OF MAGIC

Thaumaturgy has traditionally been called "low magic," since its goal (to make advantageous changes in the world) are "lower" than the more elevated quest to find spiritual fulfillment, union with the Divine, or some other lofty mystical goal. Why expend all your spiritual juice on finding a good parking spot, when you could be aiming for universal enlightenment instead?

Actually, most people who practice magic insist that theurgy is not intrinsically better than thaumaturgy. But it does seem to be a bit more psychologically integrated to aim one's spiritual intent toward manifesting Divine energies, rather than just trying to cash in on a wish or two. If thaumaturgy feels like something out of a cheap paperback book with lotto numbers and lucky days, then theurgy feels, well, more *druidic* by contrast.

In all likelihood, the ancient druids probably were just as worried about making the crops grow as they were about feeling linked with the world soul. And there seems to be a lesson in here; perhaps it's wise to balance our spiritual yearning and effort between being a giving, loving, compassionate person, and doing what it takes to make sure that our own needs, basic though they may be, are met. Selfish? Not really. Try self-loving.

THE PATH OF MAGIC

The magical notion of theurgy calls to mind the more religious notion of sacrament. A sacrament is literally a means of grace (sacred energy)—a process, action, or thing that channels Divine presence into the world. Naturally, it's a word most people know within the context of Christianity, where rituals such as baptism and Holy Communion are regarded as portals through which God's grace flows into the world.

Neopagans would argue that sacraments are a form of magic. Christians would reply that sacraments are not magic, since they are seen as initiated by God, and not by humans.

This book isn't the place to try to resolve *that* argument. But for Christians or others who find the concept of the sacrament more congenial than magic, it's a meaningful way to think of what resources are at our disposal for finding spiritual growth and fulfillment. And while druids may have never had the concept of sacrament in their spirituality, Celtic Christians certainly have. Indeed, Celtic Christianity is a sacramental faith that extends beyond the official sacraments of this or that church. In Celtic Christianity, nature herself is a sacrament— for nature reveals the grace and love of God.

THE PATH OF MAGIC

Magic is important because through it we are spiritually changed. It is a force, an energy, which flows through and affects our lives. Maybe it's a subtle change—nobody ever said transformation had to be dramatic or awe-inspiring. Sometimes, indeed, the smallest changes yield the biggest results, for they are the changes that can pay long-term dividends.

What kind of transformation can magic bring about? It can inspire faith, or hope, or trust. It can be the spiritual foundation for changes in behavior, great or small. It can inspire the kind of psychological shifts that make physical changes (such as healing) possible. And there's plenty of room for magic to involve changes with a spiritual origin as well.

If the druids are the magicians of the Celtic world, that's just a mystical way of saying they are the change agents *par excellence*. They used an arsenal of tools—science, psychology, magic, sacrifice, and history—to initiate changes in their world. Why shouldn't a seeker of Celtic wisdom today follow that model? In other words, the magical life is the opposite of being a victim or a martyr. I take responsibility for my life. When something doesn't work—I change it (or connect with someone else who can). And if all that can be changed is my attitude—even a change as humble as that can be a source of magic.

THE PATH OF MAGIC

The words *magic* and *imagination* don't appear to be etymologically related. But boy, they sure could be! As the energy of spiritual transformation, magic invites us to imagine possibilities—to see the future as it could be, and then to invest the energy of hope and choice, commitment and intention to make real what first existed only in imagination. Most teachers of magic insist that their students master such basic skills as meditation, visualization, and affirmation (using language to imagine a desired future). Each of these tools, when powered by the imagination, becomes a means for channeling spiritual energy into the world. Approached this way, magic appears less of a supernatural or occult activity, and more of a creative—yet entirely natural—tool for channeling the powers of the mind (and spirit) to catalyze positive change.

Ah, so here the link between druids-as-scientists, druids-as-psychologists, and druids-as-magicians becomes evident. The magical skills of the druids were not irrational or unscientific, but psychological in their scope and purpose. And when magic is rightly understood as a psychological rather than a supernatural tool, much of the traditional religious objection to it loses steam.

THE PATH OF MAGIC

In the popular mind, magic is often associated with spells. Go into any bookstore that carries occult or metaphysical titles, and you'll see dozens of spell books—claiming to offer just the ticket for money, romance, self-confidence, or whatever other elusive quality may be desired by the budding magician. All too often, these books are aimed at teenagers, and are designed in such a cutesy manner as to suggest that magic is, at the end of the day, just a silly little game to play—hardly a spiritual discipline to be taken seriously. The idea of casting spells seems too often linked with a superstitious, supernatural view of magic, which, when interwoven with the trendy nature of the spell books, combines to present an image of magic which is, well, pure fantasy. Maybe that makes for great marketing in the twenty-first century, but it hardly seems relevant to the Celtic tradition of the druids as master magicians. Forget the superstition and the fashionable spells. Stick with magic as a simple set of spiritual tools to carve out possibilities and attainable visions for your life.

THE PATH OF MAGIC

Instead of spells, think of magic as linked to ritual. A ritual is a formalized set of prayers, movements, and actions, designed to foster spiritual states of consciousness or a deeper sense of connection with the Divine. Noted modern magicians such as Dion Fortune and W.E. Butler describe magic as the art of changing consciousness at will; this is precisely where meditation and ritual derive their power—in the silence of meditation, or the ceremonialism of a ritual, we enter a place where both the conscious and unconscious dimensions of the mind can access its own deep wisdom. Such wisdom can be applied to cultivating the transformation and spiritual growth, which is the true heart of magic. All this, and we know that the druids of old were ritualists—they were described as presiding over all the public religious ceremonies of the Celts.

So would you like more magic in your life? You can begin by doing something as simple as lighting a candle and meditating for twenty minutes every morning. Sounds simple? You bet it is. And incredibly challenging. For such a simple practice will open up for you the chance to transform the deepest mysteries of your soul. And that is magic indeed.

THE PATH OF THE
THREE NOBLE STRAINS

Legend tells how the Dagda, the good god of the Tuatha Dé Danann, was skilled in many ways and the owner of numerous treasures. Chief among his treasures was a magical harp that would come to him when he called, and on which the Dagda could play three magical tunes, known as the "Three Noble Strains." When the Tuatha Dé Danann fought their archenemies, the Fomorians, the Dagda's harp and his personal harper were captured during the battle. Afterwards, the Dagda, accompanied by the great warrior gods Lugh and Ogma, boldly made for the Fomorian camp, where he found the harp displayed in the midst of their banquet hall. The Dagda called to his harp, and it came, killing nine Fomorian warriors in the process! When he put his hands on the harp, he began to play the Three Noble Strains, and by turns the enemy warriors were moved to profound sorrow, joyous laughter, and finally peaceful slumber. For this was the mystery of the music of the harp: that it evoked powerful feelings from all who listened.

THE PATH OF THE
THREE NOBLE STRAINS

The First Noble Strain is called *goltrai* in Irish: it is the strain of weeping. When the Dagda played this music on his harp, all who listened were moved to such depths of sorrow that could only be released through tears and lamentation. It is the music of sadness and despair, of grief and tragedy. It is the strain that can be heard in many Celtic airs and ballads, where poignant melodies or heartbreaking lyrics give voice to a people that know loss only too well.

It may be challenging to think of the music of sorrow as constituting a "noble" strain, and yet the Celtic soul understands the nobility of loss. There is a dignity that often emerges most powerfully, if tragically, at our moments of greatest sorrow. Remember that the Dagda played the *goltrai* for these warriors shortly after they were defeated in battle. The tears they shed were not artificial, but were true expressions of the deep loss held within their souls.

THE PATH OF THE
THREE NOBLE STRAINS

What can loss and sorrow teach us about wisdom? Perhaps most important of all, that such sad feelings are truly universal. Everyone has either tasted deeply of the waters of grief, or will someday. When the Buddha's parents tried to protect him from all the sorrows of the world, it was an exercise doomed to failure; although the young prince took matters in his own hands to learn about the suffering in the world, it would have been just a matter of time before the shadow-side of existence breached the fortress that surrounded him and educated him on the true measure of life's pain. Realizing how inescapable sorrow is, the Buddha taught that life is suffering, as the first of his noble truths.

Perhaps the Dagda's noble strains are not unlike the Buddha's noble truths—at least, this is so for the first of each. Life is suffering, and so music can express it perhaps more bitterly and profoundly than any other form of art. Don't believe me? Listen to the blues—perhaps the ultimate musical expression of sorrow transformed into wisdom.

THE PATH OF THE
THREE NOBLE STRAINS

When it seemed that all the tears that could be shed had fallen, the Dagda moved on to perform the *geantrai*, or the Second Noble Strain. This is the Strain of Laughter or Merriment, and its melodies were as delightful and enjoyable as the *goltrai* was sorrowful and wistful. Suddenly the warriors who moments before had teetered on the brink of despair were dancing, laughing heartily from the belly, carrying on with all the exuberant noise of a raucous party. Suddenly it seemed that every loss, every sorrow, every pain had been forgotten, submerged beneath a world of sensuality, delight, and mirth.

How could the Fomorians (or anyone) go from the deep sorrow of the first noble strain to the playful joy of the second? Surely some magical mischief was afoot, and some would say that the Dagda by this point was weaving a spell on his hapless foes. But there's another way of considering the effect of the music. Perhaps the Second Noble Strain is capable of teaching us that humor can be found most anywhere—even emerging from the pit of blackest despair. After all, isn't there something hopelessly funny about the human condition? Don't we laugh as an alternative to crying? So the Fomorians began to laugh when there was no weeping left in them.

THE PATH OF THE
THREE NOBLE STRAINS

What can joy and laughter teach us about wisdom? Is it simply about refusing to despair, even when things look really bad (as in your army just lost a pivotal battle, nine of your comrades have been killed by a flying harp, and now the harp is being used to manipulate your emotions. It can't get *too* much worse than that). Or does it suggest, as I hinted before, that there is a closer link between sorrow and joy than we might want to admit? What makes the Noble Strains so noble? Perhaps it is a simple fact that each relates to a profound feeling that is found at the heart of the human experience. Few lows can reach the despair of grief, while few highs can match the lightness of joy. And few feelings can approach the sheer peacefulness of deep slumber. But if *geantrai* lifts you up while *goltrai* brings you down, where is the unity? The answer might be found in that ancient image that appears in the Tarot: the wheel of fortune. Our sorrows do turn into joys, and our joys into sorrows. This too shall pass. So not only is joy such a lovely thing, but also it is the truest and best means of moving beyond the sorrows of despair. So enjoy yourself. It's not just a polite saying. It's a spiritual mandate. Because the opposite is almost too painful to bear.

THE PATH OF THE
THREE NOBLE STRAINS

And so now we come to the Third Noble Strain, or *suantrai*, the strain of slumber. When the Dagda played it, the enemy warriors not surprisingly all dozed off, leaving only him and his comrades alert and awake. They were able to rescue the harper, and take him and the harp away from the sleeping Fomorians.

So wouldn't this be a handy skill to have? Get out of just about any difficult situation, merely by playing soothing music that could dispatch your opponents to dreamland? But it's important to remember that this is the last of the strains. And forgive the pun, but it is important because it represents the exhaustion that comes after a straining emotional experience. The warriors had traveled rapidly from great sorrow to equally great joy. No wonder that they were ready for a nap. So technically speaking, this was not some sort of magic sedative that one could use unscrupulously for personal gain; on the contrary, it was the essential capstone of a three-part arch. For tears and laughter find their ultimate resolution in deep rest.

THE PATH OF THE
THREE NOBLE STRAINS

How, then, does restful sleep speak of wisdom? Perhaps in the same way that the darkness of Samhain, or the deathly majesty of the battle goddess the Mórrígan, speaks of wisdom. If life offers us peak emotions, then it must follow up the deal with a means to recharge the batteries. Of course, none of us wants to inhabit a world where only sorrow is known (okay, maybe some goth-kids *say* they want a world of perpetual sadness, but just give it to them and see how long they are really "happy" with it). But the truth is this: perpetual joy would be just as stultifying. The problem with "they lived happily ever after" is that it implies some sort of fantasia world where smiles are permanent and joy is a static thing. I don't know about you, but I'm in no hurry to live in such a place. Mix my joy with a few tears, thank you. And give me time to sleep off both extremes.

THE PATH OF THE
THREE NOBLE STRAINS

So the Three Noble Strains, taken as a whole, provide, naturally enough, a fine example of the power in the number three so beloved of the Celts of old. And in a way, the strains represent the wheel of the year: *geantrai* brings its delight to bear on spring and early summer, while *goltrai* governs the time of harvest and slaughter, its ennobling of loss symbolizing the coming dark time. When summer finally ends, the year spins around to the time of hibernation, or *suantrai*. And that dark time yields to the joy of another spring, and the cycle, renewed, begins yet again.

Joy does not lead to ecstasy unless we are capable of understanding the "alternative ecstasy" inspired by deep sorrow. The intensity of both requires the serenity of deep sleep. In a way, the powerful psychic states represented by the Three Noble Strains are like the three primary colors found on a color wheel. All other colors begin as measured blends of the three main ones. And so, perhaps, are all emotions, all psychological states, ultimately derived from some appropriate measure of sorrow, joy, and rest.

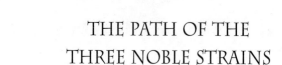

THE PATH OF THE
THREE NOBLE STRAINS

It is said that one time the Fenians were camping on the Hill of Allen, not far from Kildare. They got into a discussion about the most beautiful music of the world. One suggested that the flute made the most beautiful of music; another said the pipes, and still another, the harp. Soon the conversation turned to the music of nature. Seagulls make the loveliest music, offered one. No, the voice of seals is the loveliest of music, said another, and on and on it went. Finally someone decided to ask the group's leader, Fionn mac Cumhaill, what he thought the loveliest music was. "The finest music," mused Fionn, "is the music of what happens."

No, it's not a Zen koan (well, maybe it is, but with a distinctive Irish accent). Fionn is simply saying something along the lines of "my favorite song is whatever happens to be on the radio just now." In walking the path of the Three Noble Strains, consider how the music of sorrow, mirth and rest are related. But there's another level on which it doesn't matter how they're connected; it's not about what they share in common, but the true magic is to allow each strain to be unique. Let sorrow cry, let joy laugh, let slumber rest. And which is the most beautiful of all? Whichever one is happening.

THE PATH OF THE GRAIL

If there's one symbol related to Celtic spirituality that has transcended its cultural origins and become a universal symbol of the spiritual quest, it is the Holy Grail. Honored in poetry, legend, myth, and lore, the Grail embodies a spectrum of meanings related to mysticism, inner transformation, enlightenment, and heavenly joy. A veritable library of books exists just to help the spiritual seeker integrate the symbolism of the Grail into his or her inner life.

Much of the power of the Grail stems from the way in which it transcends cultural boundaries. The Grail is not just an element of Celtic myth, nor is it just a Christian symbol. It is both the chalice of the last supper *and* the cauldron of rebirth. This, indeed, is an important clue to the magic of the Grail: that it refuses to be boxed in by any one philosophy, religion, or tradition. It is available to all worthy seekers, regardless of the external circumstances that govern their lives.

THE PATH OF THE GRAIL

The Grail did not originate as a drinking vessel from Christ's last meal. From a Celtic perspective, the Grail began long before, as a symbol of magic and abundance at the heart of both Irish and Welsh mythologies (and probably other myths as well, although it is only those two traditions that have most clearly survived into the modern era). The origins of the Grail lie in the symbol of the cauldron—and the power of the cauldron is first seen in the Irish tale of how the Tuatha Dé Danann first çame to Eire from four mystical cities to the north: Murias, Falias, Gorias, and Finias. As we have seen, they brought with them four astounding treasures: the great Spear of Lugh, the magical Sword of Nuadu, the Stone of Destiny, and the Cauldron of the Dagda, which served endless supplies of food that could feed the entire tribe without emptying. It was the original "horn of plenty" and its origins lay in the misty magic of the otherworld—the realm of the gods.

THE PATH OF THE GRAIL

The Dagda's Cauldron symbolizes abundance, prosperity, and plenty. It represents the power of the good earth to provide sustenance beyond what is needed. To the Celts, the Dagda's Cauldron represented hope that life would not always be a struggle, or survival uncertain. The blessings of the cauldron went beyond the requirements of survival, and enabled the people to truly prosper. Indeed, some scholars have suggested that the Dagda's Cauldron be thought of as the Celtic cornucopia—the horn of plenty, the channel by which wealth and blessings enter the world. And although the cauldron is associated with the Dagda, a decidedly masculine god, it has often been seen as a supremely feminine symbol—the bowl representing the womb or the vulva. So the cauldron also suggests the blessings that flow out of the earth herself, not unlike the blessings of new life that flow from a woman's womb. Like a vulva, the cauldron signifies the portal through which life is created and sustained.

THE PATH OF THE GRAIL

Two other elements within Celtic tradition highlight this connection between the cauldron and the energies of rebirth. An image on an ancient cauldron discovered at Gundestrup, Denmark, shows warriors lining up before a godlike figure who picks up the men one at a time and lowers them into a cauldron. They then leave in the direction from which they came. This symbol is explained in an electrifying way in the story of *Branwen, Daughter of Llyr* in the *Mabinogi*. As part of her marriage dowry, Branwen's brother gave her groom, the king of Ireland, a mysterious cauldron with a powerful magical ability—any warrior killed in battle who was placed in the cauldron would be brought back to life, with the only limitation being that he could no longer speak (probably to prevent him from speaking the secrets of the otherworld). So it seems likely that the cauldron depicted on the Gundestrup Cauldron had a similar function—as a vessel of rebirth. Here, the cauldron not only bestows physical abundance, but spiritual prosperity as well—it is the channel of immortality.

THE PATH OF THE GRAIL

Remember the story of the birth of Taliesin, the bard? Like the story of the Dagda's cauldron, it is equally significant for understanding the Celtic tradition in regard to the Grail. At the heart of the story is the cauldron of Cerridwen, the witch/goddess whose potion transformed the servant boy Gwion Bach into the great bard. It was Gwion's job to stir Cerridwen's cauldron for a year and a day, only to have several drops of the magic elixir splash on his fingers as the potion was nearly done. Some versions of the story suggest that the cauldron exploded after Gwion tasted the potion; others say that the remaining liquid in the cauldron turned into poison after the boy received the benefits of the spell. The bottom line is that once again we see a Celtic cauldron dispensing miracles and wonders—in this case the gift of wisdom, prophecy, and magical abilities (Gwion's first task involved escaping Cerridwen's wrath, since she intended the potion go to her son; the newly wise servant boy fled by undergoing a series of shapeshifting transformations). Like every other mythic cauldron, Cerridwen's vessel bestows abundant blessings on those fortunate enough to taste its contents.

THE PATH OF THE GRAIL

So what do all of the Celtic magical cauldrons have to do with the Holy Grail? After all, the Grail of medieval romance (or of recent esoteric speculation) is not a cauldron, but rather a drinking vessel, specifically the cup used by Jesus when he instituted the sacrament of the Eucharist at his last supper.

The link between the Celtic cauldrons and the Christian chalice comes, naturally, through King Arthur. We can trace it back to that obscure and mysterious Welsh poem called *Preiddeu Annwn*—"The Spoils of the Otherworld"—which recounts how Arthur and a number of companions (including Taliesin) plundered the fortresses of the otherworld, seeking a mysterious cauldron. The poem is enigmatic and appears to have survived in only fragmentary form, but it says enough to suggest that, long before King Arthur and his noble knights ever rode off in search of Christ's drinking cup, they (or their mythic predecessors) launched an equally noble quest—for the Celtic cauldron of abundance, wisdom and immortality.

Is this cauldron the Holy Grail? Not exactly. For the Holy Grail came into being when two great traditions merged: Arthur's quest for the cauldron of life integrated with the Christian search for the chalice of enlightenment.

THE PATH OF THE GRAIL

Numerous books have appeared in recent years that explore the idea that the "Holy Grail" is not an object at all, but is Mary Magdalene, the mysterious disciple of Christ who, according to some legends, bore his child. It's an interesting concept, even if it is never anything other than myth. Here the "Grail" is linked directly to the womb of a sacred woman/priestess, recalling the metaphorical link between the Celtic cauldron and the life-giving body of the goddess. On one hand, the Magdalene story could be dismissed as "not Celtic" and therefore not truly part of the Celtic wisdom tradition—but since Christianity is such an important part of the Celtic story, the idea that Mary Magdalene is the Holy Grail deserves consideration. If it is only a myth, it's a myth with powerful implications. It's a myth that suggests the quest for the Holy Grail is, in fact, a quest for the Divine Feminine—for the goddess in her many forms. We find the Holy Grail when we find the Lady of Sovereignty, or the warrior spirit of the Mórrígan, or the nurturing love of Brigit. The goddess is everywhere in the Celtic world. So, too, then is the Holy Grail.

THE PATH OF THE GRAIL

Let's take the Holy Grail a step further. It beckons us to discover the goddess, and through her to connect with the energies of abundance, miracles, and eternal life. It is the symbol of enlightenment, which some say comes through the sacred marriage (of the goddess with the land, or of the soul with the Spirit of God). But just as the chalice bore the wine of Christ's blood, the womb bore the gift of new life, or the cauldron bore the treasures of abundance, so too does the Grail beckon each of us to find within ourselves a sacred "Grail"—a vessel out of which miracles are poured. Perhaps the human body is the Holy Grail, for it is the "container" which houses the soul. Or perhaps the mortal soul is the Holy Grail, housing as it does the omnipresent spirit of God/Goddess. Perhaps consciousness itself is the Grail, for it is out of the majesty of the human mind that our next leap in evolution will be borne—a leap that, some say, will enable us to shed the limitations of human flesh and truly reach for the stars.

Who knows?

THE PATH OF THE GRAIL

After Arthur plundered Annwn, and long before the heroes of *The DaVinci Code* investigated a murder in Paris, knights such as Percival or Galahad rode out in search of the Holy Grail. Several variants of the Grail quest have survived from the days of medieval romance; all are mysterious and enigmatic; none tell the entire story. The Grail holds the key to enlightenment, but it can also heal a wounded king. It can bestow eternal life, and it can restore a wasted land. It is the supreme object of the supreme quest. In the end, it may be glimpsed, but never found, held, consumed.

Today the quest continues. Some enthusiasts continue to pore through books and ponder conspiracy theories as they attempt to unravel what mysterious treasure of the Knights Templar might really be buried beneath a centuries-old chapel in Scotland. Many others are content to regard the Grail quest as metaphorical, and simply to allow the stories to inspire their ongoing spiritual life. The Grail answers no questions. It merely beckons us forward on the search.

THE PATH OF ROMANCE

The Celtic tradition is hard on love. So many love stories in the Celtic tradition seem to end badly. Men fight over women with disastrous results; fairies take mortal lovers, leading to tragic consequences. Yes, there is the occasional happy ending, but they are decidedly in the minority. If love is your passion, then the Celtic tradition seems to be dreary indeed.

But it's a mistake to take these mythic Celtic stories only at face value. Certain themes repeat themselves enough that spiritual lessons begin to emerge from beneath the drama of the individual tales. We can look at the myths of Guinevere or Deirdre or Iseult individually, and lament on how tragically each story ends. But if we stop to consider how similar these tales are, we can then look at the grand themes of cyclic renewal that inform each one.

Here's a clue: think of the characters not as individuals, but as metaphors. Each lovely lady is a stand-in for the goddess, while her suitors might represent a god (or, more likely, a king). Maybe the tales will still tug at your heart, but after all, the Celts are renowned for their love of sad stories. Yet beyond the sadness is a glimpse of the wisdom at the heart of a spirituality based in nature and the sacred land.

THE PATH OF ROMANCE

The great story of Celtic romance follows these lines: a man pursues a woman. They marry or are betrothed to marry. She then encounters a much younger man, and gives her love to him. The older man reacts in a variety of ways, from anger to jealousy to murderous rage. The story typically ends badly for all parties involved, or someone—usually the hapless woman—pays in the end.

Variations of this plot can be seen in the tales of Guinevere, Arthur and Lancelot; of Iseult, Mark and Tristan; of Gráinne, Fionn and Diarmait; and of Deirdre, Conchobar and Noíse. So why is this storyline so prominent in Celtic myth? Are Celtic women forever fighting off older guys just so the younger guys can have a chance? On one level, these stories might be seen as morality tales involving the imbalance created by older men mating with younger women; but a more compelling argument suggests that the real star of these tales is the goddess of the land—who must forever leave her older lover in order to embrace a new, younger suitor. The lover, of course, is the king—the leader of the tribe—who must age and die, while the goddess/land is perpetually renewed in the annual cycle of the seasons. So these tales of love are metaphors for the unending cycle of the generations—every new age has its own king, while the queen—the goddess— remains ever young and new.

THE PATH OF ROMANCE

Another sad story of triangular love doesn't exploit the youth/age tension, but still provides insight into the cycles of life. In the *Mabinogi*, Lleu is under a curse that prevents him from marrying a mortal woman, so the magician Gwydion fashions a wife for him out of wildflowers. This fairy maiden is exceptionally beautiful, and is called Blodeuedd ("Flower Face"). At first Lleu and his bride are happy, but one day when she spies a hunter named Gronw, she falls in love with him instead. Soon Blodeuedd and Gronw plot Lleu's murder—no easy task, for he can only be killed under extraordinary circumstances. The treacherous couple almost manage to pull off their crime, wounding Lleu so badly that he turns into an eagle and flies off. Gwydion rescues the ailing bird and heals Lleu, who a year after the attack exacts his vengeance and kills Gronw. Insight into the mythic meaning of this story can be found in the names of the two men. Lleu's name means "light," while Gronw means "staunch." They represent two alternative energies: light and dark, delicate and strong, summer and winter. Vying for the love of a woman named Flower Face, they can be seen as the two halves of the year: summer and winter, each of which can enjoy the love of the earth goddess for only six months before yielding to his rival. The goddess signifies constancy; her suitors represent the never-ending cycle of change.

THE PATH OF ROMANCE

Triangles are not always concerned with two male rivals for the love of one female. Cúchulainn's wife Emer is generally depicted as tolerant of her husband's sexual exploits; after all, demigods will be demigods. But one affair left her at her wit's end. Cúchulainn fell—hard—for an otherworldly woman named Fand, with whom he spent an entire month in enthusiastic lovemaking. Clearly this is more than just a bit of swinging fun, and Emer, for once roused to jealousy, sought Fand in order to kill her. But Cúchulainn, moved by honor, promised to be faithful to his wife, and then both women, moved by the other's love for Cúchulainn, offered to give up their claim to the hero. This unexpected turn of events found its resolution with the appearance of Manannán, Fand's husband, who took his wife away. Before leaving, he passed his cloak of magic mist between Fand and Cúchulainn, so that they would never remember even knowing one another. Once again, it's a sad story, with a resolution that may seem appropriate, but hardly joyful. It's a lovely tale about how love finds its highest expression in sacrifice, and about how love's survival sometimes requires painful, if necessary, choices.

THE PATH OF ROMANCE

Another Celtic heartbreaker comes from the legends of Fionn mac Cumhaill. Fionn's son, Oisín, was approached by the fairy princess of Tír na nÓg, Niam, who had ridden over the waves of the ocean to declare her affection for him. Exceedingly beautiful and riding a majestic steed, Niam offered not only her love to Oisín, but also an honored position in the court of the Land of Youth. Entranced by her loveliness, Oisín accepted her offer, even though it meant leaving Ireland—and all he had ever known—behind. The two lovers rode to Tír na nÓg, where they married and settled down to a life of unparalleled bliss. And so they remained for some time, until Oisín began to long for home. Against Niam's better judgment, he returned to Ireland, having promised her he would not dismount from his steed and touch the soil of his homeland. He rode over the waves, only to find Ireland diminished in size and valor, with a new religion and the exploits of Fionn mac Cumhaill having passed into legend. Indeed, three hundred years had passed! But before the sorrowful Oisín could return to Tír na nÓg, his saddle broke and he fell to the ground, where the weight of three hundred years descended upon him, leading to his rapid aging and death.

So you can't take it with you, and you can't go home again. Everything, even soul mate love, has a price. Know what you are willing to pay.

THE PATH OF ROMANCE

One of the most amazing characteristics of Celtic lore is the degree of free love—for lack of a better term—that flows between the various gods, goddesses, and heroes. Some figures, such as Meadbh and Cúchulainn, are renowned for their, ahem, vigorous sexual appetites. The fairy goddess Áine had a series of both mortal and immortal lovers, and even arranged an affair between her brother and the wife of Manannán—mainly so she and Manannán could enjoy a tryst of their own. Even the goddess Brigit, who gave her name to a militantly virginal Christian saint, had multiple lovers (for that matter, Saint Brigid had a reputation for being able to cure women who suffered from frigidity). Of course, just a cursory reading of Greek and Roman myths will reveal that the pagan Celts were not the only ones who enjoyed a polyamorous mythology; but what's remarkable about Celtic myth is the role that Christian scribes played in its transmission from oral to written form. One wonders if the original stories weren't even more frankly and unapologetically sexual, before being retold by those who had submitted to the more modest sensibilities of the new faith.

THE PATH OF ROMANCE

By now you may be wondering, "Do the Celts have *anything* positive to say about good old-fashioned, till death us do part, romance?" Fortunately, the answer is yes. Two couples in Welsh tradition in particular embody the noblest qualities of love. The regal goddess Rhiannon is wooed by Pwyll, an earthly prince, who alas was not the brightest of heroes; he fell for an easy trick in which he essentially gave away his claim to his bride. But his foolishness was more than matched by her wisdom, and so she conspired with him in a plan that took a year to execute—but that secured both their love and their marriage. Even more remarkable is the story of Culhwch and Olwen. Culhwch was under a curse that enabled him to love no one other than Olwen, the daughter of a fierce giant who had no intention of giving away his daughter's hand. Thankfully, when he saw Olwen, Culhwch was duly smitten, and willingly accepted a series of near-impossible tasks from her hostile father. After many adventures the persevering hero completed the mighty deeds, and returned triumphantly to claim his bride's hand.

THE PATH OF ROMANCE

Out of the Scottish ballad tradition comes another wonderful love story, that of Janet and Tam Lin. Tam Lin was a knight who had been whisked away to fairyland, leaving his manor Carterhaugh desolate. Janet was a young woman who willingly trespassed on the property, even though it meant an encounter with the spectral knight. Unafraid, she took him as a lover, and was soon pregnant to show for it. But the tension built when Tam Lin revealed that the fairy queen offered a sacrifice to the dark lord of the underworld once every seven years, and this year—on Samhain—Tam Lin was slated to be the appointed offering. But he enlisted Janet's help to rescue him from the clutches of the fairy queen, even though this entailed an act of extraordinary courage on her part. But Janet did all that was required of her, and in the end Tam Lin was free and the fairy queen was short of one sacrificial victim. It's a wonderful story, not the least because of how strong and well defined a character Janet is. A proud successor to Boudicca and Meadbh and the Mórrígan, Janet embodies the Celtic ideal of romantic love as not just something men offer to women, but as a dynamic where both genders play equally proactive roles.

THE PATH OF ROMANCE

Perhaps the most sweet and optimistic of Celtic love stories is a tale we've seen already: *Aislinge Óenguso* or the "Dream of Angus," also known as "Angus Óg and the Swan." Angus was a son of the Dagda, and has been called the Celtic god of love, for he assisted other lovers in their quest for romance; but this story involves his own search for happiness of the heart. The romance begins with a dream, in which Angus saw a gorgeous woman, so lovely that he was heartsick to wake up. He resolved to find his dream lover, and enlisted the aid of several gods and goddesses who search throughout the land to find this elusive maiden. Finally he discovered that she was named Cáer, and lived half her life as a swan on a lake. His test of love was to pick her out among 150 swans, and as a further sign of his devotion, he turned himself into a swan so that they might fly off together. As they flew away from her lake, they sang such heavenly music that anyone who heard their song was lulled to sleep for three days. Here, at last, we see love purely for love's sake, with no subplot about heroism or the responsibilities between the goddess and the tribe, or anything of that sort. And so what do we get? A story unabashed in its positive depiction of love.

THE PATH OF THE SPIRAL

The pre-Celtic art at Newgrange and other sacred sites from the Stone Age features a variety of abstract and symbolic designs carved into stone. Perhaps the most famous of these Neolithic designs is the Newgrange triple spiral. This can be seen on the large stone in front of the entrance into the tomb, but also on the wall by one of the three alcoves in the center of the structure. It's a deceptively simple image: three spirals in a single design, forming a sort of triangle. It suggests a powerful "three-in-one" unity-in-diversity. It may well be the single most powerful symbolic representation of the energies of both pre-Celtic and Celtic spirituality. It also handily erases the boundaries between paganism and Christianity, since both spiritual traditions revere the sacredness of the number three.

The triple goddess, the land and the sea and the sky, the three orders of bards, seers and druids—all sorts of stuff among the Celtic pagans seems to have been grouped in threes. Among Christians, of course, the three appears most prominently when referring to God: the Holy Trinity. The three in one: beautifully and simply captured in the Newgrange spirals.

THE PATH OF THE SPIRAL

The triple spiral could be seen as meaningful far beyond the strict elements of Celtic wisdom. Consider the past, the present, and the future. The body, the mind, and the soul. A thesis, its antithesis, and the synthesis. Triplicity seems linked in a real and fundamental way to stability and harmony and the resolution of conflict—and both of the great religious traditions in the Celtic world have embraced this within their symbolism. Of course, it's not just that three is so special—it is the unity of three that makes it sing. Three persons in one God. Three sisters in one Goddess. Three patron saints of Ireland (Brigid and Columba, as well as Patrick). Three otherworldly beings: ancestors, fairies and deities. And on it goes. The triple spiral of Newgrange is powerful because it is a single design. Three in one, and one in three. It seems that this could be a secret to how the entire universe works.

THE PATH OF THE SPIRAL

When you enter the heart of Newgrange—the roomy chamber sixty-five feet into the structure, accessible only by a tiny passageway—you find three alcoves set off from the main room, in each of which the remains of the dead were once ceremoniously laid. Together with the entrance passageway, the entire floor plan resembles a cross. One might speculate whether the three spirals symbolize the three alcoves. Perhaps each of these chambers, where the dead once found their final repose, is a "spiral." Granted, Newgrange does not appear to be the work of people who believed that death is the end. Far from it: the light of the winter solstice sunrise shines into the heart of the chamber, suggesting some sort of mystical relationship between ancestral remains and the sun's most southerly point. Perhaps the ancients believed the sun was the key to new life; or perhaps the ancestral spirits had to appeal to the sun to reverse its southerly movement every year. Whatever the original intent was for the builders of Newgrange, it is now long lost to us. We are left only with rooms where remains were interred, and the sun shone once a year. All symbolized, perhaps, by a triple spiral.

THE PATH OF THE SPIRAL

Could it be that the spiral symbolized life, death and rebirth? Wait—there's another sacred three. Consider the central mystery of the Christian faith, expressed in three short sentences: *Christ has died, Christ is risen, Christ will come again.* Yes, the sacred three again, this time wrapped around the heart of spiritual longing: that death is not the end. This matters whether we're talking about physical death, or the many spiritual "deaths" that occur in any life, from the death of a relationship, to the loss of face, to the many transitions small and large that give shape and meaning to our days. No, death is not the end. We live. We die. We live again. Three events, held together by a unity: by our soul, our personality, our identity so closely knit to the divine.

But how is the spiral related to this? A spiral has its own threeness: a beginning, a middle, and an end. Or if you prefer, a center, a circumference, and a path linking the two. We are born in the center, and our lives spiral outward. Eventually we reach the end point, and we retreat back to the center. Only to venture forth again.

Is this about reincarnation? That depends—Christian and pagan views on how we live after death markedly differ, so I'll dodge this particular question. But what unites the two faiths is the certainty that life, like the spiral, is eternal. It does not die.

THE PATH OF THE SPIRAL

The spiral is a labyrinth, indeed, the simplest possible labyrinth. Unlike a maze (where one can get lost and make a "wrong" turn), a labyrinth offers one path, one path only, to the center. It twists and turns and snakes back upon itself, and so too does life refuse to follow a straight path as we journey through our days. Compared to the labyrinths of Chartres or Crete, the Newgrange spirals may seem too simple: a mere circular curve that collapses in on itself until the center is reached. But the end result, the center attained, is the same in spiral or labyrinth, and who is to say that the soul's journey may not be seen to be just as simple as it is complex? The unifying factor here is the one path. Perhaps we would be less likely to agonize over our choices or be crushed by regret if we could faithfully attend to the best we can, trusting that in the end there is really only one path, one way, one journey. The choices we make, the circumstances we create for ourselves, are simply the window-dressing. Trusting in the path that lies before us may well be the most challenging—and rewarding— spiritual task we'll ever face.

THE PATH OF THE SPIRAL

The spiral is not just an odd design from prehistoric times. Explore the most glorious form of Celtic art: the illuminated manuscripts of the early Christian era—and try to count the spirals that appear on just about every decorated page. Of course, these illuminated spirals are as colorful and ornate as the Newgrange spiral is simple. Intricately accented, the spirals in manuscripts like *The Book of Kells* appear carefully integrated with all the other elements of high Celtic art: knotwork, key patterns, and zoomorphs (animal shapes), all dancing around the richly-designed letters that form the text of the manuscript.

How is it that the spiral survived as a significant artistic theme for thousands of years? Sure, the argument could be made for it simply serving as an attractive design element, with no particular or special meaning. But given how rich and symbolic Celtic art and wisdom otherwise is, such an idea would really be a cop-out. It's a fair question to ponder: what do the spirals mean? And did the ones drawn by monks in the eighth century of our era have anything to do with the ones carved in stone four millennia earlier?

THE PATH OF THE SPIRAL

We've looked at how the spiral relates to the sacred three. Now let's look at it from another angle. A spiral is made of two things: a circle and a line. Simply put, a spiral is a line, coiled up nicely within a circle. In other words, a spiral integrates the energy of masculinity (the line) with femininity (the circle). A line within a circle can be a metaphor for the seed impregnating the womb. So it's not just a yin and yang set of symbols arrayed side by side: it's the integration of these two fundamental energies, the god and the goddess in an intimate, life-giving embrace. Neither one is privileged over the other, or depicted as better or as first among equals. In the spiral, there is harmony between the sexes and they come together, in unity and peace.

Perhaps this hearkens back to the spiral as a symbol of life/death/rebirth. After all, birth first comes from conception, which requires the union of male and female (even artificial insemination had to come from somewhere). After we're born, mom and dad play a less active role in our lives; instead, our survival depends on an inner union: of reason and intuition, of magic and mysticism, of assertiveness and faith. Male and female still need to come together in the service of life. But eventually, that sacred marriage must happen within.

THE PATH OF THE SPIRAL

The Jewish and neopagan communities are among the many different cultures that enjoy dancing in a spiral. Join hands, form a line, and then coil in on the center. Reach it, and then move back out again, pulling others along behind you, just as those before you were pulling you along. Dancing a spiral is like walking a labyrinth—it embodies the spiritual ideas that rattle around in our heads, clothing them with flesh and bone and making them far more real (and meaningful) than just words or concepts. A spiral dance is fun. It's as unifying as everyone standing in a circle, but more dynamic, interesting, surprising. To make a bad pun at the expense of business-speak, it's "thinking outside the circle." And we need to be thinking outside the circles, not only about spirals but indeed about any and all symbols related to Celtic wisdom (or wisdom in general). A spiral can mean many things—and perhaps its most important meaning for any one of us is the meaning we give it ourselves. If a simple little design can symbolize death and rebirth or the union of masculine and feminine energies, what greater riches lie in the stories and myths and legends of the Celts (or of anyone else)?

THE PATH OF THE SPIRAL

Pictures of galaxies reveal that at least some of them are spiral shaped. Perhaps the universe as a whole is a spiral. The union of circle and line, center and path seems to replicate itself again and again in our cosmos. Think of a nautilus. A whirlpool. A spider's web. A hurricane. Although *spiral* and *spirit* have different etymological pedigrees, they're close enough to each other to make it at least worthwhile to consider the pun.

I think everyone should try to find ways to make spirals in their lives. If you're an artist, that's easy. Paint them, draw them, and doodle them in your notebooks. Others may have to be more creative. Plant a garden in a spiral, buy clothes with spiral designs, or bake a cake and make a spiral design in the icing. Use your imagination. But however you find ways to "spiralize" your life, make it even more Celtic: do it in threes.

THE PATH OF IMBAS AND AWEN

A medieval Irish writer named Cormac described a method of divination called *imbas forosnai* (illuminating poetic knowledge). Imbas, or poetic knowledge, is a special category of prophetic insight attained by the highest of bards and seers. *Imbas forosnai* involves a ritual for attaining this divinatory knowledge, which may have had its roots in ancient shamanic ceremonies. The seer-poet seeking the guidance of the imbas would chew the raw flesh of a sacred animal—a dog, a cat, or a pig—but rather than swallowing the meat, would remove it from his mouth and speak a special incantation over the flesh. Following this ceremony, he would lie down and sleep in a specific, ceremonial position, with the palms of his hands held over his eyes. Others would watch him as he slept, to ensure that he remained in the proper position, undisturbed. After about three days, he would know whether or not the sacred, illuminating knowledge had been granted to him or not.

Numerous key figures in Irish mythology prophesy through the imbas, including Scáthach (Cúchulainn's mentor) and Fionn mac Cumhaill.

THE PATH OF IMBAS AND AWEN

The Welsh tradition includes a concept similar to the *imbas forosnai*—that of the *awenyddion*, or poetic inspiration. Both prophets and poets could use this skill, enabling them to speak with the eloquence of divine knowledge or the sheer beauty of poetry. The concept of *awen* has become popular in the Celtic wisdom tradition, referring to the gift of sacred inspiration available to the dedicated poet or prophet from the otherworld. Such is the skill that empowered the voices and songs of great bards like Taliesin or great seers like Merlin.

The awen could be thought of in terms of light or love, or for that matter as a poetic equivalent of neart—as an energy that flows to and through the bard who channels it. It is the catalyst that enables an ordinary mortal to speak the words of eternity, to give shape to the deepest yearning and knowing of the soul, to allow the wisdom of Spirit to find form through a mortal's mouth. Such a sacred energy would be available to all, yet accessible only to those who prepared spiritually and professionally to receive and share it.

THE PATH OF IMBAS AND AWEN

Are imbas and awen the same thing? Well, we can never get into the mind of the ancient druids, but they seem similar enough to warrant consideration in this way: they represent Irish and Welsh understandings of an important aspect of Celtic spirituality—the reliance on divine inspiration for both poetic skill and intuitive vision. Furthermore, it is the same kind of inspiration that results in both poetry *and* prophecy. It has been said that if you sleep on a cairn (an ancient burial mound) in a Celtic land, you will die, go mad, or become a poet. Perhaps madness is related to prophecy, for after all, how can we finite mortal beings truly comprehend the depth of divine knowledge and foresight without it literally "blowing our fuses"?

One of the earliest tales of Merlin describes him as going mad after witnessing a horrific battle. In a similar manner, the goddess known as the Mórrígan spoke a frightening prophecy of a grim, graceless future after the shock of the great battle in which the Tribe of the Goddess Dana defeated the Fomorians. It seems that the shock of battle served a function similar to a night on a cairn—it brought forth death, madness, and poetic inspiration.

THE PATH OF IMBAS AND AWEN

Is all poetry inspired? Certainly not. But all poetry has the potential to be inspired—just as it has the potential to inspire. The *logos* mysticism of early Christianity declares, "In the beginning was the word." Language can be one of the most powerful forms of creativity, and it can also be a force for community-building and peacemaking ("the pen is mightier than the sword"). Consider Brigit's triple function as the goddess of poetry, of midwifery and herbalism, and of the blacksmith's forge. The transforming power of the word stands alongside the transforming power of healing, and the transforming power of technology. Poetry is inspired—and inspires—whenever it serves to create something new in the world. Perhaps this is the test of prophecy as well—it is a "true" prophecy not in how well it predicts the future, but rather in how powerful a force it engenders to help *create* the future.

THE PATH OF IMBAS AND AWEN

Can we cultivate the forces of imbas or awen in our lives? The druid revivalists believe so—they often include prayers for the blessings of imbas or awen in their rituals. Opening up the power of poetic/prophetic inspiration is, in Celtic terms, not unlike opening up to God's or the Holy Spirit's blessings in more mainstream religions. And perhaps the analogy continues: just as a mystic of almost any faith will insist that we cannot *force* God's blessings to flow, but can only prepare ourselves to receive them; in a similar way, the powerful energy of sacred inspiration cannot be beckoned like an obedient puppy dog. It is a force wild, untamed, free, as powerful as the great elements of land, sea and sky. Our job in approaching imbas and awen is to create within ourselves a worthy home for such otherworldly blessings.

So we cannot really cultivate inspiration itself—but we can cultivate ourselves in our yearning to receive. And while I don't recommend chewing the raw meat of domestic animals or especially pork, we can always make plans to sleep on a cairn (even if it is just an "inner cairn" found within the depths of our souls).

THE PATH OF IMBAS AND AWEN

If we open ourselves in prayer and meditation to the blessings of the Divine, and we seek to manifest poetic and prophetic inspiration in our lives, then what do we do with it, once we get it (assuming we get it)? An obvious place to begin is the composing of poetry. No, this doesn't mean you have to become a staff writer for a greeting card company (remember, not *all* poetry is inspired). Your poetry may not even be strictly a matter of words on a page. The internet, video, and audio recording tools all provide powerful ways in which we can express ourselves poetically, using sound and color as well as words. And such poetry need not be created with an eye to publication (although there's nothing wrong with seeking to disseminate your work). What, finally, separates ordinary poetry from the inspired kind? Ask yourself these questions: how does your poetry contribute to a transformed world? What forces are at work in your words, to help shape a visionary future? How does the voice of eternity and the otherworld flow through your words (and that doesn't mean you have to write specifically "spiritual" poems. Perhaps the less self-consciously spiritual your poetry is, the more likely the imbas will be to flow to and through it). Keep these questions in mind—but most important of all, keep writing. Imbas, like any spiritual gift, is akin to a muscle; it must be exercised to reach full strength.

THE PATH OF IMBAS AND AWEN

Alongside the word of poetry, divine inspiration also leads to the more direct, and unmediated word of prophecy. Put aside old notions of Jeremiah railing against the Jerusalem elite (or for that matter, of your local fundamentalist preacher with a bullhorn downtown near the train station). Even put aside any ideas of hoary old Merlin offering his words of wisdom to the receptive young king of Camelot. To give voice to prophecy may be as simple and humble a task as speaking the truth—even, in the words of Maggie Kuhn, "if your voice shakes." It may be nothing more special than making sure that there are always alternatives—always more than one way of looking at things, of making value judgments, of setting up a game plan. What makes it prophecy is largely the same energies that make a poem inspired—the energies of vision, of possibility, of healing, and of transformation. Of course, in the true spirit of imbas, the ultimate way to express your intuition of divine guidance is through poetry. Yes, art can change the world. That's the secret of the imbas.

THE PATH OF IMBAS AND AWEN

You can't measure the imbas or the awen. It's not as if the poet/prophet who has been touched by the divine in this manner can suddenly finish an epic poem in three hours or demonstrate that 90 percent of their predictions come true within three weeks. That's just not how it works. The presence of divine inspiration is something revealed slowly, over time (even the ancient druids took three days to decide if the imbas had been granted; remember that three is a sacred number, and so in this case it probably just means "they took their sweet time"). Ultimately, inspiration reveals itself by the way it makes a difference in the world—and that can be a process that takes years, centuries, millennia. Energies set into motion by Jesus and the Buddha and Mohammed are, after thousands of years, still making an obvious difference in the world. How many others have inspired transformation in less dramatic or obvious, but no less real, ways? And who's to say that the inspired visionaries of our age will not have just as big an impact themselves, as the centuries to come unfold?

THE PATH OF IMBAS AND AWEN

Perhaps the best strategy is simply not to worry about whether you've "got" the imbas or not. If you seek to be a poet or a prophet, live the life of meditation, of contemplation, of devotion. Speak your truth and compose your poetry. Live in a way that is dedicated to love, to healing, to hope for a better tomorrow. And then allow the energies to flow, as they will. Don't try to be "special" or "important." Just do your best.

If you invite the imbas into your life, you will die. Maybe not physically for now (yes, we'll all do that eventually), but initially the imbas will simply slay your sense of being in control and having to be the important one. Then, you will go mad. Not necessarily to the point of needing meds, but perhaps to the point where all the symbols and values and meaning in your life seem to suddenly fall away, leaving only your naked soul, alone and dependant upon the grace of eternity to survive. At that point, you will be invited to rebirth, to slowly rebuilding your sanity. And how will you go about doing that? Through poetry, of course...

THE PATH OF SACRIFICE

Several of the ancient writers who discuss the druids make comments about their function as the priests who preside over sacrifice. "Druids are in charge of public and private sacrifices," Julius Caesar explains, and goes on to point out that the worst thing that could happen to a member of Celtic society was to be banned from participating in the sacrificial rites. Clearly, such ceremonies played a central and important part in the spiritual life of the ancient Celts.

But just what kind of sacrifices were the druids involved in? Sacrifice is a loaded word nowadays, implying either some sort of self-negating act, or worse yet, barbaric rituals where animals or even humans were slaughtered to appease superstitious fears regarding a bloodthirsty deity. Clearly, such images of sacrifice make it an idea distasteful to the extreme.

But there's more to sacrifice than bloodshed or self-victimization. The word itself is a simple Latin compound that means, "to make holy." If the druids were involved in rituals that created the energy of holiness, then that sounds like something worth knowing about. And perhaps Celtic wisdom today can be a path where each individual person can participate in the process of sacrifice—that is to say, of making the world a holier place.

THE PATH OF SACRIFICE

Some time ago, I told a good friend that I was interested in druidism. This particular man was very active in the neopagan witchcraft community, so I thought he would certainly understand and appreciate my desire to pursue Celtic wisdom. But he surprised me. Despite his knowledge of pagan spirituality, all he could ask me was, "Didn't the druids perform human sacrifice?"

Druidism and human sacrifice have been linked since the days of Julius Caesar. Erroneous ideas about Celtic sacrifice include Caesar's vivid description of animals and men immolated in giant wicker cages. A century later, Tacitus claimed that the druids of Britain considered it "a duty to cover their altars with the blood of captives and to consult their deities through human entrails."

Did the druids practice human sacrifice? Although the archaeological evidence for it is limited and mysterious, there does in fact exist evidence suggestive of the practice. In a world where Romans made it a sport to watch gladiators kill one another or Christians killed by lions, perhaps such barbaric practices are to be expected. Still, that the Celts weren't the only ancient culture to shed blood as part of their rituals does not change the fact that violent sacrifice is now utterly unacceptable. But can the concept of sacrifice—nonviolent, of course—still play a role in Celtic wisdom today?

THE PATH OF SACRIFICE

On August 1, 1984, a body was discovered preserved in peat in a bog called Lindow Moss, near Manchester, England. Police investigators quickly determined this was not a criminal case, but a matter for archaeologists—the body, well preserved in the peat, was centuries old. Investigation revealed that "Lindow Man," as the figure came to be known, did not die of natural causes—but had been clubbed, garroted, and had his throat cut. A triple execution. Then his body, naked except for an armband of fox skin, was dumped into the bog, where it lay for probably close to two thousand years. The man was well-groomed, probably belonging to the upper classes of society. While it's possible this could be a criminal execution, why would the ancients have gone to the trouble of the triple form of killing? The evidence certainly suggests a ceremonial death—a human sacrifice.

Scholars Anne Ross and Don Robins wrote a fascinating book called *The Life and Death of a Druid Prince* in which they recount the story of the discovery of Lindow Man, the investigation into the remains, and speculation over the nature of the death. While some of their ideas are strictly conjectural, the evidence that someone in ancient England saw fit to kill others for religious purposes is fairly strong. The take-away: to explore Celtic paganism, one must deal with the question of human sacrifice.

THE PATH OF SACRIFICE

Lindow Man's stomach contained evidence of a last meal, including mistletoe and burnt bannock. This undigested food, along with his nakedness, his fox armband, and the crouching position in which his body came to its final rest could all be significant in terms of the rituals surrounding the end of Lindow Man's life. But can we ever know for sure what happened? Alas, no. Ross and Robins speculate that Lindow Man may have been a human sacrifice to ask the gods for protection against the march of the Roman Empire. It's plausible enough, but it can only remain a theory. Meanwhile, it's important to consider that only a few other archaeological remains found in the Celtic world could, like Lindow Man, be interpreted as evidence of ritual sacrifice. For this reason, many scholars insist that Celtic sacrifice may not have been a common practice—it may have been something the ancients did only under extreme circumstances.

Still, that doesn't erase the basic question that we of the modern world must ask. How can we follow a spiritual path where ritual killings were accepted? What could modern druidism look like, evolved beyond such barbaric practices?

THE PATH OF SACRIFICE

The ritual of *tarbfheis* or the "bull feast" is an interesting clue to the role that sacrifice plays in the Celtic world. The ceremony involves divination to determine the future king. A bull was sacrificed, and the druid or seer would eat the animal's meat before sleeping; the new king would be revealed in a dream. A similar practice, *taghairm*, included the seer sleeping in the skin of the sacrificial animal.

So sacrifice, at least in terms of the bull feast, appears linked to the practice of divination or seership. Which is to say, it's linked to the practice of fostering communication between this world and the otherworld. In the *tarbfheis*, it's not just the druid who enjoys the feast—it's also the helping spirits, to whom the sacrifice is made, and who will reveal the desired information to the diviner as he or she sleeps.

So a sacrifice is more than just trying to make an angry god happy. Indeed, the idea of propitiation (basically, "buying off" a deity) may not be that relevant to Celtic sacrifice at all. In other words, a sacrifice is not about paying off a debt. It would be more akin to giving a gift to strengthen a relationship.

THE PATH OF SACRIFICE

Mohandas Gandhi is said to have devised a list of modern "social sins." One of those sins is "worship without sacrifice." Surely Gandhi, the towering champion of nonviolence and peaceful means of conflict resolution, was not suggesting that society needs bloodletting as part of our religious observance! True enough, that's nowhere near Gandhi's intent. The sacrifice that he saw as so essential is that which separates religion-as-lip-service from religion-as-committed-activity. In other words, sacrifice is that moment where a person actually walks the talk, or puts money on the line. A sacrifice may mean a gift of cash, or of time, or of in-kind goods and services. What matters is that the gift is given.

American neopaganism is filled with people who insist that it is wrong for religious leaders to be paid for their services to their communities. Meanwhile, many of the movement's leaders suffer from burnout or feel taken advantage of by people who participate in rituals but make no effort (either financially or by volunteering) to support the group. Sadly, this is not unique to neopaganism. For some reason, our culture operates with the idea that it's a good thing to get something for nothing. That is the opposite of the Celtic way, which is based on mutual exchange—and sacrifice—as the heart of soulful living.

THE PATH OF SACRIFICE

Modern druid groups have made efforts to incorporate sacrifice into the spiritual ceremonies. Sometimes this entails literal offerings—such as dairy products, herbs, oils, flowers, even silver or trinkets. Like the gifts left at holy wells in the Celtic lands, these gifts offered in a ceremonial way to the spirit world are meant to convey love, devotion, respect, and the humble requesting of assistance and blessing. Others feel that such physical offerings are wasteful, but still emphasize the concept of gift-giving, concentrating on poetry, art, dance, and devotional energy as non-physical gifts given to the non-physical spirits.

Modern druids do not shed blood. Most would say that animal or human sacrifice is simply an ancient practice found in many cultures, and almost universally abandoned as a sign of ethical and psychological progress. Since modern Celtic spirituality approaches the spirit world optimistically, there is no sense that sacrifice is "required"—blood or otherwise. And so only nonviolent sacrifices, are ever offered, and only in a spirit of a freely given gift.

THE PATH OF SACRIFICE

The Christian religion can shed some light on the role of sacrifice in the Celtic world. Many Celts are Catholic—a branch of Christianity that regards Holy Communion as a form of sacrifice. But even Protestant Christians have a sense of Christianity as requiring a "living sacrifice"—a ceremonial sense of offering one's body and soul to God, as a living, breathing, functioning gift. Presumably, God has better use for us living than dead. This could also be seen as an inner sacrifice—a concept that could be relevant to Celts of all spiritual and religious persuasions. Here, sacrifice is an offering in the fullest sense of the word—an offering of one's own entire being, consecrated to the good purposes of the spiritual life. Such a sacrifice might entail surrendering a bad habit, offering time for volunteer work or some other spiritually beneficial activity, or simply choosing to relate to others from a place of kindness and understanding—hospitality, in short.

If worship without sacrifice is a mistake—a "miss" in the target-practice of life—then the best way to hit the bull's-eye would be to give the best of possible gifts: our very selves.

THE PATH OF SACRIFICE

When you meet someone you like, often you make the effort to spend time with him or her. And not only will you carve out time to be together, you'll also give the person gifts as thoughtful expressions of your kind regard. This can be the proverbial candy and flowers of traditional romance, or various items that reflect a shared hobby or interest, or a significant gift to express a profound, heartfelt love. In all these cases, giving (and receiving) gifts serves one primary function: it builds and strengthens relationships.

So it is with sacrifice. Celtic wisdom points out that we live in a world populated by spiritual beings: ancestors, fairies, angels, gods and goddesses, and the ultimate presence of the creator. Each of these entities represents a possible meaningful relationship, in which we can learn more about ourselves, grow mentally and physically, and foster a greater sense of purpose and power in our lives. But spiritual relationships are like physical relationships. If we want to get to know the spirits in our lives more intimately, we need to spend time with them (prayer and ritual are great places to start) and we need to build the relationship. Offering ceremonial, sacrificial gifts is the key to making this happen.

THE PATH OF THE FUTURE

On the surface, Celtic spirituality seems to be more about the past than the future. After all, the glory days of the Celts were some two to two-and-a-half millennia ago. For too long now the Celts have clung to the edge of Europe, or have dispersed to lands far and wide where they have been little more than interesting subcultures—ethnic communities in the great melting pot that is the modern world.

Look closer, and the picture gets bleaker still. Every Celtic language is, to a greater or lesser extent, threatened. Sure, Welsh and Breton aren't dead yet, and God bless Ireland for its public commitment to the Irish language. But even though political and social opposition to the languages has eased up, economic forces and the omnipresent power of the mass media mean that the surviving Celtic tongues could very well die out in a few generations' time.

And with the languages would go untold treasures—stories that have never been told in any other tongue; ways of thinking, ways of seeing, patterns of spiritual and cultural identity. These things can never be measured on a spreadsheet, and so the corporate world sees no reason to halt the erosion of the unique Celtic consciousness. But to those of us for whom a culture is a haven for spiritual wisdom, such a loss is unthinkable.

So the future seems bleak. But as long as a child lives who speaks the old tongues, there is hope for a Celtic future.

THE PATH OF THE FUTURE

L anguage, culture, and identity are not static things that can be measured, catalogued and stored for a future generation to examine. They are living aspects of the human experience. Think about Shakespeare and the King James Bible—how much the powerful English language has changed in a mere four hundred years. The Celtic tongues are no different in their ongoing process of transformation and renewal.

This is a comforting thought to hold when we consider the future. No, the Celtic world as you and I know it will not survive. But neither will the American, English, French, nor any other culture. If there's one quality in the future we can count on, it's transformation. The stuff of magic. Druids were magicians—in other words, they were agents of transformation. They did not fight the shifts and innovations that the future always revealed; it's reasonable to assume they embraced such changes.

And so we can embrace change today. What is important about the future of the Celtic world is not whether it will survive, but for us to consider in what ways it will survive. What is most important about Celtic wisdom? What do we most want to pass on to our children and grandchildren? These are the important questions.

THE PATH OF THE FUTURE

We are told that the ancient druids saw death as the midpoint of a long life; that they believed in reincarnation; that they were so confident about the soul's survival of bodily death that they encouraged their warriors to be fearless regarding death. In the mythology we find lovely images, such as that of Tír na nÓg or the Summerland, of otherworldly paradises where souls may travel beyond their death.

Part of what makes the future scary is death. That's something about the future we all share. The day will come when there is a moment beyond our ability to experience it. How do we approach such an eventuality? With despair, or trust? Clearly, the path of the Celt is one of trust. Death leads to rebirth, in some form or fashion. And so it will be with the Celtic world in its entirety. The Celts survived the loss of independence in Gaul, then in Britain, then in the rest of the British Isles. They survived the coming of the Vikings, the Normans, the English, and the French. Each of these historic events represented a death of the old order. And yet, rebirth of some form or fashion always followed. The Celts will survive. Just as each one of us will survive. Death may appropriately be placed at the bottom of our to-do list. But it is nothing to fear.

THE PATH OF THE FUTURE

What does hope look like, when spoken with a Gaelic or Welsh accent?

There are several ways to appreciate a Celtic perspective on hope. Remember how the Gaelic words for sovereignty is *flaitheas* and the word for generosity is the closely related *flaithiúil*? Now consider *flaithis*—a word that means "heaven." Freedom is related to hospitality and both concepts are related to heavenly hope. The hope of the Celts lies not in individual feats of bravery; powerful though he was, Cúchulainn died young and tragically, failing to save his homeland from invasion. As important as the hero's valor may be, ultimately true hope lies in the community and the bonds of kinship and honor that hold it together. You can't have hospitality without both a giver and a receiver; sovereignty also implies relationship, for freedom is meaningless without someone to be free from (or with whom the freedom is shared). And so, too, heaven is not a solitary, solipsistic journey into never-ending subjectivity, but rather the ultimate hope that community, like the individual soul, will survive all death and all transformation. Heaven is heaven precisely because we will never be abandoned.

THE PATH OF THE FUTURE

Hope for the future is linked with memory, and so one of the functions of the bard is to create hope—hope through the alternative visions praised in story and song. For while memory can be a tool to honor the great tragedies of the past, in its most primal form it begins in a sense of all being right with the world. A tragic memory makes sense only because we also have memory of that which is not tragic; it is because we know love and happiness that we find so much sorrow in lacking them. So we remember the possibilities of life: community, and love, and peace, and happiness. And in the remembering, we find the template of our hoping. There is a future for Celtic wisdom precisely because it has such a noble past.

We know the past through memory and story; how then do we know the future? Perhaps it is known through prophecy and dreams, but also through vision and planning. The future is ours to create. Several stories in Celtic myth tell of ghosts who come back from the dead to recount stories of old, or of ancient survivors of ages past who live long enough to tell their story to a future generation. Why are such stories so precious? Because there is a link between the past and the future. When we know our past, we can more readily design our truest and best future.

THE PATH OF THE FUTURE

But if the bards remind us of the future possibilities encoded in the stories of the past, the seers more directly call us into the future. For theirs is the realm of prophecy, divination, and the not-yet-manifest. Bards may be said to hold up a mirror, seeing the future reflected in the past; seers by contrast hold up a telescope by which glimpses of the future might be obtained. Prophets like Thomas the Rhymer or the Brahan Seer described events decades or even centuries before they came to pass. The grim end-of-the-world prophecies of the Mórrígan have not yet been fulfilled (and may they never!). Which raises another question: can prophecy be dodged, like a bullet? I think the answer must be yes, for several reasons. First, if prophecy is carved in stone, then we have no free will. Secondly, even the best seer has the human capacity to err. And finally, a world without possibility is a world without hope. So the seers can tantalize us with their hints about tomorrow, but remember: hope always trumps even the sunniest fortune telling. It can always be better than it sounds.

THE PATH OF THE FUTURE

The mortally wounded King Arthur was carried from his final battlefield to Avalon, where he rests to await his return at the hour of England's most dire need. He is the once and future king. Merlin, likewise, is trapped in Nimue's enchanting embrace, there to remain until the end of time. The fairies live in suspension, waiting until the end of all things to discover their eternal destiny. Some say the fairies have no hope; others say they must work out their salvation like the rest of us.

Part of what makes the future bearable is the idea that even it will someday end. The sun will supernova and the earth will return to the primal flame. Arthur will return, Merlin will be set free, and the fairies will finally get tickets to their next destination. If you're a Christian, you believe that at that point the elect will receive their eternal reward. If you prefer a neopagan view of things, then perhaps you affirm that the cycle will begin yet again, only after a period of universe-wide cataclysm.

Every ending has a new beginning of some sort. But sometimes it's a good thing just to honor the ending for what it is.

THE PATH OF THE FUTURE

I once spoke with an astrologer who looked at my horoscope and made all sorts of wonderful predictions about what an amazing difference I would make in the world. I thanked her for the reading, but I think she missed the boat. When I look at the future, I don't want to see it in terms of ever bigger and better feats and achievements, kind of like how this year's blockbuster movies have to have even more explosions and special effects than ever (until next year, of course). I like the story in Celtic myth about the land where a river or a fence separated two pastures. In one pasture grazed black sheep; in the other all the sheep were white. Every now and then one sheep wanders over the river or past the fence, from one pasture to the other. When it does, it changes color to match the sheep it has joined—and another sheep invariably makes the opposite journey, likewise changing color as it makes the transition. And thus, balance is achieved. Our culture is so concerned about growth; about bigger/better/faster/richer. The Celts didn't see things in such a way, preferring instead to emphasize balance and equilibrium over never-ending expansion and growth. I rather think a balanced future is less overwhelming than one where everything just keeps getting louder and faster.

THE PATH OF THE FUTURE

Well, the story of the black and white sheep might even be a story about the future and the present. For the future is in the present and the present is in the future. After all, the future exists primarily in our hopes and dreams and visions. We nurture the future in our hearts and minds, which exist here and now. So the future is in the present. And the only thing that makes the future comprehensible to us is our place in it. The future is something we can understand and relate to—otherwise it's meaningless. So the present (i.e., us) is always a part of the future (at least the future we envision). No one worries about five hundred years from now—at least, not for very long. But we all are curious about ten years from now, because most of us will still be around, and we can't wait to see how it all turns out.

But actually, we all *can* wait. Every moment between now and whenever it is we're curious about, is precious. Every moment is a miracle of possibilities. Every moment invites us to be fully alive. The more deeply we allow ourselves to sink into each and every precious present moment, the less the future even matters. As more than one wise person has pointed out, it will take care of itself.

THE PATH OF THE DIASPORA

Seen from the long view of history, perhaps the one quality that has characterized the Celts the most consistently over the centuries has been mobility. The earliest signs of Celtic culture come from archaeological finds in Austria and Switzerland, but historians hold a variety of opinions as to where the Celts come from—some arguing that the original home of the Celts was farther to the east, perhaps Asia Minor near the Black Sea. By the time the Celts had a strong enough presence on the world stage to command the attention of their unimpressed Mediterranean neighbors, their heartland was Gaul—more or less modern-day France. But Celtic adventurers (or at least, those willing to adopt Celtic culture) settled as far afield as Turkey, Spain, and the British Isles. When the fortunes of the Celts suffered at first under the Romans and later the Saxons and Normans, they retreated until their backs were against the ocean. And from their coastline homes, the Celts proceeded to explore the world, eventually settling in the Americas and Australia. These final destinations in the Celtic travelogue have—with very few exceptions—failed to establish a Celtic society, even as a subculture. But the Celtic spirit lives on, even if only as an ethnic identity. This is the story of the Celtic diaspora.

THE PATH OF THE DIASPORA

Diaspora is a Greek word, meaning, "to scatter about." It is used to describe the experience of people with an ethnic or cultural identity who, usually because of collective tragedy, become dispersed over a large geographical area away from their ancestral home. Thus, we can speak of the Jewish diaspora or the African diaspora. In a similar way, the Celts are a diaspora people, thanks to economic displacement and the cruelty of crop failure and subsequent famine.

Today, it is estimated that as many as a third of United States citizens can trace at least part of their ancestry back to Ireland or one of the other Celtic nations. Canada and Australia have similar significant Celtic populations. In Cape Breton, Nova Scotia, not only did the highlanders arrive but they brought their language, resulting in a thriving Gaelic community that rivals its counterpart in Scotland. Of course, most people in the Celtic diaspora don't have their ancestral language, and their link to the homeland is often more romantic or fanciful than truly significant in their lives. Still, if you organize a festival of Celtic music or a highland games competition in the U.S., expect a large turnout. To the people of the Celtic diaspora, having a Celtic identity matters. But the question is, just how does it matter?

THE PATH OF THE DIASPORA

Americans often have a bit of a checkered reputation back in the ancestral Celtic lands. Many of us equate being "Celtic" with being "pagan," using notions of Wicca and magic that are far more English than Celtic in nature. We speed around the Irish or Welsh countryside in our hired cars until we see a stone circle or some other prehistoric monument— and before you can say "Great Goddess," we're spooking the livestock with an impromptu ritual at the site, having conveniently forgotten to ask the landowner for permission to trespass. Perhaps most charming/annoying of all is how we gush when we meet a "real Celt," not stopping to consider that to the person we're gushing over, their identity as an Irishman or Scotsman is far more important. And while we can't get enough of traditional storytelling or touristy souvenirs, our eyes glaze over at the thought of how economic and cultural forces (many of which are exported from America) are threatening to destroy the vestigial remnants of real Celtic language and culture.

Of course, culture is organic, and changes over space and time. Celtic tradition will somehow adapt itself to the brave new world of mass media—a world where millions think of themselves as Celtic even though they couldn't translate *uisce gu leor*.

THE PATH OF THE DIASPORA

British scholar Marion Bowman has coined a phrase—"Cardiac Celt"—to describe a person, often a descendant of the Celtic diaspora, who has little or no direct connection to traditional Celtic culture, but who feels a powerful emotional or intuitive tug toward images and symbols of the Celtic world. These "Celts of the heart" have responded to the romanticism that has been part of the "Celtic experience" ever since writers from Walter Scott to W.B. Yeats exploited the traditions and identity of their homeland as a way of self-consciously rejecting a more dominant (read: English) culture. For Cardiac Celts, the dominant paradigm that needs subverting is just as likely to be American consumerism as British imperialism. The point is, the fairy-world of the Celts is a mystical haven where all that is unsavory and unloved about the "real world" can simply be escaped from, behind a mist, as it were. Alas, the problem with escapist romanticism is that, while it might be a temporary way for those doing the escaping to feel good about themselves (or about the culture they are supposedly "experiencing," even if only in their imagination), it does little to really change things. And so the problems that need to be escaped from simply remain unchallenged.

THE PATH OF THE DIASPORA

Of course, Cardiac Celts can be quite sophisticated in their exploration of the Celtic world. Thanks to the Internet, resources abound where eager students can learn at least a conversational smattering of Celtic languages, and numerous translations and retellings of Celtic myth and lore are regularly published (or available for free download online). Indeed, one of the most fascinating things to watch online (I've seen this more than once) is a chat-room or mail-list argument between two self-taught "Celtic reconstructionists" who use their divergent interpretation of mythology and folklore as benchmarks for an "I'm more Celtic than you are" contest. Actually, it's a bit pathetic, especially when the subject being debated is religion—for nowhere do spiritual values (like community, kindness, or compassion) ever seem to enter into the debate. Lacking the security of a truly grounded cultural matrix, the Cardiac Celts must forever prove to one another their right to be included among the Celtic elect—and then defend their place on the cybernetic hierarchy of Celtic correctness. Meanwhile, the language and traditional cultural practices continue to decline in rural areas where most people still don't even have in-home access to the Internet.

THE PATH OF THE DIASPORA

There's nothing wrong with trying to integrate Celtic language, literature, or values into a postmodern spirituality in a place like America or Australia. Whether your particular "flavor" of Celtic identity is bound up with a nation or region (Scotland, Wales, Cornwall), an art form (music, dance, highland games) or a spiritual orientation (Celtic Christianity, Celtic Wicca, neopaganism, druidism, Celtic reconstructionism), if you live outside of Western Europe you are probably getting it "wrong" in all sorts of ways. Which is simply to say that someone from a land where the language is surviving by the skin of its teeth will see in you little more than a hobbyist with a charming (or annoying, depending on your personality) interest in *their* culture, *their* heritage, *their* tradition. In fact, what will largely determine whether you are charming or annoying is the extent to which you acknowledge that, as a child of the diaspora, you are not so much a "Celt" as a cultural tourist who specializes in the Celtic world.

THE PATH OF THE DIASPORA

Can there be a genuine Celtic experience in the lands of the diaspora? Setting aside Cape Breton, the answer to this question depends largely on how much we believe language shapes and directs culture. I tend to be conservative on this point, so it seems to me, you cannot have Celtic culture without Celtic language. And no, a group of hobbyists who get together once a week to practice their Irish over a pint at the local pub doesn't count. But others may arguably take a more liberal view. If we can keep at least some elements of the heritage alive—storytelling, music and dance, mysticism, poetry—and create communities where this kind of culture can be celebrated and passed down to our children, then at least Celtic ethnicity survives, if not a cohesive Celtic culture. And I suppose as long as tourists from around the world continue to descend upon Ireland and the other Celtic lands, there will be those in the old country who will do what they can to help us Cardiac Celts keep our interest alive. So some form of Celtic experience will likely be with us forever— alongside those who struggle to preserve a Native American experience, or a Jewish experience, or any other of countless marginalized cultures and ethnicities.

THE PATH OF THE DIASPORA

The establishment of a free Irish state nearly a century ago, along with more recent movements toward Scottish and Welsh home rule, have been encouraging signs in the uncertain future of Celtic identity. Sovereignty may, ultimately, be even more important than the survival of the languages when it comes to preserving the Celtic world. On a day-to-day basis, Irish independence or Scottish home rule mean little to the Cardiac Celts of the diaspora. But the key to the survival of Celtic identity outside the European seaboard cannot depend on sovereignty or language, since neither of those issues are even remotely relevant to the Celtic experience in Australia or North America (again, excepting Cape Breton). What will keep the Celtic fires burning in the diaspora is access to a living Celtic culture back in the homeland. This is why so many Americans have made the understandable, if inexcusable, mistake of supporting terrorists in Northern Ireland. For too many Americans, the *idea* of a fully independent Ireland is far more persuasive than any real effort to understand the complexity of issues that divide the people of that troubled province. Once again, romanticism trumps thoughtful understanding—for on a romanticized, spiritual level, Irish freedom seems to make a difference for Cardiac Celts who want their chosen cultural mask to actually mean something.

THE PATH OF THE DIASPORA

After one particularly heated conversation several years ago with an outspoken Irishwoman about the quality of my insight into the spiritual traditions of her homeland, I've taken to thinking of my spiritual path not as "Celtic," but as "Celtic-American." It seemed not only more honest and accurate, but the best way to honor the fact that, as a fourth-generation American son of a Scottish immigrant, ultimately my only real claim to the Celtic tradition is the extent to which my knowledge of and appreciation for the culture shape my identity as an American. And so I believe it must be for all Cardiac Celts of the diaspora. Celtic mythology, spirituality, cultural and national identity—all these elements of culture can make a real difference in our lives, no matter where we live. But they do not excuse us from the messy business of trying to make the world a better place, which often means dealing with concerns and issues that are as un-Celtic as can be. But if my sense of myself as being as much shaped by my Celtic ancestry as by my American citizenship can help me choose how to relate to others, how to spend my money, how to give my time back to my community, and how to orient my spiritual beliefs and practices, then it is of inestimable value. And that's true even if I'll never get comfortable driving on the left side of the road.

THE PATH OF THE OGHAM

One way to approach Celtic wisdom involves the use of the Ogham, an ancient method of writing that has been linked to traditional and mythic lore.

The Ogham is a cipher—symbols that represent letters in the Roman alphabet. Earliest examples of Ogham script were carved on stones used to mark graves, property lines, or historical sites. But the script also appears in medieval manuscripts, where it is suggested that the various characters may embody deep spiritual symbolism. Legend holds that the Ogham was created by Ogma, a god renowned as a great champion but also known for his eloquence and literary skill.

Each character in the Ogham script is associated with a tree or other plant, and conveys a rich symbolism: oak is related to strength; willow is related to intuition; and so forth. The Ogham could be used like the Norse runes, as a tool for deciphering omens. But the Ogham is not a fortune-telling device; the symbolism associated with each tree/plant is general and spiritually oriented rather than geared toward the ordinary, mundane world. The Ogham doesn't predict the future, but rather suggests ways to access inner guidance to shape life in spiritually positive ways.

THE PATH OF THE OGHAM

Birch often grows at the edges of forestland; thus it is known as a tree that stands between two worlds. Likewise, it sits at the entrance to the Ogham itself, and is the first of the twenty plants and trees associated with the script. Symbolically, the birch is the tree of beginnings, thresholds, and initiations.

Perhaps it is a cliché to say that life is full of initiations and new beginnings, and yet often we pay precious little attention to the threshold moments in life. We tend to be creatures of routine, and find change (except when it's our own idea) to be stressful, bothersome, or downright traumatic. The birch reminds us that initiation is not just a clichéd part of life; it *is* life, fully lived.

Initiation often is defined as some sort of mysterious, ritualistic life-transition in which nothing is ever again the same. And yes, such world-shattering transformations do happen. But far more common are the tiny shifts that occur in the unadorned moments of our lives. A single wrong turn can put a traveler a thousand miles away from her destination; so too the tiniest initiations often yield the hugest consequences.

Any new beginning requires energy and effort. We have to take responsibility for generating and shaping the life we desire. Otherwise, if we choose to go through life "by default," we end up shaped by our circumstances or by plain dumb luck. Either way, we change. The question is, who's doing the changing?

THE PATH OF THE OGHAM

The second of the Ogham trees, rowan, has a longstanding reputation as a ward against malevolent psychic and spiritual forces. It sports white flowers and red berries, a symbol of otherworldly energies. While a massive tree like the oak represents strength in its most down-to-earth, this-worldly form, the rowan implies a different kind of strength, related more to the inner landscape and invisible forces against which conventional strength affords no defense.

But the lore of the rowan tree leads to this question: how do we really protect ourselves from that which cannot be seen? It's a perennial spiritual question, and one that virtually every religious or magical system answers on some level. For many, protection is a benefit of invoking the name of God, or Christ, or the Virgin Mary, or the angels of the four directions. Others might choose a more abstract approach, visualizing golden-white light flowing about them almost like a comforting shield. For others, a prayer or incantation of reassuring words (like Patrick's Lorica) can be the best tool for calling in energies of safety and security.

In the end, all these techniques share a common willingness to believe in the forces of good, and in your eligibility to receive such beneficent help—and then taking responsibility to issue the call when needed. You are as secure in the spiritual world as you choose to be.

THE PATH OF THE OGHAM

Alder, third in the Tree Ogham, is a hard wood that is especially resistant to the rotting effects of moisture. Many of the foundations in waterlogged Venice are made of alder; back in the Celtic lands, it had a reputation as a fine wood for the making of shields. Celtic lore also notes that alder is an excellent wood for making milk buckets—integrating its sturdiness with its liquid-resistant quality.

So this is the tree of foundation and stability. Its symbolism within the Ogham suggests that every plan, idea, or strategy must be built on solid, immovable ground. Jesus' wry comments about building on sand rather than rock are not unrelated to the alder's symbolic meaning.

Consider the many projects in your life, whether work-related, financial, artistic, or family-oriented. Life is about making things happen, and making them happen efficiently and well. Before opening night, a play must be rehearsed many times. Any project, no matter how large or small, whether it will involve lots of money or just a grateful smile, requires careful preparation and a thoughtful game plan. Not only is it important to have your goal in mind, but it's perhaps even more necessary to have a good sense of what the starting line looks like. Many races are lost in the first ten seconds, even though others are won in the last ten. In other words, building a strong foundation is not the only key to success. But it's an important start.

THE PATH OF THE OGHAM

Water is often regarded as a symbol of the unconscious—the depths of the ocean make a fitting metaphor for the depths of the mind. And so, of all the Ogham plants, the willow's reputation as one of the thirstiest trees makes it the natural symbol for intuition and the ability to access wisdom from deep within the psyche.

Contemplation has been described as an ecstatic state in which one's finite consciousness experiences a sense of merging with a greater identity, as deep and vast as the ocean itself. Approaching the depths of the mind and soul with a contemplative stillness is very much like giving a large body of water time to slowly find peace and stillness. And just as the ocean seems always to surge and heave with endless energy, so too does the conscious mind never seem to relinquish its spidery webs of thought and distraction. That is not a bad thing; after all, it is the function of the mind to think just as it is the function of the heart to beat. But the quest for contemplative stillness is ultimately the quest for the deep spaces between thoughts—whether such thinking pounds with a storm's rapid fury or moves in a placid, leisurely rhythm.

The wisdom that whispers from deep within often expresses itself in wispy delicate feelings and thoughts, not unlike the branches of the willow. Listen carefully for the quiet voice of God; like the rustle of a breeze in the willow's branches.

THE PATH OF THE OGHAM

According to Norse tradition, the great world tree, Yggdrasil, is an ash, a magnificent tree that knits together all of the nine worlds that make up the cosmos. The great god Odin once hung himself as a sacrifice for nine days from the branches of the great ash, at the end of which time he was given secret knowledge in the form of the runes.

Odin's closest cognate in the Celtic traditions is the Welsh trickster-druid Gwydion—and it's hard to decide if he's really likeable. He's not above trickery, and not just for harmless pranks, either—in one story he helps his brother seduce a virgin whose service to the king is compromised by the seduction. Even worse, the "trick" he uses to distract the king is to cause a war! Eventually all this is found out and Gwydion and his brother endure a humiliating punishment, but it's unclear if he is ever truly repentant. To his credit, he becomes a champion and mentor to one of the more important gods, Lleu.

Like this mysterious and ambiguous figure, the ash is the Ogham tree that stands for bringing different energies together in service of a greater whole. It is the tree that symbolizes the idea of "the whole being greater than the sum of its parts." And like Odin's nine-day ordeal, it suggests that sometimes we must be willing to make a sacrifice in order to obtain that great, unifying good.

THE PATH OF THE OGHAM

Like the rowan tree, the hawthorn has white blossoms with red berries, thereby marking it as a tree with otherworldly associations. The sixth Ogham tree has a longstanding reputation as a fairy tree, particularly when found growing alone on a windswept hill. Irish folklore abounds with stories of such fairy trees cut down, always leading to disappointment, if not downright tragedy, for those who did the cutting. It is said that a fairy tree was cut down when construction began on the plant that manufactured the DeLorean automobile—one of the most spectacular of failed businesses in recent memory.

Within the Ogham, hawthorn represents obstacles, difficulties, and the need for restraint and self-control. It's an apt symbol for our society, which is obsessed with rights and desires but suffers from collective amnesia when it comes to such matters as duty and discipline. Spirituality (whether Celtic or otherwise) is not some sort of inner drama about getting everything we want. And anyone who suggests otherwise is probably just trying to sell you something.

The thorns of the hawthorn remind us that life brings pain as well as pleasure. Spiritual wisdom is not just a matter of minimizing the pain to increase the pleasure. On a deeper and more eternal level, it's about recognizing the gifts and lessons that all of life has to bring us: the bad times as well as the good.

THE PATH OF THE OGHAM

The oak—seventh tree of the Ogham—may not be the largest or tallest of trees, but when mature it is still an impressive sight, with a gargantuan trunk supporting myriad leafy branches. The king of Celtic trees, the oak appears solid and strong—which is what it represents in the Ogham.

The Irish town of Kildare (home to Saint Brigid and, before her, the goddess Brigit) takes its name from the Gaelic *Cill Dara,* or "church of the oak." Tradition holds that at the time of the saint, a mighty oak tree graced the crest of the hill where the cathedral stands today; it was said that no weapon could be set against the trunk of this magnificent tree (echoing how both the goddess and the saint of Kildare were champions of peace). This tree was in all likelihood venerated by the pagans before the coming of Christianity.

Echoes of the old word for oak (*duir* in Irish) also appear in words like en*dur*ance and *dur*ation; it may well be that even the word *door* has a link to the king of trees. It's interesting to ponder the link between the strongest of trees and the utility of a door. True strength doesn't simply stand solid and still, but rather it facilitates movement and change. Doors are powerful precisely because they create a boundary when necessary, and yet admit passage as needed. The greatest strength is that which knows when to be flexible and yield.

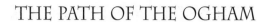

THE PATH OF THE OGHAM

In folklore, two mythic figures—the Oak King and the Holly King—perpetually struggle for dominance, a metaphor for the cyclical march of the seasons. At the winter solstice, the Oak King triumphs and reigns over the waxing half of the year, when the days grow ever longer. But then at the summer solstice, another struggle ensues and the Holly King emerges victorious, to reign during the waning months as the days shorten. Until the next winter solstice, of course, when the cycle begins again.

So the evergreen holly tree balances out the oak with its cycle of new leaves in the spring leading to fallen leaves in the autumn. And as the eighth of the Ogham trees, holly stands for maintaining balance and equilibrium. Its prickly leaves also symbolize self-defense, symbolizing justice and the necessity to fight for what is right.

The Celtic tradition has its peaceniks like Brigid, but it is also a warrior path, and therefore honors those who set and defend necessary boundaries. As some clever soul once pointed out, if you stand for nothing, you'll fall for anything. The holly calls us to strap on our armor and take a stand for eternal values and virtues—those that never go out of season. It also reminds us not to give up, even when we suffer temporary setbacks. After all, the Oak King may win on the darkest day of the year, but within six months the Holly King must again take a stand.

THE PATH OF THE OGHAM

Irish legend tells of a magical pool of deep crystal-clear water called the Well of Segais. Nine hazel trees surrounded the pool, and ancient salmon swam in its depths. When the trees bore their nuts, they fell one by one into the pool, where the salmon swam to the surface to eat; when a fish ate of the nuts, red spots formed on its otherwise silvery white skin. It may well have been one of the salmon from Segais that the young Fionn mac Cumhaill ate in order to gain his superhuman knowledge, wisdom, and insight.

The fourteenth-century English mystic Julian of Norwich saw in a vision something she described as "a little thing, the size of a hazelnut." This little thing was the entire universe in miniature. She was given in her vision a "God's-eye" view of all things, so that she could understand that the universe exists because God made it, God loves it, and God keeps it. From this little "hazelnut," Julian received profound and life-altering wisdom.

So the hazel, ninth tree in the Ogham, represents knowledge and enlightenment—not merely the knowledge that feels smug in its own smartness, but rather the mental and spiritual insight that combines awareness and intellect with virtue to chart a course toward a healthy, good, and balanced life.

THE PATH OF THE OGHAM

When King Arthur fell in battle, he did not die but was carried by angels (or fairies) to Avalon—the isle of the apples. Perhaps this is just a metaphor for heaven, or perhaps it is a lovely way of describing the land of fairy, where the great king is resting and recuperating and preparing for his return at the hour of Britain's greatest need. Either way, it is a place outside time; a place where Arthur's weary body and soul are nourished by the life-nurturing qualities of the beautiful red fruit. Avalon may have originated in the pagan tradition of *Emain Abhlach*, an island said to be ruled by the sea god Manannán and home to a magical orchard of apple trees. The fruit from these trees conferred immortality to those fortunate enough to eat of them.

The tenth tree of the Ogham symbolizes both beauty and eternity. As the heavenly fruit of the otherworld, it represents health ("an apple a day keeps the doctor away") and happiness. And yet the apple is a reminder that we are not yet in paradise, not yet enjoying the fullness of beauty that may only truly be found on the other side of the veil. So in that sense the apple is also the fruit of choice—calling us to be mindful in our many choices great and small, so that the future we create for ourselves be one that truly honors our potential as conduits of the eternal values of truth, goodness, and beauty.

THE PATH OF THE OGHAM

The vine is the eleventh plant in the Ogham, but of the twenty species represented it is the one least connected to the British Isles. Although efforts were made to establish vineyards in the Celtic islands beginning in Roman Britain, it's just not a native plant. For this reason, some authorities suggest that the "vine" actually refers to the blackberry bush.

Either way, the energies associated with this Ogham character are the same: both relate to intoxication. It's the "party Ogham," symbolizing celebration, joy, and the exultation of the harvest. It also suggests candor and truth telling; after all, wine has this amusing tendency to cause the dropping of inhibitions!

The wisdom of the intoxicating beverage recalls the great queen of Irish legend, Meadbh. Her intoxicating beverage was offered to the newly-crowned king, whose sacred union with her symbolized the essential relationship between humanity and land. But she also told the truth—for the land would prosper only when a king was just.

As an Ogham symbol, the vine reminds us of the wisdom in celebrating our triumphs and successes; and it subtly affirms the power of truth telling. When we nurture within ourselves a spirit of celebration and joy, perhaps it is easier to let others know exactly where we stand. Then, even when our views are unpopular, at least they are emerging from a place of spiritual and emotional strength.

THE PATH OF THE OGHAM

Of all the sacred trees and plants of the Ogham, the ivy is the one I am most likely to think uncharitable thoughts about, as I struggle to pull its grasping tendrils off the trees in my yard. Tenacious and persistent, ivy stands for the stick-to-it quality that we sometimes need in order to prevail when circumstances are not entirely favorable. It symbolizes drive, ambition, the will to succeed, and the energy to reach and achieve goals. It's a quality that is highly prized in our culture, and is a truly necessary aspect of maturity, freedom, and autonomy. Invoke the energies of the ivy whenever you need an extra "oomph" to keep on keepin' on.

The shadow side of ivy is, naturally, quite similar to the shadow side of ambition. It can easily veer into ruthlessness or overly aggressive effort. Its natural tenacity can breed a prideful arrogance that can create opposition just as easily as it overcomes it. The take-no-prisoners approach to life can lead to success, but it can also engender loneliness and isolation. Just as the leaves and vines of ivy ultimately become deeply intertwined, this plant calls us to remember that our tenacity must be balanced by all the other great values of Celtic wisdom: community, hospitality, honor, and kinship. After all, what's the point of being a winner if you have no one to share in your prize?

THE PATH OF THE OGHAM

The thirteenth Ogham character is sometimes said to represent the reed; at other times the broom. Either way, it symbolizes order and the restoration of order. The reed is related to writing and music, thus linking to such concepts as harmony and memory; it relates to the order of beautiful sound or of preserved words. On the other hand, the broom plant is of course related to cleaning and sweeping. In this way, the "order" this Ogham character symbolizes is not only abstract and artistic, but also very much down-to-earth and practical as well.

My wife and I are both avid collectors of many and varied things. Therefore, several times a year we have to go through the house, cleaning and organizing and banishing the clutter. What invariably happens at those cleaning times is a process of remembering: we encounter an important this or that which has been lying unnoticed beneath some other important this or that. So the decluttering process is not only about cleanliness and order, but it has a positive function as well: we create harmony by re-connecting with important if forgotten objects or ideas.

Ultimately, you create the harmony in your life. To sit around and passively wait for the symphony to start may result in nothing ever happening. It's better to recognize the places in our lives where harmony seems missing, and to take responsibility for calling it into being.

THE PATH OF THE OGHAM

The fourteenth of the Ogham trees is often seen as the most magical of the lot. Not magic in the sense of pulling rabbits out of hats, or even in the sense of Harry Potter whipping up a spell with his wand (which was made of yew, at any rate). No, the magic of the blackthorn is the magic of understanding, and working with, forces that are larger than you are. Forces of destiny, of fate, of what the Norse call *wyrd*—the web of life, the way things simply are. New agers love to talk about creating their own reality. That's great, but if you jump out of a window expecting to create flight, it will last about 3 seconds, and then you kiss the ground.

As a thorn tree, blackthorn implies that the forces of fate are not always kind and generous. The magic of the blackthorn helps you learn to make the most of what you've got, of thriving within your limits, and sometimes—but only sometimes—transcending them. This Ogham tree is not about giving up or giving in; but rather working creatively within any situation so that you need never settle for being a victim or a martyr.

Thorns wound. And sometimes life wounds as well. A wound can kill, but it can also mark a powerful turning point for those willing to learn from their disappointments and setbacks. Wounds are related to wonder; to experience life's wonder, sometimes we have to bump up against the walls in our world, even if it means getting a bloody nose.

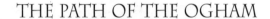

THE PATH OF THE OGHAM

Elder, fifteenth of the Ogham trees, is like other fairy trees marked by a short, thick stature, with white blossoms and red berries. The summertime flowers have five petals and the berries are used to make elderberry wine. The divinatory energies associated with this tree cover a wide terrain: it has been called a tree of healing and transformation, but has also been linked with embarrassment or shame. While the blackthorn relates to the forces of fate that lie outside our control, the elder points to how we react to the larger-than-life forces when they impact us. Do we flow with their energies in order to take advantage of the natural order of things? Or do we struggle against the way things are, often to our later regret? The energy of this tree suggests being mindful when encountering spiritual forces in life. Just as traditionally no Celt with any sense would harm a fairy tree, so even in our hyper-cynical and skeptical world, there is a rightness in relating to otherworldly forces with an appropriate spirit of reverence and awe.

THE PATH OF THE OGHAM

The fir is not the tallest tree in the British Isles, nor even the tallest species in the Tree Ogham, but the sixteenth tree in the series is nevertheless related to loftiness of vision and taking the high road. Not that the fir is a short tree, mind you—this tall, straight evergreen can reach heights of 100 feet, certainly respectable as a symbol of elevated consciousness. So in the symbolism of the Ogham, the fir is all about the big picture—not getting bogged down in details, or in petty conflicts, or in anything less than full and ultimate potential. It is the Ogham of peak experience, implying the highest and best possible integration of emotion and well-being. It is the light bulb that goes off when a new idea occurs; it is a watchman finding an advantageous position from which the movements of friends and foes alike may be monitored. Finally, there's a pun linked with the fir, for the tree of great height is all about feeling "high," not so much in a druggy sense but in the more natural, holistic sense of being "high on life."

THE PATH OF THE OGHAM

Travel around the British Isles and you'll likely notice that gorse (also called furze) is everywhere, an abundant shrub that covers ground like a luxurious carpet. It is thorny and therefore symbolically linked with hawthorn and blackthorn; and yet its traditional meaning within the Tree Ogham has more to do with prosperity than with danger. Medieval texts provide contradictory ways of thinking about the plant: on the one hand linking it with the warrior spirit, on the other hand praising its gentleness. Paul Rhys Mountfort suggests that it is linked with sexuality, an idea that ties the fertility of eros together with the fecundity of a prosperous life.

Abundance, fertility, eros, fecundity ... these are concepts of growth, expansion, bursting beyond limits and manifesting miracles. And so this is the energy that gorse symbolically represents. Meditate on this humble little shrub with its golden yellow flowers, and—spiritually speaking—allow yourself to trust in blessings and prosperity filling your life and the lives of those you love with joys and delights. It's the energy of "there's plenty to go around"—no need to live by the fear of scarcity, but rather to confidently embrace faith that there is enough to go around—enough life, enough food, enough love, enough miracles.

THE PATH OF THE OGHAM

Gorse is the Ogham plant signifying sexuality and eros, and so the gorgeous heather follows it as the symbol of love, of relationship, of intimacy and emotional healing. This fragrant and beautiful plant is, like gorse, a groundcover rather than a tree. It is the plant on which the lovers Diarmait and Gráinne first consummated their relationship, while traditional folksongs like "Wild Mountain Thyme" suggest that the "blooming heather" is a place where lovers meet.

For so many people, the two biggest areas in which life can provide either pleasure or pain are the realms of finances and of love. Psychics and psychiatrists alike hear an endless litany of challenges, issues, conflicts, sorrows, and anxieties over money and sex. So the two shrubs that appear in the Tree Ogham are modest symbols of these two close-to-the-heart issues. And how fitting that such "big" issues in life are represented by such homely and down-to-earth (literally) plants—that don't even deserve to be called trees, even though they are part of the Tree Ogham. With these two humble shrubs, the Ogham may be a subtle reminder that the concerns that our human egos think are so major, from the perspective of spirit may actually be quite minor indeed.

THE PATH OF THE OGHAM

The white aspen, or poplar, is a hardy and resistant tree. Its leaves are delicate and dynamic, moving at the slightest of breezes and appearing energetic or anxious, depending on your point of view. Perhaps the subtle movement could signify spiritual presence—or perhaps it could signify fear, and the soul's need for courage.

In a warrior tradition like the Celtic, the mastery of fear is an essential key to wisdom. Psychologist Susan Jeffers wrote a self-help book with a title that sums it up: *Feel the Fear and Do it Anyway*. Erasing fear is about as feasible as erasing thought or stopping a beating heart. To feel no fear is to be not alive. The Celtic tradition accepts and even embraces fear, not for its own sake but as a simple and pure manifestation of energy—energy that could be re-channeled to hope, or courage, or envisioning a more positive future. We can feel fear, know fear, and befriend fear, but we do not have to either repress it, or give in to it. Indeed, Jeffers suggests that a benefit of fear is that it helps us see when we're growing and moving beyond our comfort zone. Such a concept could be the heart of what the poplar represents in the Tree Ogham. The nineteenth tree is not about avoiding fear—but recognizing what it means and how it accompanies us on the path of courage.

THE PATH OF THE OGHAM

Hoary yew trees grace many churchyards and graveyards in the British Isles; they are dense evergreens with an unmistakable aura of solemn dignity about them.

Legends abound as to why yews are commonly found in cemeteries: one theory holds that as a tree sacred to the druids, yews and the ground on which they stood were considered holy long before the "new religion" of Christianity came along and built its temples in their shadow. Others simply consider the tree to be the botanical equivalent to the grim reaper, a symbol of death so potent that no other tree would ever be nearly at home growing among the remains of the dead. Whatever the origins of the romance or legend surrounding the yew, as the twentieth and final tree of the Ogham it clearly stands not only for endings and death, but also for rebirth and regeneration.

Seekers of Celtic wisdom can invoke the energies of the yew whenever there is a chapter in life that needs to come to a close. But as we contemplate the yew, let's remember that death, to the druids, was but the midpoint of a long life, and that it is only in the releasing and clearing energies of death that room is created for new life. Thus the cycle goes full circle, and every ending is a sacrificial and reverent act, opening up the possibility of yet another new beginning.

THE PATH OF THE MYSTIC

What, ultimately, is the point behind Celtic wisdom? Is it just a way to take pride in our Irish, Scottish, or other Celtic ancestry? Does it truly represent an alternative doorway into spirituality—different from the official teachings of the churches, or the values of society? Can the Celtic path help us to be more wise; more loving and compassionate; more empowered? Can it inspire us to be better people? For that matter, can it make us happy?

I think the answer to all these questions is a qualified yes. The qualification is this: ultimately, the Celtic path, like any wisdom tradition, is what you make of it. Many neopagan traditions insist that spiritual truth ultimately must be found within. Compare that to Jesus saying, "the kingdom of God is within you." These are universal spiritual truths, as applicable to the Celtic path as to any other.

So it is what you make of it. You are left with the task of deciding for yourself what you wish to cultivate within yourself, spiritually speaking. Your soul is like the fertile land of Ireland—and your spirituality is the seed you plant in that moist earth. The crop you grow includes your values, your beliefs, your life experiences, and your relationships. To all this, Celtic spirituality—like any wisdom tradition—is the fertilizer (okay, no jokes, please). It is the web of stories and visions and dreams to nurture your deepest self.

THE PATH OF THE MYSTIC

If you are like me and like many others who love the Celtic way, you may find that the farther you walk down this path, the more questions remain unanswered—indeed, it seems that for every question that does find a reply, three new ones occur. The Celtic way, like all journeys of the heart, is a way of mystery. Part of the frustrating joy is that mystery opens up to mystery, and hidden places reveal deeper darknesses within and below. Celtic tradition is full of strange stories about warriors or heroines who are lost in the mist, or explore subterranean wonderlands, or face fearsome beasts in the blackest part of night. Each of these could be seen as metaphors for the unconscious, or for the womb, or for the goddess. Yet each of these represents the fertile ground or matrix from which new life emerges (matrix, after all, is Latin for womb).

Christian mystics have long spoken of such profound images as the cloud of unknowing or the dark night of the soul. Such imagery would not be out of place in the Celtic world. Perhaps your journey toward spiritual fulfillment is a quest for the light, but remember: all light emerges out of darkness. So befriend your unanswered questions. They are the fuel for your continued journey.

THE PATH OF THE MYSTIC

The metaphors of darkness, or of questioning, or of "unknowing," allude to the poetic and visionary tradition of western mystical spirituality. Although mysticism is not particularly associated with the Celtic world, the ideas of medieval mystics like Saint John of the Cross or Julian of Norwich all point to universal spiritual experiences that resonate with the wisdom of the Celts. The darkness within the burial chambers of Newgrange; the solitude of the lonely hermit-monks of Skellig Michael, the remote monastery located on a remote Atlantic island; the many paradoxes and unanswered questions that the legends of the goddesses and heroes of old have left behind—these are symbols of the profound and central place that *mystery* has within the Celtic tradition.

"Mystic" is a word often overused and misused; it means a person who has been initiated into spiritual mysteries. In classical culture, this was a formal religious process; many modern occult and neopagan groups have tried to revive this practice of initiating people into the "mysteries" (the great unanswerable questions of life and the soul). But a mystic need not be someone who has gone through an official ceremony or ritual. Anyone who has profoundly and in a life-transforming way embraced the great spiritual questions of life has begun to walk the mystic path—a path at the heart of the Celtic tradition.

THE PATH OF THE MYSTIC

Many sacred spaces in the world—not only the Celtic world, but throughout the earth—are places of profound silence. Sure, there may be tourists buzzing about, or even the sound of a farmer's tractor in the distance; but places like the Hill of Tara, the Chalice Well, the Standing Stones of Callanish, Tintagel, or countless others often seem to literally buzz with an energy, a feeling, a depth that can only be described in terms of silence, of presence, of Spirit. Like mysticism, this silent presence is not unique to the Celtic world—but arguably the chief value of Celtic wisdom is its ability to sensitize us to this silent song of intimacy and closeness to the Divine. This is something that ultimately cannot be put into words (hey, "it's a mystery") but if I can paint a verbal picture of it, even in broad strokes, perhaps you can relate it to a mysterious moment or moments in your life when all duality, all separation, all sense of anything other than Spirit just ... fell away. That comes to everyone in different ways—some frequently, some dramatically, some rarely, some in the most ordinary and commonplace of ways. Do not judge your spiritual experiences—but do allow them to unfold in your life.

THE PATH OF THE MYSTIC

Near the village of Gort in County Galway is a lovely park called Coole, the former grounds of the home of Lady Gregory, the famed Irish author and patroness of the arts. In the grounds, still alive in the early 21st century, is a beech tree on which numerous of Lady Gregory's most distinguished friends and acquaintances carved their initials. William Butler Yeats, George Bernard Shaw, John Millington Synge, and Lady Gregory herself are among those who left their mark—literally—on this beautiful tree. It's a splendid testament to the community of visionary artists (read: bards) whose contribution to Irish literature in the late-nineteenth and early-twentieth centuries helped forge the consciousness of a land that would regain its independence in their lifetime. A splendid monument—and yet, a living tree that will someday die, and eventually be lost to future generations.

Celtic wisdom, so intimately entwined with storytelling and personal experience, is something like that tree. It is not truly captured in a book, or a statue, or even a stone circle or beautifully landscaped holy well. It lives only in beating hearts and pensive minds. Thankfully, it has a better chance of survival than the Coole beech—as long as we are willing to share our stories, and truly listen to one another. We all have encountered mystery, each in our own unique way. Like the Celtic tradition, our dance with mystery will survive only if we open our mouths (and our ears).

THE PATH OF THE MYSTIC

For mystics (of any religion), spirituality is not something we read about in a book, or watch as someone else experiences it. It is experience of our own. Some cynics have suggested that mysticism is just a strategy for finding happiness through religion. Maybe so—but few mystics would say that's the entire story. The happiness of the mystic isn't just a matter of feeling good, or feeling "right with God," or having a sense of connection with the Goddess. It's not just about moments of divine illumination, when one experiences ecstasy or world-shattering enlightenment. No, the happiness of the mystic arises from choices and commitments made in response to the mysteries of life. Choosing faith in light of death. Choosing hope in light of birth. Choosing love and compassion in light of suffering. Choosing hospitality and honor, in light of the stories of our ancestors and how they make us feel connected to something larger than ourselves. Choosing to trust the future, no matter how uncertain it may be. None of these choices guarantee happiness—at least, not on the surface. But each one can help to make life radiant with meaning. For this is the goal of the mystic: to embrace life's mysteries, and in the darkness and the unknowing, to find meaning.

THE PATH OF THE MYSTIC

Brigid inspired generations of nuns to tend a sacred flame, seeing in it a metaphor for the light that burns in each one of us. Lugh encouraged a community to trust that light enough to fight for what is right. Patrick brought news of a new faith to a land where he had once been a slave—and in doing so, practiced forgiveness and fought for a world where slavery would be obsolete. Rhiannon never stopped telling her story, feeling grief at her sadness but also exulting in her joys. Angus Óg remained faithful to love, even when it threatened to break his heart. Columcille accepted the consequences of his own actions, and turned the tragedies of his life into new opportunities for service. These saints and gods, figures both historical and mythical, each invite us in a unique way to embrace the mysteries. None of them have all the answers—for that matter, none of them have all the questions! But they do all represent openings, pathways, thresholds into a life deeply and truly and faithfully lived. Such a life is the life of wisdom.

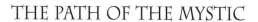

THE PATH OF THE MYSTIC

Every ending is also a beginning. The yew tree, the final symbol in the tree Ogham, represents death and eternity, but also immortality and rebirth. The ancient druids taught that death is the mid-point of a long life. In other words every ending ultimately leads on to something else.

A year spent with Celtic wisdom leads to another year: maybe a year taking a deeper look at the myths and legends and stories; maybe a year for moving on to something else. Wherever our path will take us, the cycle continues. Remember what I said in one of the first meditations in this book: you could explore the same elements of Celtic spirituality that I do, and come away with an entirely different understanding of what it all means. And for this, I think, we should be grateful.

At the heart of the darkness in Newgrange, the winter solstice sunrise shines in a blaze of otherworldly glory. And so it is, that the darkest of places is but a womb, waiting to give birth to a new light, a new dawn, a new possibility. Pray for the grace to remember this, the next time life visits you with sorrow. "This, too, shall pass."

THE PATH OF THE MYSTIC

Bliain agus lá is Gaelic for "a year and a day." It's a common literary figure in Celtic lore; the hero of a story might wait a year and a day before being able to complete a task, or win the hand of a promised lover, or meet an adversary in battle.

Why a year and a day? Perhaps it goes back to when the 365-day calendar was first being used. Originally, a year would have been measured by lunar cycles. Assuming a lunar month lasted 28 days, a year would be 13 moons x 28 = 364 days. You'd need to add a day to equal the solar year, hence "a year and a day." Alas, it's not very convincing, not only because the solar year vacillates between 365 and 366 days, but also because a lunar month is often 29 or 30 days long.

Actually, I prefer a simpler definition: a year and a day means "this time next year." From January 1 of one year to January 1 of the next includes one full year (January 1–December 31) and the extra day (the following January 1).

All this is hairsplitting. What's more important is to consider a year (and a day) as an appropriate time to allow major periods of growth and transformation to occur in your life. Forget our fast-food, gotta-have-it-now culture. If you want to learn the ways of wisdom, take your time. Take at least a year and a day (to just get started). Go slow.

ACKNOWLEDGEMENTS

Thanks to all sorts of wonderful and lovely people who have supported this book (and its author) in ways large and small—for insights, encouragement, debate, stories, humorous emails, and various other manners of contact, including (but not limited to) Candace Apple, Greg Brandenburgh, Fiona Brown, Cari Buziak, Joel Crawford, Steve Fischer (and everyone at Thorsons), Phil Foster, Kathryn Hinds, Jon Kasik, Gwen Knighton, Joe Raftery, Bev Richardson, Linda Roghaar, Laura Sheahan, Sylvia Sultenfuss, and everyone at Brigid's Well. Most of all, thanks with love to Fran and Rhiannon, who get to put up with me at deadline time (and beyond). If I've left anyone out, my deepest apologies—as the Celts of old used to say, I'll pay you back in the otherworld.

BIBLIOGRAPHY

Bowman, Marion, "Cardiac Celts," in *Paganism Today*, Graham Harvey and Charlotte Hardman, eds. London: Thorsons, 1995.

Carmichael, Alexander. *Carmina Gadelica*. Edinburgh: Floris Books, 1992.

Carr-Gomm, Philip and Stephanie. *The Druid Animal Oracle*. New York: Simon and Schuster, 1994.

Ellis, Peter Berresford. *The Druids*. Grand Rapids: William B. Eerdmans, 1995.

Evans-Wentz, W.Y. *The Fairy-Faith in Celtic Countries*. New York: University Books, 1966.

Green, Miranda. *Dictionary of Celtic Myth and Legend*. New York: Thames and Hudson, 1992.

Green, Miranda. *The Gods of the Celts*. Surrey: Bramley Books, 1986.

Kondratiev, Alexei. *The Apple Branch*. Dublin: Collins Press, 1998.

MacKillop, James. *Dictionary of Celtic Mythology*. Oxford: Oxford University Press, 1998.

MacLennan, Malcolm. *Gaelic Dictionary: Gaelic-English, English-Gaelic*. Edinburgh: John Grant, 1925.

McColman, Carl. *The Complete Idiot's Guide to Celtic Wisdom*. New York: Alpha Books, 2003.

Monaghan, Patricia. *The Red-Haired Girl from the Bog*. Novato: New World Library, 2003.

Mountfort, Paul Rhys. *Ogam*. London: Rider, 2001.

Ó Duinn, Seán, OSB, *Where Three Streams Meet: Celtic Spirituality*. Dublin: The Columba Press, 2000.

Ó Ríordain, John J., C.Ss.R., *The Music of What Happens*, Dublin: The Columba Press, 1996.

Rees, Alwyn, and Brinley Rees. *Celtic Heritage*. New York: Grove Press, 1961.

Toulson, Shirley. *The Celtic Year*. Rockport, MA: Element, 1993.

INDEX